Chekhov

"THE VAUDEVILLES"
and other short works

A Smith and Kraus Book
Published by Smith and Kraus, Inc.
PO Box 127, Lyme, NH 03768

Copyright ©1998 Carol Rocamora
All rights reserved
Manufactured in the United States of America

Cover and Text Design by Julia Hill, Freedom Hill Design
Cover illustration: Signed self portrait by Anton Chekhov, courtesy of
the State Museum of Literature, Chekhov Museum, Moscow

First Edition: February 1998
10 9 8 7 6 5 4 3 2 1

The Library of Congress Cataloging-In-Publication Data

Chekhov, Anton Pavlovich, 1860–1904.
[Plays. English. Selections]

Chekhov: the vaudevilles: a collection of one-act plays /
translated by Carol Rocamora. —1st ed.
p. cm. — (Great translations series)
Includes bibliographical references.
ISBN 1-57525-127-2

1. Chekhov, Anton Pavlovich, 1860–1904—Translations into English.
I. Rocamora, Carol. II. Title. III. Series: Great translations for actors series.

PG3456.A19R63   1998
891.72'3—dc21   97-42181

Chekhov

"THE VAUDEVILLES"

and other short works

Translated by Carol Rocamora

Great Translations Series

SK
A Smith and Kraus Book

"First I get my patients laughing,
and only then do I begin to treat them."

from Chekhov's letter to Leykin, 5/20/84

Contents

Preface

Chekhov, the dramatist, is known primarily for the four major plays which he wrote at the end of his short lifetime — *The Seagull (1896), Uncle Vanya (1899), The Three Sisters (1901),* and *The Cherry Orchard (1904).* These mature works are the window to the soul of this extraordinary writer and man, and the gentle and poetic expression of his remarkable *weltanschauung.*

If these later plays reveal the mature Chekhov, then the one-act plays written between 1885–1891 are a delightful revelation of the youthful, exuberant Chekhov in his twenties. They are also a reflection of the vibrant theatre life of Moscow in the 1880s, a period when Chekhov's literary star was rising, when he felt free to experiment with a variety of dramatic forms. It was a time when Chekhov was in love — with life and with the theatre, a gay and happy time, before consumption cast its long shadow over his life. To experience the "vaudevilles," as Chekhov loved to call them, is to fall under the spell of this charming young writer, and to catch a glimpse of him at a period of his life so full of energy and hope.

The purpose of this collection of translations is to rediscover and to celebrate the comedic short plays by an extraordinary young dramatist. And also, for those who know and love the later plays, this collection provides an opportunity to enjoy Chekhov's masquerade in comedic dress, while catching a glimpse behind the humorous mask of a darker demeanor to come.

Included in this collection are (in chronological order): *On the High Road* (1885), *On the Harmful Effects of Tobacco* (1886–1902), *Swan Song* (1887), *The Bear* (1888), *The Proposal* (1888), *Tatyana Repina* (1889), *The Tragedian in Spite of Himself* (1889), *The Wedding* (1889), *The Jubilee* (1891), and *The Night before the Trial* (1890s). In addition, a *feuilleton* entitled *In Moscow* (1891) has been added, as a fitting epilogue to this collection. It has also been included, should theatre artists wish to perform it as a monologue.

While the four major plays are well-known and widely performed on the English-speaking stage, only a few of the ten short plays in this collection are seen here with frequency — most notably *The Bear* and *The Proposal.*

Productions such as Meyerhold's famous *Thirty-Three Swoons (1935)* in Russia, a grouping of Chekhov's one-acts, are not nearly as popular in this country as are productions of the full-length plays. An additional purpose of this collection, therefore, is to familiarize English-speaking theatre artists with Chekhov's lesser-known one-act plays, which, while they may present some challenges for our contemporary stage, are nonetheless delightful and production-worthy in their own right. In whatever combination, they can provide a wonderful "Chekhov Evening" of theatre, such as the one Tolstoy saw in December, 1900, where, according to Olga Knipper, he "laughed his head off" *(Knipper to Chekhov, 12/16/00).*

This collection also includes a glossary and pronunciation guide for the benefit of theatre artists, as well as a chronology of his works, a biographical chronology, and bibliography. An introduction is also provided to offer a perspective on the place of the short plays in Chekhov's larger literary oeuvre, and to address the issues of form and tone with which he was experimenting.

Above all, these translations are for the pure pleasure of theatre artists, audiences, students, and lovers of dramatic literature. They have been newly translated to be read, performed, and enjoyed.

ACKNOWLEDGMENTS

For the preparation of these translations, I am indebted to the International Theatre Institute, which supported my travel to Moscow in 1992 to research my translations of Chekhov's major full-length plays. It was on that trip that I saw *The Bear* and *The Proposal* performed in a delightful vaudevillian evening entitled *Choy-to Ty vo Frakye?* ("Why Are You Wearing Tails?") at the Theatre for Contemporary Drama in Moscow, and fell in love with Chekhov's vaudevilles. I am also indebted to the CEC International Partners, which supported my return trip to Moscow in June, 1997. My special thanks to my colleague at the Moscow Art Theatre, Dr. Anatoly Smeliansky, who hosted my visits; to Anne Denlinger and the Bryn Mawr College Library, for their resources; and to my colleague, Dr. George Pahomov, for his valuable advice. Further thanks to Janet Neipris and all my colleagues and students at New York University's Tisch School of the Arts, for their meaningful support; to my students Todd Ferrari and Ian Gould, who first performed some of the texts included in this collection with great dedication; and to Laura Rappaport Blaha and Matt Cheney, for their assistance.

For the preparation of the introduction to this collection, I wish to acknowledge the sources listed in the bibliography, most notably the biographical studies of Chekhov by Ernest J. Simmons, Henri Troyat, and David Magarshak as well as Vera Gottlieb's scholarly study of *Chekhov and the Vaudeville.*

Notes from
the Translator

While Chekhov subtitled his short plays as farces, one-act plays, dramatic scenes, and monologues, he enjoyed referring to them collectively in his correspondence as "vaudevilles." Even though all of the short plays included herein do not conform to the conventions of that popular theatre genre of the day, I have nonetheless used "vaudevilles" as the unifying title for this collection, as he did. To understand why he did so — that is to say, the Chekhovian spirit in which he used the term "vaudeville" — is to further appreciate the significance of the short plays in his larger literary oeuvre. These reasons will be explored in the introduction to this collection.

The ten one-act plays included in this collection are written in a variety of styles, as Chekhov's various subtitles suggest. All — with the exception of the earliest one *(On the High Road)* — are comedic. I have presented them in the order in which they were written. (Note: *On the Harmful Effects of Tobacco* was revised five times from 1886 to 1902. I have placed it in the chronology according to the date of the earliest version; my translation, however, is of the final — 1902 — version.)

I have included in this collection one short work by Chekhov that he did not write for the stage, but that, however, lends itself as a fitting epilogue — both artistically and biographically — to the collection and to the period of Chekhov's life in which these plays were written. It is a *feuilleton,* published in the journal *Novoe Vremya* in 1891, entitled *In Moscow* — although it is frequently referred to as "A Moscow Hamlet", a name the narrator gives himself. It lends itself well to the stage as a dramatic monologue. I have translated it faithfully, as Chekhov wrote it, so that the actor who wishes to perform it will know the author's intent. I leave any modification or adaptation which the actor finds necessary to his discretion.

A special translator's note: *The Night before the Trial* was written sometime in the 1890s (actual date unknown, but assumed by most biographers and literary historians to be 1891), and is unfinished. It appears that Chekhov was in the process of adapting his short story of the same title into a vaudeville, but never actually completed it, for reasons unknown. I have taken the liberty of completing the play according to Chekhov's short story, so that theatre artists who read this collection might also be able to perform it. For those artists, please rest assured that I have provided an ending that is faithful to his prose version. (The one liberty taken has been to provide unity of time and place for the ending of the play with what preceded it — since the short story ends the next day in a different scene, and since with all the other vaudevilles, Chekhov observed these unities.) I do hope that the adapted ending will prove useful, and that the author would have approved.

Chekhov wrote these short plays at the height of a lively and youthful period of experimentation as a dramatist. For this reason, there are many wonderful, rich, and colorful features to his dramatic language. Each of the plays in this collection has its own very distinct "personality" and vocabulary, and thus requires special attention. Dog pedigrees, dueling procedures, and land settlements are only a few of the many vocabularies in which Chekhov is fluent here, and therefore require the translator to be. Two present special challenges for the contemporary translator. In the case of *The Wedding,* I have sought to make "General" Revunov-Karaulov's technical sailing terminology as understandable as possible for a contemporary American audience while retaining the accuracy and the appropriate historical flavor, which is the source of the humor in Chekhov's usage. In this regard, I wish to thank William Peterson, Senior Curator of the Mystic Seaport Museum, whom I consulted with respect to historical sailing terminology. In the case of the Russian Orthodox marriage ceremony in *Tatyana Repina,* I have consulted both the King James Version of the *New Testament* and an edition of *The Service Book of the Holy Orthodox-Catholic Apostolic Church* (compiled and translated by Isabel Florence Hapgood, New York, Associated Press, 1922), for the passages of the church liturgy which Chekhov included in his play, so that they too will be both accurate and recognizable to English-speaking audiences who are familiar with religious services and their standard texts.

In this collection, I have striven to create living translations for the purposes of reading and performance, which are both faithful to the original Russian language, while at the same time fluid for the contemporary actor and accessible to modern, English-speaking audiences. I have retained the formal use of the Russian names and patronymics, a challenge for the contemporary English-speaking actor — even more so with the short plays than with the full-length ones, since here Chekhov displays a parodist's delight in naming his characters. Once mastered, however, these names greatly enhance the fun and the flavor of the texts in translation. A pronunciation guide is included at the end of the collection for the actor's usage, as well as a glossary for the many historic and literary allusions that enrich these short plays.

In general, a modified form of the popular standard transliteration system has been used in these translations, in both the texts and the bibliography. Where there are exceptions, it is for the purpose of making it easier for the actor's use.

A final *mea culpa* to the author for any unintentional liberties or inadvertent errors, which might not do these delightful texts justice. The original language is rich and extremely challenging for the translator. I have striven to be faithful to the original, and have sought to show his texts the respect and reverence they deserve.

Introduction

Chekhov's prose writings occupy the dominant place in his literary oeuvre. Indeed, the thirty volumes of his complete collected works contain almost five hundred short stories, as well as over four thousand personal letters of inestimable literary and autobiographical value. It is a remarkable outpouring of prose for a man who only lived to be forty-four years of age, and who suffered from consumption most of his adult life.

In contrast to this enormous outpouring of prose, the body of his dramatic writing seems infinitessimally smaller — only seven full-length plays (an eighth, his first, is lost to us), ten one-act plays (approximately five more youthful efforts have also been lost), and a handful of parodic skits that were meant as practical jokes rather than as performance pieces. And yet the influence of his remarkable plays on twentieth-century world theatre has been incalculable.

Chekhov's one-act plays — the "vaudevilles," as he liked to refer to them in his correspondence — lie like jewels in the lap of this vast literary oeuvre… or, rather, like baubles, if we are to practice his preferred custom of trivializing the popular genre that he subsequently elevated to an art form. While they constitute a minuscule part of this literary outpouring, they are treasures, and their value, considered as a body of work (however small), is enormous, in terms of pure theatrical entertainment, as well as an appreciation of the spirit of this extraordinary writer.

For Anton Pavlovich Chekhov (1860–1904) — doctor, humanist, humorist, Russian, aesthete, literary philosopher, practical joker, and astute observer of human behavior — the vaudeville was the perfect form with which to make his debut as a young playwright in the glamorous Moscow theatre world that he held both in awe and contempt. The vaudeville, a Russified version of the French comedic genre, was a highly popular theatrical form *comme il faut* of the Moscow stage in the 1880s (and the only one that could get past the censors of the day), and the comedic muse was already with the young Dr. Chekhov in this decade, when he was turning out literally dozens of humorous short stories a year, garnering for him fame, a monthly assignment with the best "thick journals" of the day, an income, and the status of "darling" of the Moscow *literati*. The vaudevilles came naturally to him — they were easy and pleasurable, and brought him the same success he received for his short stories — praise, fame,

1

economic remuneration, and critical accolades. Yet through these "stage confections," an astute and determined young dramatist was at work, investigating characters and themes that would later mature and gain complexity in the later plays. And behind the hilarity and antics, a darker *weltanschauung* was developing, of the truths and absurdities of the human condition.

Chekhov wrote ten one-act plays in a variety of forms and styles. They are included in this collection. They were written during the second half of the Moscow period (1880–90) — a decade which brought Chekhov fame as a short story writer, primarily, but also a decade in which the passion to become a serious dramatist was burning within him. (Several other texts from that period also survive today: comedic "skits" that Chekhov wrote as parodies and jokes for special occasions, and were not meant to be performed. There are also at least a half-dozen other skits or vaudevilles Chekhov wrote in the Taganrog period and the very early Moscow period, according to his brother, Mikhail; regretably, these texts have been lost to us.)

Thus, while the "vaudevilles" repreesent a miniscule part of his larger literary oeuvre, as a whole they are a treasure. We read and perform them for pure enjoyment, for their incomparable humor, for a flavor of the Moscow theatre scene of the 1880s, for an appreciation of Chekhov's consummate craft, and above all — for a recognition of the comedic and tragic duality in his work, which would later mature in his four major plays, wherein he found the special dramatic balance of these elements that is known the world over as "Chekhovian."

CHEKHOV, THE YOUNG DRAMATIST

While his critical success, his national fame, and his livelihood came from the remarkable outpouring of the short stories, the most passionate love of Chekhov's life — complex and conflicted though it may have been, and unrequited, as he saw it — was for the theatre. It was in writing for the theatre that Chekhov experienced his greatest joy and deepest frustration. For while the comedic muse was always with him, it was as a serious playwright that he wanted to be considered.

Chekhov's dramatic oeuvre readily divides itself into four periods, corresponding to his places of residence: 1) 1860–1879: the Taganrog period — named so for Chekhov's place of birth and residence with his family during his youthful years. During this period, he wrote one full-length play and several comedic skits, which survive in title only; 2) 1880–1890: the Moscow period, during which he wrote three full-length plays: *Platonov* (1880–81), *Ivanov*

(1887), and *The Wood Demon* (1889), and the short plays included in this collection; 3) 1890–1900 and 4) 1900–1904: the Melikhovo and Yalta periods respectively, during which Chekhov, the mature dramatist, wrote his four major plays: *The Seagull, Uncle Vanya, The Three Sisters,* and *The Cherry Orchard.*

Chekhov wrote all of the short plays included in this collection from 1885–1891 (from the ages twenty-five to thirty-one), those highly charged years when his involvement with the Moscow and St. Petersburg theatre was at its height, and when his fame as a successful prose writer was soaring. It was owing to the widening gap between his passion to be taken seriously as a dramatist and what he perceived to be the public and the literary world's inability to understand his dramatic intent — as well as a frustration with what he felt were his immature abilities as a dramatist — that prompted almost a six-year hiatus in serious playwrighting, from 1889–1895. It was during this period, with his humanitarian journey to the island of Sakhalin, his slowly declining health, his move to his "estate" at Melikhovo, and his distancing from Moscow and the theatre world, that he gained the perspective and maturity to write the four major plays — the final ones of his tragically short life.

Choosing the appropriate literary terminology to identify Chekhov's one-act plays has presented a challenge for literary history and criticism. Chekhov subtitled all his plays, both one-act and full-length — an issue about which he was extremely sensitive in the case of the major plays, where he insisted that they be perceived and interpreted in accordance with these subtitles. Of the ten one-act plays in this collection, four, he subtitled as "shutki," which can be translated as "farces" (it also means "jokes"); two, he subtitled as "dramatic studies"; one, a "drama"; one, a "one-act play"; and one, a "monologue." They are written in a wide variety of styles and content. The unifying factor is that all — with the clear exception of one, *On the High Road* — contain comedic elements, and to varying degrees are delightfully funny.

What is interesting to note is that Chekhov himself simply referred to them all as "vaudevilles" in his correspondence, even the more serious ones. This seems to suggest that he wished the public (including the critics and the *literati*) to consider his plays to be light, diverting entertainment of inconsequential literary value, again, according to the conventions of the contemporary Russian vaudeville. However, his short plays do not conform to the conventions of the vaudeville as it appeared on the Russian stage in the 1880s. This suggests that Chekhov may have had another agenda in calling his plays "vaudevilles." By setting up an expectation in his public of certain conventions, Chekhov gave himself the freedom to poke fun at existing theatrical genres, and also to experiment within the perimeters of comedy to create his own "new forms" for the stage.

Just as he insisted that his mature, full-length plays were comedies, Chekhov persisted in referring to his one-acts as "vaudevilles." Furthermore, he went to great lengths in his letters to make us believe that he did not take his vaudeville-writing seriously. And yet, looking back on his dramatic oeuvre as a whole, the vaudevilles are far more than delightful entertainment. They were a critical stage of experimentation in Chekhov's development as a serious dramatist, where he explored the compatability of comedic and tragic elements within a given dramatic form. Later on in the introduction, we shall explore how Chekhov used the subterfuge of this popular generic classification quite deftly for his own special, "Chekhovian" purposes.

THE TAGANROG PERIOD: 1860–79

> "I haven't received a letter either from Moscow, or from my parents, or from you. And it's so boring here! How are you! Please write! There's nothing new in Taganrog, absolutely nothing! [...] I'm bored to death! I went to the Taganrog theatre the other day, and compared it with your theatre in Moscow. What a difference! And what a difference between Moscow and Taganrog! As soon as I finish school, I'll fly to Moscow on wings. I do love Moscow so much!"
>
> *to cousin Mikhail, 11/4/77*

We know from early reminiscences of his brother, Aleksandr, as well as from Chekhov's biographers, that parlor theatrics were a part of family life in Taganrog — a welcome respite from the otherwise harsh upbringing that the six Chekhov children endured at the hands of a domineering and rigid father. In addition to compulsory service in their father's shop after school (where he often struck the children), they also had the burden of church choir practice imposed upon them by their father in the early morning hours, leaving hardly any time for school work. There were five brothers and one sister — Anton was the third child — and they eagerly welcomed the theatrical diversions instigated by Anton. According to the reminiscences of Mikhail, Chekhov's youngest brother, Anton would "direct" his siblings in these domestic productions, which always featured Anton in one of the leading roles.

After the family had moved north to Moscow to avoid bankruptcy due to his father's failed enterprise, Anton was left behind to finish school in Taganrog (in the south of Russia, on the Azov Sea). During those years, Mikhail reports, he frequented the theatre, and was particularly interested in French plays. We also know from Mikhail's memoirs that during this time he began experimenting with the vaudeville form. Mikhail refers to a serious full-length drama he wrote entitled *Fatherless,* as well as several vaudevilles, with titles such as *Laugh It Off If You Can, Why the Hen Clucks,* and *Scythe Strikes Stone,* which he sent to his eagerly awaiting brothers in Moscow. Anton harbored hopes that his eldest brother, Aleksandr, might submit them for publication in the city that was the theatrical mecca of his youthful imagination. Actually, Aleksandr had readings of these plays at the family's tiny flat in Moscow, and sent his younger brother a "critique" offered by his newly acquired literary friends. Mikhail kept those works in safekeeping, but when Anton arrived in Moscow, he tore the drama to pieces. The fate of the unproduced vaudevilles is unknown — Mikhail speculates that the manuscripts may have been lost during Anton's constant moving from place to place during the early Moscow years.

It is significant to note, then, in terms of his development as a dramatist, that between the ages of sixteen and nineteen (1876–79) Chekhov had already written a full-length play and a handful of short comedic works, and that his heart and energies already belonged to the theatre.

THE MOSCOW PERIOD: 1880–1890

> "Do you know how I write my little stories? Here!" He glanced at the table, took the first object that caught his eye — an ashtray — put it in front of me, and said: "Tomorrow, if you like, I'll have a story entitled "The Ashtray." And his eyes lit up with gaiety. Already, images, situations, adventures were floating in his mind, images which had not yet assumed their form, but the humorous muse was already upon him."
>
> *from Korolenko,* Anton Pavlovich Chekhov

> "I cannot recall one single story on which I worked more than a day; *The Huntsman,* which you liked, was even written in a bathhouse! As reporters dash off their notes about fires, so I write my stories, mechanically, unconsciously…"
>
> *to Grigorovich, 3/28/86*

In 1879, Chekhov moved to Moscow to join his family and to enter medical school. The Moscow period (1880-1890) is distinguished as the period, corresponding to Chekhov's twenties, when he wrote the vast majority of his five hundred short stories. What began as a pleasurable pastime — a skill which came naturally and easily — developed into an extraordinary career as a short story writer, from which Chekhov gained critical fame, literary and social recognition, and enough remuneration to support his entire family.

During the period of the early 1880s, the Chekhov family lived in a basement apartment in the Drachovka quarter of Moscow. Chekhov describes his dire circumstances during a period when he was attending medical school, trying to support his family by writing humorous sketches, scurrying from journal to journal to find those who would accept his work, and receiving three kopeks a line for his writings. Sometimes the editors would offer him free theatre tickets or a pair of trousers instead of the promised royalties.

> "...in the next room howls the child of a distant relative who is living with us now, in another room father reads to mother aloud from *Angel of My Memory*...Someone has wound up a music box, and I hear *La Belle Helène*...I feel like running away to the country, but it's already one in the morning...There couldn't be more vile conditions than these for a writer. My bed is occupied by a relative who's just arrived, who keeps on trying to start a conversation with me about medicine. [...] The conditions are incomparable."
>
> *to Leykin, 8/21–24/83*

Somehow, in this chaotic period, Chekhov managed to graduate from medical school and launch a literary career. His rise to fame as a short story writer was meteoric. During the Moscow years he contributed over four hundred sketches, *feuilletons*, pastiches, and stories to almost a dozen periodicals, under a variety of pseudonyms, including "Antosha Chekhonte," "My Brother's Brother," "A Doctor without Patients," "A Man without a Spleen," and "Don Antonio Chekhonte," among others. Four major collections of his short stories: *Tales of Melpomena (1884), Motley Stories (1885), At Twilight (1887),* and *Stories (1888)* were published — the latter two collections by the prestigious publisher Suvorin, Chekhov's mentor and friend. His fame and popularity as a short story writer during the Moscow period culminated with his being awarded the Pushkin prize (1888), and his election to the prestigious Society of Lovers of Russian Literature (1889).

It is difficult to imagine, in this maelstrom of activity, how Chekhov — a young man in his twenties, living with his parents and five siblings, surrounded by family chaos — could have sustained this stunning successful literary career *and* maintained a career as a doctor as well.

> "I am a physician, and I have become absorbed in my medical work, so that no one has been more troubled than I by the proverb about chasing two hares…I am only twenty-six years old. Perhaps I shall still manage to accomplish something, although time flies by so rapidly."
>
> *to Grigorovich, 3/28/86*

> "Medicine is my lawful wife, and literature is my mistress. When I tire of one, I spend the night with the other. While this may be chaotic, at least it's not as boring, and anyway, neither one loses anything by my duplicity. If I didn't have medicine, I'd never devote my spare time and thoughts to literature. I lack discipline."
>
> *to Suvorin, 9/11/88*

In 1886, due to his increasing financial success with his short story writing, Chekhov was able to afford to rent a house for his family on Sadovo-Kudrinskaya Street — his rose-colored "chest of drawers," as he referred to it. This bright-colored, charming little house still stands today, with the sign "A. P. Chekhov: Doctor" on the door, and one can visit the small front room on the first floor, where he admitted patients and also managed, somehow, to write all his stories and the one-act plays.

> "And now, when I recall […] the small sitting room with Chekhov's old mother presiding over the samovar, the affectionate smiles of his sister and brothers, and the atmosphere of a warm, close-knit family surrounding a charming and talented young man with such a joyous outlook on life — I have the feeling it was the happiest, indeed the last happy period in the life of the family as a whole, an idyllic time on the threshold of the drama about to unfold…In Chekhov's expression and demeanor at that time, I seem to remember a sort of duality: There was the carefree Antosha Chekhonte, happy, successful, ready to laugh at the "intellectual caretaker" who advises the kitchen-help to read books, at the barber who, while cutting a client's hair, learns that his sweetheart is going to marry another man, and leaves the client's head unfinished…Images hovered over him, they crowded around him, amusing him…And yet, at

the same time, a perceptible change was taking place...Chekhov himself, as well as his family, could not help realizing that in Antosha's hands lay not only an amusing plaything, useful to the family, but a great gift which might bring with it serious responsibility."

from Korolenko, Anton Pavlovich Chekhov

It is important to note that in 1884, during this period of intense activity, the young Dr. Chekhov, at the age of twenty-four, suffered his first lung hemmorhage, and in 1886, a second one. It was later, with his brother Nikolai's death from consumption in 1889, that the truth began to dawn on him about his own possible diagnosis.

It is therefore difficult to imagine how, during all the turmoil of the Moscow period, the young Dr. Chekhov somehow managed to launch his career as a dramatist! It is, no doubt, testimony to his love for the theatre, which prevailed over all his other activities, and even — for this short time, at least — over the threatening shadow of a serious illness.

The Moscow period is distinguished as an exciting and vigorous period of experimentation for Chekhov, the young dramatist, when he explored with intense determination both the short and long forms, the comedic and the dramatic. During this period, Chekhov wrote three full-length plays and the ten comedic one-act plays included in this collection — an experimental period crucial to his development, which helped him find his mature voice as a dramatist in the unique, and final, four major plays.

The Early Moscow Years: 1880–1885

The Dramatist

A man walks into a doctor's office — a dull-looking type with lustreless eyes and a congested appearance. Judging by the size of his size of his nose and the moody expression on his face, this individual is clearly no stranger to alcoholic beverages, chronic headcolds, and the habit of philosophizing. He sits in the chair and complains of shortness of breath, reflux, heartburn, and an unpleasant taste in his mouth.

"What is your occupation," asks the doctor.

"I am a dramatist!" the individual declares, not without pride.

The doctor, filled with respect for his patient, smiles deferentially.

"What an unusual occupation…" he mutters. "Since that kind of work is purely cerebral, it must be very stressful work."

"Oh, I sup-po-o-ose so…"

"…I'd like to ask you to describe your lifestyle… …your general activities…"

"Fine…" says the playwright. "Well, sir, I get up at about noon …And the very first thing I do is smoke a cigarette and drink two glasses of vodka, sometimes three…I might even take a fourth, depending on how much I drank the day before…"

"Sounds like you drink a lot."

"What do you mean, a lot? What is a lot?…Anyway…after breakfast I drink beer or wine, depending on my finances…Then I go to a tavern…I play a game of billiards…And that's how I pass the time until six o'clock, when it's time to eat again…After dinner, I go to the theatre…"

"Ah…and the theatre, no doubt, gets you agitated!"

"Terrrrrribly! It annoys and upsets me, but all my friends are there, and we drink! So I have a vodka with one, and some red wine with a second, and beer with a third — and by the third act I can hardly stand up…And God only knows how bad *that* is for your nerves…After the theatre I go to 'Salon's' or to some masked ball at 'Rrrodon's'…I'm lucky if I get to bed before morning… Sometimes I'm out all night for a week at a time…Sometimes I don't come home for a month, I forget my own address…"

"Sooo, when do you write your plays?"

"My plays? What do you mean?" the dramatist shrugs his shoulders. "It depends…"

"Would you mind describing your process of playwrighting…"

"Oh…well, first of all, sir, I get a hold of some French or German farce, either by chance or through friends — I don't have time to keep up with all the literature. And if it's any good, then I take it to my sister's or I hire a student for five rubles…Anyway, someone does a translation of it, and I sort of "fix it up" so that it comes out Russian-style…you know, instead of foreign names, I substitute Russian ones, etcetera etcetera. That's all…But how difficult it is! Oh, how difficult!"

The dull individual rolls his eyes and sighs…Meanwhile, the doctor starts tapping, and listening, and feeling, and groping…

1886

The early Moscow period (1880–1885) was indeed one of frenetic activity and intense creativity for Chekhov. And yet, during these early years, busy with the study of medicine, the writing of short stories, and the caring for his family, Chekhov's passion for the theatre increased. At last, he was in Moscow! He could now plunge into the glamorous theatre world of his childhood dreams.

In 1881, Sarah Bernhardt visited Moscow, and Chekhov wrote a review of her performance for a Moscow journal. While he criticized her acting technique, the passion with which he wrote is evident, and the event clarified his own views on the need for a naturalistic style of acting for the Russian stage — a need that, according to Stanislavsky, Chekhov answered one and one-half decades later, by writing his major plays. In 1882, at the age of twenty-two, Chekhov wrote an ecstatic review of *Hamlet* — a play that was to have a profound impact on his development as a dramatist. In this review he called out passionately for Shakespeare to be performed everywhere, so that fresh air might be let in on the stagnant Russian stage.

No sooner did the young Chekhov arrive in Moscow (in 1879, at age nineteen) to join his family and to enter medical school, than he began work on a full-length play. This earliest — and untitled — surviving full-length play, written in 1880–81, which we now refer to as *Platonov*, was never performed during his lifetime. He submitted it to Yermolova, a leading lady at the Maly Theatre, presumably because the Maly was the preeminent theatre of Moscow in the 1880s, and the young Chekhov had set his sights on the most prestigious and glamorous theatrical possibilities. Her rejection of the play prompted the angry Chekhov to tear it up. (Fortunately, his siblings saved the rough draft.) *Platonov* is considered unproducible, for all practical purposes, in its unwieldy, one hundred sixty-four page original state. It is valued today primarily as source material for some of the characterizations and themes of the later plays (versions of *Platonov* are performed from time to time in contemporary European theatre, and Michael Frayn's recent adaptation, *Wild Honey,* is presented today on the English-speaking stage). In terms of his development as a dramatist, however, its significance lies in the fact that Chekhov wrote it while in medical school and under "extreme" domestic conditions — evidence of his passion and determination to be a serious dramatist. At twenty, he was already at work on developing what would be the themes of the later plays.

After *Platonov*, from 1881–85, while Chekhov's career as a writer was focused on the writing of comedic short stories, he also wrote a handful of vaudevilles. Chekhov's brother Mikhail reports that one, entitled *The Nobleman*, was banned by the censors. Mikhail further reports that another, entitled *The Cleanshaven Secretary with the Pistol,* concerns an American prince who takes a poem to an editor and causes a scene when it is rejected! Neither of these two texts remain today. From this early period, a sketch did survive entitled *Impure Tragedians and Leprous Dramatists: A Terribly—Horribly—Scandalously—Desperate Trrrragedy*, published in 1884 in the journal *Budilnik* under one of Chekhov's pseudonyms, "The Brother of My Brother." It is a parody of the drama *Impure and Leprous*, written by K. Tarnovsky (who had translated it from the German). This "theatrical joke" — with its cast of dozens including little green devils, witches and the King of Sweden, beginning with an epilogue followed by six acts, all in the space of four pages! — was written for the joy of parody and the amusement of its anonymous author, and was not meant for production.

Though we have no further information regarding the content of any of the other one-acts during the early Moscow years, their titles suggest that Chekhov was guided by his irrepressible comedic muse, as well as by the popular literary conventions of the day which he parodies in a sketch entitled *Those Things Most Frequently Encountered in Novels, Stories, and Other Such Things* (1880). And we also know that, while he was busy earning money to support his family through the writing of his short stories, as well as studying medicine, his heart continued to be set on the theatre.

The Prolific Moscow Years: 1895–1891

> "When I'm all 'written out,' then I'm going to write vaudevilles and live on them. I believe I could write a hundred a year. Subjects for vaudevilles spout out of me like oil from the depths of Baku."
>
> *to Suvorin, 12/23/88*

> "So now I'm a very popular vaudevillist, am I! My God, how they grab them! If in all my life I somehow succeed in scribbling a dozen empty trifles, I'll thank God for it…This season, I'll write a vaudeville, and that will keep me happy till the summer. Now, is that what you call work?"
>
> *to Leontyev, 11/2/88*

> "Among all the Russians now writing successfully, I am the most light-minded and the least serious; actually, I am now on probation, so to speak; to put it poetically, I loved my pure muse, but I didn't

respect her, I was unfaithful to her, I led her into places which were
unsuitable for her."

to Korolenko, 10/17/87

The chronology of the ten one-act plays written from 1885–1891, against
the backdrop of his other literary efforts, tells a fascinating story in and of itself.
It shows that Chekhov experimented alternatingly with the comedic and tragic,
the short form and the long form. This alternating pattern suggests a duality
within Chekhov himself, and the experimentation with both form and tone was
crucial to his development as a serious writer.

By 1885, the middle of the Moscow period (and the date of the first short
play in this collection), Chekhov's virtuosity and productivity with the short
story form was dazzling. He was writing literally dozens per year in the mid-'80s,
and his popularity was soaring. In the year 1885 alone, he wrote over one hundred short stories! In 1884, *Tales of Melpomena*, the first collection of humorous stories by Antosha Chekhonte, was published. In 1885, the second
collection, *Motley Stories,* was published. In 1885, Chekhov also met Suvorin,
the editor of St. Petersburg's influential *Novoe Vremya (New Times)* and began
one of the most important relationships of his literary career as well as an intimate correspondence containing his most compelling letters about life, art, and
literature.

The fact that the first short play of the Moscow period in this collection,
On the High Road (1885), is entitled a "dramatic study," that it contains elements of tragedy and melodrama, and that it was written during a time of
tremendous output of the comedic short stories — strongly indicates Chekhov's
continuing determination to try his hand at serious drama. This is also reflected
by a number of serious short stories he wrote during this period, as well. *On the
High Road* is an adaptation of an earlier short story, *In Autumn* (1883). It is the
only one-act play of this period devoid of comedic elements. It was presented
to the censorial board in May, 1885, and rejected for performance in September
as being too depressing and sordid in theme and therefore unsuitable for performance. Mikhail, Chekhov's brother, reports that on the copy of the rejected
play the censor had written the word "barin" (meaning "master," "gentleman")
in blue pencil — referring to the principal character in the play. Mikhail spec-
ulated that it was considered improper by the censors to represent a desperate,
drunken "barin" onstage. It was not published during Chekhov's lifetime.

Chekhov returned to the comedic vein for his next attempt at writing a
play in the short form — a pattern of taking refuge in comedy after serious dramatic attempts that was to repeat itself throughout his career. Perhaps it was

because of his experience with the censorial board over *On the High Road*, or perhaps he had more confidence holding the pen of "Antosha Chekhonte," whose work he knew would be published. In any event, this time he chose to write in the monologue form. He wrote *On the Harmful Effects of Tobacco* on February 14, 1886, and described it in the playfully trivializing tone which characterized all commentary about his one-act plays:

> "I've just finished my monologue *On the Harmful Effects of Tobacco* which in my heart of hearts was meant for the comedic actor Gradov-Sokolov. Having only two and a half hours at my disposal, I spoiled this monologue and…sent it, not to the devil, but to the *Petersburg Gazette*. My intentions were honorable, but the execution turned out to be 'horriblissimo'!"
>
> *to Bilibin, 2/14/86*

This first draft was published only two weeks later in the *Petersburg Gazette*, on February 17, 1886, under the name of "Antosha Chekhonte."

What is fascinating to note is that, over the next sixteen years, Chekhov returned to this monologue no less than *five times* to write yet another draft of it — an act prompted each time not by external influences such as criticism but rather by some powerful internal urge to revisit the theme of this remarkable little play. That is to say, as his illness progressed, as his life darkened, as his insights into the meaning of life and his understanding of human nature and the human condition matured, and as the Russia around him was slowly, inexorably moving toward its ultimate destiny, the one play that he returned to again and again to rewrite and refine according to his developing *weltanschauung* was this little monologue, *On the Harmful Effects of Tobacco*. In this repeated act, there is a profound insight to be gained into the soul of the dramatist, and the tragicomedic vision of life he was developing. With each revision, the originally comedic material is overshadowed by the tragic. It is as if this rewriting process were a metaphor for the spirit of the dramatist himself.

With his consistently characteristic offhandedness, Chekhov announced his next one-act play, in a letter to Maria Kisileva. In it, he himself explains his reasons for writing in the short form.

> "I've written a four-page play. The running time is probably fifteen to twenty minutes. It's the shortest drama on earth. The famous actor Davydov is going to perform it; he's working at the Korsh Theatre now. It will be published in *The Season*, and so it will get

around. [...] My play took me an hour and five minutes to write.
I started another one, but I didn't finish it; I just don't have the
time."

to Kisileva, 1/14/87

The play, entitled *Calchas*, was adapted by Chekhov from his short story
Calchas (1886), and was completed by January 14, 1887, the date of the above
letter. (Calchas is a minor character in Shakespeare's *Troilus and Cressida*). The
play was first performed at the Korsh in Moscow on February 19, 1888. He
made subsequent revisions of it later on that year and retitled it *Swan Song* for
its second production at the Maly Theatre, starring its leading actor, Lensky.
(Again, it is significant to note that, as with *On the Harmful Effects of Tobacco*,
the first draft of *Swan Song* was largely light and comedic, but with the revisions, Chekhov sought to deepen the tone and fill out the characterizations.)

"A few days ago Jean Shcheglov brought you my one-act play
Calchas or *Swan Song*. Would you please have it read by the literary
committee [Dramatic and Literary Committee of the Imperial
Theatres] and approved [for performances on the Imperial Stage]?
The play has little merit and I do not think it important in any way,
but Lensky wants to act in it, no matter what, at the Maly Theatre.
So therefore I ask you, not as much on my behalf as on his. If it's
not approved, then you will catch hell from Lucifer and his angels
in the other world. [...] If I were ever a member of that committee,
I'd veto it ruthlessly."

to Pleshcheev, 10/17/88

"I have changed the title of *Calchas* to *Swan Song*. It's a long, bittersweet title, but I could not think of another one, however hard I
tried. Forgive me that I've spent so much time on this play. The fact
of the matter is that it's had to pass through two purgatories: the
censor and the [literary] committee. If it weren't for the censor,
you'd have had it in your hands long ago."

to Lensky, 10/26/88

For Chekhov, 1887–1889 would be the period of his life marking his most
intense involvement with the theatre. His passion found expression in a veritable outpouring of writing, both of plays and of letters, and his extensive correspondence of the period dealt eloquently and compellingly with a variety of

topics pertaining to life, art, literature, drama, and the state of the Russian theatre. The catalyst for this prolific period was the writing of *Ivanov* — the event that opened the floodgates of theatre activity for him. The Korsh Theatre expressed a desire to commission a full-length drama from Chekhov in September, 1887.

> "I have already been to the Korsh Theatre twice, and on both occasions Korsh tried to persuade me to write a play for him. I answered: with pleasure. The actors assured me that I would write a good one because I'm able to play on people's nerves. I responded: *merci*. And, of course, I will *not* write a play…I don't want to have anything to do with theatres, nor with the public, for that matter. To hell with them!"
>
> *to Kisileva, 9/13/87*

And yet, within a month, he presented the Korsh Theatre with *Ivanov!* He boasted of writing it in ten days, and was proud that the Korsh found no errors in it (and that they even admired his stage directions!). Chekhov was highly excited — at last, his first serious drama was to be staged. Even the devoted Aleksandr wearied of reading about *Ivanov* in his brother's feverish letters. Chekhov grew so agitated over what he reported to be the actors' wild and uncontrollable behavior at rehearsals that his friends advised him to keep away. When opening night finally arrived on November 19, 1887, despite Chekhov's reports of ad-libbing and drunkenness in the company, there were many curtain calls between the acts, and at the end, there was an uproar in the audience. Chekhov was thrilled! In a letter to Aleksander, he ecstatically reported that

> "…at the first performance there was such excitement in the audience and backstage, the likes of which the prompter hadn't seen in all his thirty-two years in the theatre. The sensation, the stir, the racket, the applause, the booing! In the buffet a fistfight broke out, and in the gallery, the students wanted to throw somebody else out, and the police had to evict them all. There was general pandemonium. Our sister almost fainted…[…] Am I boring you with all this? I believe that I've been psychotic the whole month of November."
>
> Yours, Schiller Shakespearovich Goethe"
> *(to Aleksandr, 11/24/87)*

Chekhov's popularity had reached its zenith. He was finally receiving the recognition he craved as a serious dramatist, and his signature of "Schiller Shakespearovich Goethe" to the above letter attests to his tremendous excitement. News reached him that he was being considered for the Pushkin Prize, society ladies were pursuing him, the distinguished artist Repin invited him to his studio, he was wined and dined by the *literati*...Chekhov was living the life in the theatre he had dreamed of.

The 1888 and 1889 seasons were ones of even more feverish theatrical activity for Chekhov. In a little over a year and a half, from February, 1888 to October, 1889, Chekhov wrote five of his vaudevilles: *The Bear, The Proposal, Tatyana Repina, The Tragedian in Spite of Himself,* and *The Wedding.* During that period, he also rewrote *Ivanov, Calchas* (now retitled *Swan Song*), and *On the Harmful Effects of Tobacco.*

The very same month that *Swan Song* also opened at the Korsh (2/19/88) Chekhov sat down and wrote *The Bear.*

> "Having nothing better to do, I have written a trival little farce in
> the French style called *The Bear*... Alas! When they find out at the
> *Northern Herald* that I write vaudevilles, I'll become their *bête noir.*
> What am I to do? Can I help it if my hands are itching to write pure
> 'tra-la-la'?"
>
> *to Polonsky, 2/22/88*

Chekhov wrote it for Solovtsov, his good friend and star actor at the Korsh. Chekhov had seen Solovtsov in a French vaudeville, *Les Jirons de Cadillac* (written in 1865 by Pierre Berton), which was playing that year in Moscow. In this play, an elegant lady offers to marry her boorish (but warm-hearted) suitor, provided that he control his penchant for uttering profanities. Though he fails her test, she is charmed, and accepts his offer by uttering one of his own great oaths. Solovtsov was huge, with a booming voice, and Chekhov liked him so much that he decided to write the part of a "Russian Bear" for him. After Suvorin published *The Bear* in the *Novoe Vremya (New Times)* in August, the play received a negative report from the censor, which deplored the triviality of the subject matter but permitted it to be performed, subject to the expunging of certain "rude" language. It received its debut on October 28, 1888, at the Korsh Theatre in Moscow, with Solovtsov as the "Bear," and was a resounding success. Chekhov was ecstatic!

"Now about *The Bear*. Solovtsov [Smirnov] played the role phenomenally. Rybchinskaya [Popova] did just fine; she was lovely. There was continuous and uproarious laughter throughout; the monologues were interrupted by applause. After the first and second performances, the author and the actors were called out for the curtain call. All the dear critics, except for Vasilyev, praised it ... After the first performance we had an unfortunate incident. The coffeepot killed my *Bear*. Rybchinskaya was drinking coffee, and the coffee pot burst from too much steam and scalded her face. Glama played her role at the second performance, and she was fine. But then she left for St. Petersburg, and so my furry teddy bear died, unfortunately. It didn't even live to be three days old. Rybchinskaya promises to be well by Sunday."

to Leontyev, 11/2/88

"Well, I've succeeded in writing a foolish vaudeville, which because of its foolishness is a big success. Vasilyev [a critic] [...] tore it to pieces, but the public is in seventh heaven. They can't stop laughing in the theatre."

to Kiseleva, 11/2/88

"At the Korsh, the public is roaring with laughter [at *The Bear*], they can't stop, even though Solovtsov and Rybchinskaya aren't acting well at all. My sister and I could play it better."

to Suvorin, 11/7/88

"My *Bear* is a huge success in Moscow, although the he-bear and the she-bear are playing their roles rather badly."

to Pleshcheev, 11/10/88

The Bear would prove to be the most popular play of his career, and one that produced him a steady income for years to come. (It was, parenthetically, the play of Chekhov that Tolstoy liked the most! As for his full-length plays, Tolstoy once allegedly told Chekhov: "Shakespeare wrote badly, but you write worse.")

"I live on the charity of my *Bear* and Suvorin, who has bought me for a hundred rubles' worth of stories for his "Cheap Library." Heaven preserve them both."

to Pleshcheev, 1/15/89

"My *Bear* should really be called the "milch cow." It has brought me more money than any of my short stories. Oh, the public!"

to Sakharovoy, 1/13/89

"A gypsy would not have gotten as much [money] from a live bear as I got from a dead one. I've received five hundred rubles for my beast."

to Suvorin, 3/6/89

"I am waiting for them to finish threshing and sell the rye, and till then I shall live on my *Bear* and on mushrooms…"

to Suvorin, 8/16/92

Delighted with the success of *The Bear*, Chekhov sat down and wrote *The Proposal* a few months later (October, 1888), the next vaudeville of this prolific period. It was published in December, and premiered in St. Petersburg on April 12, 1889, where it also became extremely popular.

"I've scribbled a worthless little vaudeville especially for the provinces called *The Proposal,* and sent it to the censor. […] If, my angel, you happen to be at the censor's, then tell [them] that […] I humbly beseech the censorial "hydra" not to keep the vaudeville in quarantine. It's a wretched, vulgar, boring little skit, but it will be fine for the provinces…I won't put it on in the capitals [Moscow and St. Petersburg], though."

to Leontyev, 11/7/88

It was performed before the tsar at Tsarskoe Selo, his summer residence, in August, 1889.

"They wrote me that Svobodin was superb in *The Proposal*, which was put on at the Tsarskoe Selo; he and Varlamov managed to get something out of a bad little play, which prompted even the tsar to pay me a compliment in public. I await the order of Stanislav and appointment as a member of the State Council."

to Leontyev, 8/29/88

"…Davydov wants to play in *The Proposal* at the Alexandrinsky Theatre, at least that's what he told me. Ask him. If he's not counting on it, then I give you *carte blanche*. Make of my notoriously stupid play what you like; roll cigarettes out of it for all I care."

to Leontyev, 3/11/89

Meanwhile, in the midst of all this frantic activity, Chekhov was revising *Ivanov* for its upcoming Petersburg production, and was frustrated with the process. (He now referred to the play as "Bolvanov" — meaning "dummy".) He was deeply relieved when he finished these revisions at the end of 1888.

> "I have just completed my "Bolvanov" and am sending it to you. I'm sick of it…[…] At least now my Mr. Ivanov is much more intelligible. The finale does not entirely satisfy me (except for the shot, everything pales), but I console myself with the thought that it is not yet in final form. […] I give you my word that never again shall I write such an intellectual and vile play as *Ivanov*."

to Suvorin, 12/19/88

Ivanov opened again in St. Petersburg in January 31, 1889. By that time, Chekhov had grown to dislike it deeply. Despite the positive reviews for his rewritten version, Chekhov felt that the public did not understand his hero, and that the intelligentsia did not accept the play. He was growing increasingly insecure about his own abilities as a serious dramatist. Again, Chekhov sought refuge and release from this anxiety in the writing of his short comedies.

> "I still lack a political, religious, and philosophical world view — it keeps changing every month, so I'll have to limit myself to the description of how my heroes love, marry, give birth, die, and how they speak."

to Grigorovich, 10/9/88

At the end of this theatre-filled year of 1888, Chekhov helped to advise his publisher, Suvorin, on the dramaturgy and the production at the Maly Theatre of Suvorin's own new play, *Tatyana Repina*, a four-act, reportedly turgid melodrama. Suvorin had based his play on a true story (occuring in 1881) of the well-known Russian actress Eulalia Kadmina, who actually poisoned herself intentionally so that she could die onstage in a production of Ostrovsky's *Vasilisa Meletyeva* in Kharkov — and all this to punish her unfaithful lover who was present in the audience. She was playing the role of the wife of Ivan the Terrible in Ostrovsky's play, which called for her character to be poisoned.

According to reports, she died onstage in terrible agony, and the audience was overwhelmed by what was thought to be her remarkable acting, until at last the performers as well as the spectators realized what had actually happened! Mikhail Chekhov, who subsequently saw a performance of Suvorin's play at the Maly in Moscow, with Yermolova playing Tatyana Repina, reported that the audience was so agitated that many ladies went into hysterics, and the actors could hardly be heard.

According to Mikhail, his brother Anton was a great connoisseur of church literature. He knew the Bible perfectly and was familiar with the unusually ornate texts of the church ritual, from his days of compulsory church attendance in Taganrog imposed by his father. In fact, says Mikhail, Chekhov kept a small library of church ritual and service books. Just for his own amusement, he sat down with the text of the marriage service, and wrote a one-act play whose action was a continuation of Suvorin's *Tatyana Repina!* Intending it as a practical joke, he presented it as a gift to Suvorin.

> "I enclose…the very cheap and useless present that I promised you. I shall be bored by your dictionaries, so you may as well be bored by my present. I wrote it in a hurry, in only one sitting, so it's absolutely worthless. As for my using your title, you'd better take me to court. Don't show it to *anyone*, and throw it in the fire when you've finished it. Or else throw it in the fire unread."
>
> *to Suvorin, 3/6/89*

Chekhov's play was never produced (he knew it wouldn't have been, anyway — a play calling for a religious rite to be staged would never have passed the censors!) but Suvorin had two bound copies made exclusively, containing both his and Chekhov's versions — one for himself and one for his protégé, the practical jokester.

The St. Petersburg production of *Ivanov* had opened in January, 1889, and brought positive reviews, but Chekhov was still not satisfied. He continued taking refuge in the short comedic one-acts. In 1889, Chekhov wrote two more vaudevilles, both adaptations of short stories. On May 4, he completed *The Tragedian in Spite of Himself* for the famous St. Petersburg actor K. A. Varlamov (1848–1915). The story from which he adapted the play is *One of Many* (1887).

> "Last night I suddenly remembered promising Varlamov to write him a vaudeville. I wrote it today, and I've already sent it off. What a harvesting is going on here! And you write that I've grown lazy!"
>
> *to Suvorin, 5/4/89*

> "A day or two ago, I remembered promising Varlamov last winter to turn one of my stories into a play. I sat straight down and did it — rather badly. From a story on a stale and trite theme, a stale and feeble farce is born. It's called *The Tragedian in Spite of Himself*."
>
> *to Leontyev, 5/6/89*

By now well-prepared, Chekhov edited it for the censors. It was first published in the journal *Artist* in April, 1890. It received its first performance on October 1, 1889, in St. Petersburg.

By this time, Chekhov was feeling the cumulative effects of his vaudevilles' popularity — and delighting in all the theatrical intrigue.

> "...I am invited everywhere; they wine and dine me all over town as if I were a general at a wedding; my sister is indignant since she is invited everywhere because she is the sister of a writer. No one wants to love us for our ordinary selves. And therefore, it follows that if tomorrow we should appear as mere mortals in the eyes of our good friends, they will cease to love us and will merely pity us."
>
> *to Suvorin, 11/24–25/88*

> "There is a whole revolution going on with my vaudevilles. *The Proposal* has been playing at Gorevaya's [Theatre] — and I took it out of the repertoire; The Korsh Theatre is fighting with the Abramov Theatre over *The Bear* — the former is claiming exclusive rights to the play to no avail, while at the latter, Solovtsov [the actor] says that *The Bear* belongs to him, since he's performed in it one thousand eight hundred and seventeen times. Even the devil couldn't sort this one out! Meanwhile, the Maly Theatre is offended that *Ivanov* is playing at the Korsh Theatre, and Lensky [the actor] hasn't been to see me yet — he's probably angry with me. What a mess you've got on your hands, o statesman of the theatre!"
>
> *to Leontyev, 9/18/89*

He next wrote *The Wedding*, in October 1889. It is an amalgam of three earlier stories: *The Marriage Season* (1881), *Marrying for Money* (1884), and *A Wedding with a General* (1884). Chekhov may also have had this one-act play in mind after the experience of living for a year (1885) with his family in quarters above which was a flat often rented out for weddings. His brothers and friends would amuse themselves by improvising a wedding party and dancing to the music, while a real wedding was taking place in the flat above! *The Wedding* also satisfied Chekhov's love of poking fun at the merchant class, with which he was all too familiar from his childhood in Taganrog. He had written a series of humorous articles that appeared in a monthly Moscow journal, *Oskolki (Fragments)*, poking fun at various aspects of Moscow society — including the passion that merchants have for generals and civil servants, without whom, according to Chekhov, they couldn't possibly hold their weddings and other social occasions. He submitted the play to the censors, who required changes that included the omission of a prolonged kiss!

The Wedding was produced several times by amateur, provincial theatres, and eventually made its way to Moscow, where the Society of Arts and Literature included a performance of it in a "Chekhov Evening" on December 16, 1900, which also included *The Bear* (a month before *The Three Sisters* premiered). According to reports by Olga Knipper, Tolstoy attended the evening and laughed heartily during both *The Wedding* and *The Bear* (obviously, an important literary occasion!). It then was performed at the Alexandrinsky Theatre in St. Petersburg in 1902, on the same stage where *The Seagull* had been hissed and booed at six years earlier, in 1896.

Meanwhile, throughout 1889, Chekhov worked intermittently on his third full-length play, *The Wood Demon*. He described it as a "big comedy-novel" with "nice, healthy people," a "lyrical" style, and a "happy ending" (to Pleshcheev, 9/30/89). In the letter, he also said that he was seeking to achieve "literary significance" — a sign that again he was experimenting. While it was not wholly successful dramaturgically, the play's value is that it served as a draft for at least one-half of *Uncle Vanya* seven years later. The *Wood Demon* was rejected by the Alexandrinsky Theatre because of its copious dialogue and absence of action, according to the theatre's literary committee. He was advised to confine his literary efforts to the writing of short stories.

Chekhov was secretly hurt by the Alexandrinsky Theatre's rejection. His dear friend Solovtsov (*The Bear*) loved *The Wood Demon*, however, and thanks to him, the Moscow Abramov Theatre produced it. It opened on December 27, 1889, and received uniformly discouraging reviews. Chekhov was deeply embittered. The years 1887–89, with his constant involvement with the theatre, had been the happiest of his life. He was the theatrical toast of Moscow, and had achieved success and recognition. Now, however, Chekhov sank into disenchantment, disillusionment, and self-doubt as to his true purpose — to be a serious writer of full-length plays. He had reached a point of spiritual *ennui*.

"I don't have much passion. Add to this the following psychopathic symptom: over the past two years, and for no particular reason, I've grown tired of seeing my works in print, have become indifferent to reviews, to talks on literature, to gossip, successes, failures, big fees — in short, I've turned into an utter fool. There is a sort of stagnation in my soul."

to Suvorin, 5/4/89

That year (1889), a cartoon appeared in the literary journal *Oskolki (Fragments)*. The drawing depicted Chekhov driving a cart drawn by three figures — Ivanov, a bear, and a wood demon. The cart stood at a crossroads whose signs indicate "Road to Prose" and "Road to Drama." The reports were that Chekhov took it good-naturedly, but it must have confirmed what he felt so acutely to be the public's misunderstanding of his true intent.

This three-year period of whirlwind theatre activity (1887–89) had brought Chekhov enormous popularity and recognition, placing him in the front ranks of Russian writers by the age of twenty-eight. In 1888 he was awarded the prestigious Pushkin prize (and with it, five hundred rubles) by the Imperial Academy of Sciences in Petersburg. In 1889 he was elected to the Society of Lovers of Russian Literature. But none of this could assuage the frustration at not yet finding his serious dramatic voice.

"…everything I have written, everything I received the prize for, will live no more than ten years in people's memories."

to Suvorin, 10/10/88

"I did not know how to write a play…If on paper my characters [in *Ivanov*] have not come out alive and clear, the fault is not in them but in my inability to express my thoughts. It means that it is still too early for me to start writing plays."

to Suvorin, 12/30/88

"I think that if I were to live another forty years, and read, read, read, and learn to write talentedly — i.e., concisely — at the end of that time I would fire on you all with so great a cannon that the heavens would tremble. But for now I am but a Lilliputian, like the rest."

to Suvorin, 4/8/89

In June, 1889, Chekhov's brother Nikolai died of consumption. Despite his own two lung hemorrhages in 1884 and 1886, the great successes had temporarily obscured a growing concern about his own health. Now, however, his own brother had died of the illness that, as a doctor, he must have suspected he also might have. This possibility was too threatening to face. Enervated by the days he spent by Nikolai's bedside, and acutely disappointed by *Ivanov* and *The Wood Demon*, he longed to escape.

The year 1890 marks the end of the glorious Moscow period — when, disenchanted with "*le tout Moscou*," as he called it, and with the shadow of consumption ever lengthening over him, Chekhov left Moscow to undertake the arduous overland journal to the Pacific Coast, to visit the Isle of Sakhalin and study the penal codes there. Chekhov, the doctor and humanitarian, was prescribing Chekhov, the young dramatist, with a temporary cure for his *ennui*.

> The thought of Moscow with its cold climate, bad plays, buffets, and Russian "ideas" frightens me. I wish I could spend the winter far, far away.
>
> *to Pleshcheev, 8/13/88*

Transition: 1890–91

> "In January I'm turning thirty. Hail, lonely old age; burn, useless life."
>
> *to Suvorin, 12/7/89*

Chekhov returned only twice more to the vaudeville form (not including his final revision of *On the Harmful Effects of Tobacco*, an effort with special meaning that will be addressed later in this introduction). Back in Moscow after Sakhalin and a brief visit to Europe, Chekhov wrote *The Jubilee*, an adaptation of his short story, *A Helpless Creature* (1887). He completed it in December, 1891, and its elements of biting satire reveal a darker Chekhov than the one who wrote the earlier vaudevilles. The censors approved it that same month, and it was published in February, 1892.

His final, unfinished vaudeville, *The Night before the Trial*, was written sometime in the 1890s. Literary historians are unsure of the date; some place it in 1891. Chekhov based it on the story of the same name (written in 1886), and did not complete it. This unfinished piece shows a vaudevillian style and spirit similar to that of *The Bear* and *The Proposal*.

The fact that he never completed it suggests that while Chekhov loved writing vaudevilles, the early '90s was a peculiar period of metamorphosis for him. His mood was changing. The hiatus between *The Wood Demon* (1889), the last full-length play of the Moscow period, and the writing of *The Seagull* (1895), the first of the major plays of the Melikhovo and Yalta periods, was six years. During that time Chekhov experienced an intense disenchantment with Moscow life. Deeply dissatisfied with his revision of *Ivanov*, ashamed of *The Wood Demon* (he asked that it never be published), saddened by the loss of his brother, burdened by living with his family, Moscow became the personification of his *ennui*.

After his long journey to Sakhalin and subsequent visit to Europe, he was only back in Moscow for a short period before he purchased his "estate" in Melikhovo (March, 1892), where he intended to retreat from Moscow and his family and write. The impulse to write vaudevilles had been tied to the excitement and the immediacy of Moscow theatre life. With the process of separating out from Moscow, the prolific period of writing vaudevilles was past. He was no longer "Antosha Chekhonte," nor did he really want to be "Schiller Shakespearovitch Goethe." And he was not yet sure of the direction of the dramatist Anton Chekhov.

The same month in which Chekhov wrote *The Jubilee*, he wrote a *feuilleton* entitled *In Moscow,* which was published in *Novoe Vremya* under a pseudonym on December 7, 1891. Having just returned from Sakhalin, his disgust with the Russian intelligentsia and with Moscow life seemed to have intensified. This "article," as it was so called, is unique in the Chekhovian oeuvre — while written like an essay, it reads almost like a dramatic monologue. With its chilly, ennui-laden perspective, one hears Chekhov's own voice of disaffection with Moscow life. It sounds like his own "swan song" to a period and a place in his life he had outgrown. Like a disenchanted lover, Chekhov felt that his merry mistress, the theatre, had deceived him, and Moscow, the place of his love affair, was too much of a reminder. And thus, he was saying good-bye to the object of his intense affections: a gay and frivolous period in his life and literature that now no longer suited his darkening *weltanschauung*. And with no regret...

> "...sketches, *feuilletons,* nonsense, vaudevilles, boring stories, masses of mistakes and absurdities, pounds of paper I've scribbled on, an academic prize, the life of a Potemkin — and out of all of this not even one line that, to my mind, contains any serious literary value. A mass of forced labor, and not one moment of serious work. [...] How I long to hide away somewhere for five years or so and do some serious, painstaking work. I need to study, learn everything

from scratch, because as a writer I'm a complete and utter ignora-
mus; I need to write conscientiously, with feeling and intelligence,
not five reams a month but one ream every five months."

to Suvorin, 12/20/89 (approx.)

•   •   •

CHEKHOV AND THE VAUDEVILLE GENRE

"We need new forms, we must have new forms, and if we don't,
then we may as well have nothing at all."

Konstantin Gavrilovich Treplev in The Seagull, *Act I*

When the young playwright Konstantin Gavrilovich Treplev explodes with
rage in Act I of *The Seagull* over the ridicule of his play, Arkadina's spontaneous
response to her son is that he himself had told her that it was only a "shutka"
(meaning "farce," or "joke"), so what else could he expect from his audience?
Though we do not hear Treplev describe his play as such firsthand, we can take
his mother's word for it, for it is not unlike the practices of Treplev's own cre-
ator, the dramatist Chekhov himself, to trivialize his efforts by employing a
non-serious dramatic form, thereby misleading his audience as to his true inten-
tions — as well as protecting himself from failure in the attempt to create new
forms for the theatre.

Like his character Treplev, Anton Chekhov fervently longed to make his
mark on the Russian theatre scene with "new forms." With his first two serious
attempts, however, he knew he was not yet ready to write full-length plays "of
literary significance," as he put it. The vaudeville was the most popular form of
comedy in the Russian theatre, and Chekhov, who knew the vaudeville from his
youthful days in Taganrog, was drawn to it naturally, with a sense of ease and
confidence.

And so it happened that it was not initially through the writing of serious,
full-length plays, but rather through the short comedic plays, that Chekhov created new forms for a theatre he loved, and for a theatre that so desperately
needed them.

"The contemporary theatre is like a rash, a bad urban disease. It is necessary to sweep away this disease with a broom; to like it is not healthy. You'll start arguing with me and repeating the same old saying: the theatre is a school, it educates, and so on and so on…But I'll tell you what I see: the present theatre is not above the crowd — on the contrary, the life of the crowd is above the theatre, more clever than the theatre, even! Therefore, that means the theatre is not a school, but something else…"

to Leontyev 11/7/88

"The modern theatre is a world of confusion. Nonsense, stupidity, and idle talk."

to Leontyev, 11/11/88

"The conviction that the 'eighties' have not produced a single writer may in itself provide material enough for five volumes…"

to Suvorin, 12/23/88

The Moscow theatre scene of the 1880s was one characterized by conventionalism, conservatism, and creative torpor. There were two kinds of theatres at the time: the Imperial Theatre, and the privately owned theatres of Moscow and St. Petersburg. According to the description of Moscow theatre life by Nemirovich-Danchenko (a co-founder of the Moscow Art Theatre in this same decade), even the offerings of the Maly, Moscow's preeminent theatre, at the height of its fame in the 1880s, had become stale and conventional. The repertoire was predictable, dominated primarily by Ostrovsky, a prolific Russian dramatist of the mid-nineteenth century, and established European classics by dramatists such as Schiller and Hugo. As far as new plays were concerned, there were several writers-in-residence at the Maly whose task it was to write expressly for the company's leading actors and actresses (Yermolova, who had rejected *Platonov*, was one of the company). If they fulfilled this priority, these playwrights' positions were secure, and they had only to inform the resident director when a new play would be ready and how to cast it, and it appeared in the repertoire. But these were not the great dramatists of the day, as Nemirovich pointed out. And there was no artistic leadership — the theatre was run by an administrator appointed by the government, not an artist, and the stage director had no creative power or function.

The Russian theatre was stagnating in the 1880s, Nemirovich-Danchenko lamented. There were no visionaries on the horizon to lead the Russian theatre into new artistic territory. And there was no system of identifying, nurturing and developing serious new dramatists for the stage. To Nemirovich's complaints about the Maly, Chekhov added his own observations about the other Moscow theatres — the mediocrity of the new playwrights; the low level of production values; the uneducated, ill-prepared and often inebriated actors. Later, in the first of the four major plays, *The Seagull*, the young playwright Treplev would summarize the Russian theatre of the 1880s as Chekhov saw it:

> "Every evening, when the curtain goes up, and there, under the bright lights, in a room with three walls, those celebrated artists, those high priests of our sacred art, when they play it all out before us, how we mortals eat, and drink, and love, and go around wearing our clothes and leading our lives; when out of this vulgar scenario we are served up some kind of message or moral, however meagre, ready for our daily domestic consumption; when after its one thousandth incarnation all these plays seem to me to be the same, time after time after time the same, then I flee — I flee, like Maupassant fled the Eiffel Tower, because it outraged him how enormously trite it was."
>
> *Konstantin Gavrilovich Treplev in* The Seagull, *Act, I*

As for the theatre of the Russian provinces in the 1880s — the theatre of Treplev's actress-mother, Arkadina, in *The Seagull*, the repertoire in which she performed consisted of revivals of foreign plays, second-rate "formula" plays, melodramas, farces, and vaudevilles.

The Vaudeville Tradition

It was to the vaudeville that Chekhov naturally gravitated. By the 1880s, when the young Chekhov arrived in Moscow, the vaudeville (i.e., Russian adaptations of the French genre) was one of the most popular forms on the Moscow stage. This "rage" for the vaudeville, so to speak, had been developing in Russia since the end of the previous century, when the vaudeville had arrived from France. (A full accounting of the origin and development of the Russian vaudeville can be found in Vera Gottlieb's study, *Chekhov and the Vaudeville* [see bibliography].)

The French vaudeville itself was a popular, eclectic "low comedy" form, with elements of song, dance, burlesque, farce, and satire (the word "vaudeville" may be derived from *voix de villes* — "song of the city streets"). It had its origins in the little theatres of the Paris fairs, and by the end of the seventeeth century, was a recognized comedic genre. In the eighteenth century, the popular vaudeville resembled musical comedy or light opera, often parodying plays of the legitimate French theatre.

By the end of the eighteenth and beginning of the nineteenth century, translations and adaptations of French vaudevilles began to appear on the Russian stage. Also at that time, during the reign of Tsar Nicholas I (1825–1855), a stern censorial board was created for the theatre. This presented a unique challenge for contemporary Russian dramatists, who found that they could circumvent this daunting obstacle with the vaudeville form, since only plays of pure entertainment value could escape the censorship. Thus, contemporary Russian writers began to write vaudevilles so that their work could be produced, even well-known writers such as Krylov and Griboedov. And so the vaudeville, ironically, became one of the few outlets for the serious new dramatist in Russia.

The vaudeville flooded the Russian stage in the 1830s and 1840s. By midnineteenth century, it had progressed from a curtain-raiser into a one-act play in its own right, and became a staple form of theatrical entertainment in the Russian theatre's repertoire, as well as a "star vehicle." An example of the vaudeville's enormous popularity was that, in 1840, according to Gottlieb's study, ten out of the twenty-five plays in that season's repertoire at the famous Aleksandrinsky Theatre in St. Petersburg were vaudevilles. No wonder that, by 1896, when *The Seagull* had its ill-starred premiere at the Aleksandrinsky, its audience was outraged that the tradition of light comedic and broadly popular fare was spoiled by this incomprehensible new piece of "symbolic decadence!"

When Chekhov arrived in Moscow, the Russian vaudeville was just as he described it in his sketch *The Dramatist* (see page eight of this introduction) — that is, generally translated from French and German vaudevilles (and not very good ones) with superficial themes, little moral and social content, and no "Russian" flavor other than the characters' names which had been substituted for the foreign ones. The musical and dance elements of the eighteenth century vaudeville had gradually faded away, as well as the couplets. The Russian vaudeville of the 1880s was based on a fairly fixed formula according to the following conventions: stock settings (landowners' mansions); stock characters (landowners, damsels-in-distress, the odd relative, the old servant, etc.); formulaic plots (a couple-in-love overcoming obstacles, with a relative or servant as sidekick or foil); and rapid-paced action, culminating in the happy ending. By this time, the Russian vaudeville, a popular form for almost a century, was in a state of ossification.

The stagnant Russian theatre of the 1880s was ready for new forms and new voices. The timing of Chekhov's arrival on the scene was opportune.

Chekhov's Contribution to the Vaudeville

> "It is much easier to write a play about Socrates than about a young girl or a cook. Which merely shows that I do not consider the writing of vaudevilles a frivolous occupation. Nor do you consider it as such, much as you may pretend that it is nothing but a lot of frivolous nonsense. If the vaudeville is nonsense, then a five-act play by such a man as Burenin is nonsense."
>
> *to Suvorin, 1/2/94*

In his letters, Chekhov referred to all his short comedies as "vodevily" (vaudevilles), whether he subtitled them "farces" *(The Bear, The Proposal, The Tragedian in Spite of Himself, The Jubilee)*, "dramatic studies" *(Swan Song)*, "monologues" *(On the Harmful Effects of Tobacco)* or "one-act plays" *(The Wedding)*. (He clearly subtitled *Tatyana Repina* "a drama" as a practical joke!)

Chekhov's consistent use of the term "vaudeville" seems to indicate his true intention — to set up audience expectations to be entertained and amused according to certain existing theatrical conventions, and to inform the censors, the critics, and the *literati* that the author was presenting a popular, second-rate theatrical form that was not to be taken seriously. This literary subterfuge, or disguise, appealed to the practical joker in him. On one level, he was indeed writing vaudevilles, whose purpose was to entertain, divert, and amuse. This provided a smokescreen, a handy camoflauge for the young humorist, to have the freedom and flexibility to experiment with the short theatrical form without serious consequences, as he was finding his dramatist's voice. It also provided him with the opportunity to surprise and delight the public by subverting the conventional form with innovative dramatic techniques and devices. And it was thus that Chekhov elevated a conventional, stale, second-rate form into an art form, thereby contributing something fresh, new, and exciting for the contemporary Russian theatre.

Chekhov's familiarity with the contemporary Russian theatre prompted him to want to break away from its stale conventions.

"One cannot keep serving up the same types, the same towns, the same ladies' bustles, over and over again. After all, besides bustles and summerhouse husbands, there are still plenty of comic and interesting things in Russia."

to Pleshcheev, 10/4/88

"...the vaudeville...must contain criticism on the current state of the theatre, for without criticism, our vaudeville won't have any meaning."

to Lazarev-Gruzinsky, 11/15/87

Through the hitherto-innocuous vaudeville, Chekhov was able to accomplish a great deal. Through parody, he created new innovative variations for the vaudeville's conventions — and still preserved the ability to entertain and delight. He introduced truly Russian themes to the vaudeville, so that rather than remain a Russified French genre, it became truly Russian. He satirized Russian ways of life and institutions. And, most innovatively, he introduced into the vaudeville genre both comedic *and* serious elements. In short, he revived a stale and stagnant Russian theatre through the most unexpected of vehicles.

With regard to conventional vaudevillian plot, for example, Chekhov introduced the innovation of parodic treatment to the formulas traditionally involving lovers, marriage, land, and dowry. *The Bear* and *The Proposal* are clear examples of Chekhov's elevation of a second-rate form to pure art. By scrupulously presenting the "textbook vaudeville" formula, complete with two lovers at the center, a third character-as-foil (an ancient servant and an obsequious parent, respectively), he essentially parodizes the form — and then subverts it as well by providing totally unexpected twists to the expected conventional characters and plots. In the case of *The Bear*, the would-be lovers become dueling opponents, and their seconds are farmhands. In the case of *The Proposal*, a) the fiancée doesn't even know of her suitor's intent; and, b) even when she does, a proposal never actually takes place; c) the father, desperate for the denouement, has to *coerce* them to kiss! And yet, when both plays end happily — i.e., according to convention — the audience thrills at the plot twists and gyrations, and the dazzling technique with which Chekhov has brought all this about!

Chekhov loved to subvert the plots of his vaudevilles, by setting up expectations that he never delivers upon, but rather changes midstream. Nothing ever happens as planned or expected. Thus, Nyukhin never actually delivers the lecture he is supposed to give in *On the Harmful Effects of Tobacco*. The speech we all are waiting for in *The Jubilee* is never completed. Instead of consoling

Tochakov, the errandboy/husband in *Tragedian*, his confidant Murashkin ends up asking Tolchakov to perform an errand for *him* as well. And "Dr. Zaytsev," the rogue in *The Night before the Trial*, finds that his hopes for a "one-night stand" have been thwarted by his "intended's" husband, who turns out to be the public prosecutor he has to face at his own trial the next day. And so on and so on...

With regard to stock vaudevillian characters, the playful Chekhov could not resist the Gogolian convention of naming his characters suggestively, as the roots of his characters' names indicate: thus, Chubukov (from "pipe"), Lomov ("break"), Tolchakov ("push"), Svetlovidov ("light" and "see"), Zmeyukina ("snake"), Revunov ("howl"), Karaulov (the cry of "help!"); Aplombov ("aplomb"), Nyunin ("whimper"), Mozgovoy ("brain"), Shipuchin ("fizzy"), Khirin ("withered"), Murashkin ("small insect"), etc. This was a practice Chekhov would repeat more selectively in his later, mature plays.

At the same time, he also introduced significant innovations to the stock vaudevillian characterizations, by taking conventional "types" and, either through parody or subversion, humanizing them. In *The Bear,* for example, Chekhov subverts "the grieving widow-type" and transforms her into a dimple-cheeked beauty who in turn becomes a pistol-brandishing feminist. In *The Proposal*, Chekhov subverts "the eligible young lady-type" into a shrewd, apron-clad estate-manager capable of threshing whole meadows herself, who fights fiercely with her neighbor over land rights and dog pedigrees, while the conventional "suitor-type" is a whining hypochondriac. In *The Tragedian in Spite of Himself,* Tolchakov, the henpecked husband, becomes homicidal — and we empathize with him.

Using short stories as resource material, Chekhov introduced full human characters to the vaudeville. The schoolteacher, one of Chekhov's favorite characters throughout his prose writings, who begins as a pathetic object of ridicule in *On the Harmful Effects of Tobacco*, becomes transformed into a figure of courage and nobility in his desperate attempt at freedom from the shackles of his tyrannized existence. The Russian-style Pagliacci, Svetlovidov — the pathetic spear-carrier in *Swan Song* — breaks out into inspired recitations from *Hamlet* and *King Lear.* In these two characterizations, there are elements of the absurd — Gogol's legacy. However, by preserving their sense of dignity, Chekhov also adds an element of the tragic. These unexpected, fully human characterizations in the context of conventional forms are fresh and new, and the results are deeply moving. And the laughter which Chekhov provokes is that of surprise, tenderness, compassion, and recognition of the sad truths of human nature.

Chekhov brought a new sense of the absurd to the vaudeville by exaggerating the conventional usage of extreme behavior and physical action. There is not only the obligatory "one," but rather a dozen fainting-spells per twenty-minute vaudeville in *The Bear* and *The Proposal*. Characters draw weapons, break furniture, curse, pray, swoon, chase each other around the room, collapse into armchairs and call out for "water!" every half-page! Physical ailments abound in Dr. Chekhov's vaudevilles — extreme itching *(The Night before the Trial);* twitchings-of-the-eye *(Tobacco);* breathlessness *(Tragedian);* exhaustion *(The Bear* and *Tragedia*n); dizziness *(Tragedian* and *Tatyana Repina);* migraine *(The Wedding);* gout *(The Jubilee);* indigestion *(The Jubilee* and *Tragedian);* anxiety attacks *(The Bear* and *The Proposal);* uncontrollable rage reactions *(The Bear* and *Tragedian);* leg, shoulder, head and chest pains, shortness of breath, heart palpitations, temporary paralysis, imaginary loss of limb, seeing stars *(The Proposal)* — and to top it all, a doctor-imposter prescribing dubious cures for a variety of ills *(The Night before the Trial)!* The malaise that Dr. Chekhov treats is hypochondria, and his patient is the ordinary man, unable to cope with the everyday pressures and disappointments in life. Dr. Chekhov treats this hypochondria with a literary dosage of hyperbole, thus providing tragicomedic insight into the human condition.

Chekhov also introduced the artistic and innovative usage of language to the vaudeville. Whether it be technical sailing terminology *(The Wedding),* Orthodox Russian church liturgy *(Tatyana Repina),* types of dueling pistols *(The Bear),* or terms of land ownership *(The Proposal),* the intricacy of the language in the context of the fast-paced vaudeville provides a hilarious non-sequitur effect. It complicates the forward-moving action, sets new obstacles in its path, promotes misunderstandings — in short, heightens the comedy.

Chekhov further contributed to the vaudeville form, which still bore the stamp of its French origins, by endowing it with a "Russian-ness." His mis-en-scènes are rich in Russian flavor. For example, *The Tragedian in Spite of Himself* depicts the dilemmas of Russian "dacha" life, and provides Chekhov with a ripe opportunity to satirize the institutions of marriage and middle-class family ways. *The Bear* and *The Proposal* both contain details of provincial estate life that are unmistakeably Russian. Similarly, the filth-and-bug-infested inn of *The Night before the Trial*, the church scene in *Tatyana Repina*, the banquet scene in *The Wedding* — all are distinctly Russian. Chekhov responded to the two-century-old mania of slavish and superficial Francophilia by making *la vaudeville russe* truly Russian.

Chekhov's vaudevilles were also topical. Poking fun at feminism, a fashionable topic of the 1880s *(The Bear);* exposing the greed and narrow-mindedness of the middle class *(The Wedding* and *Tragedian);* portraying the inhumanity of the banking institutions and the blind self-importance of its officials *(The Jubilee)* — all are examples of Chekhov's satire of contemporary Russian life in a vaude-villian context.

With all these innovations, Chekhov succeeded in elevating the vaudeville, an acknowledged second-rate genre, into an art form — providing supreme entertainment, as well as insight into the human condition. And through this experimentation, Chekhov reaffirmed the classical strength of comedy as a vehicle of serious expression of thought. This he accomplished with great *élan*, and the joy of a practical joker.

CHEKHOV AND THE TRAGICOMEDIC

> "No matter how hard I try to be serious, it just doesn't come out that way, I'm always alternating the serious with the trivial."
>
> *to Polonsky, 2/2/88*

> "This isn't a vaudeville, it's a tragedy!"
>
> *Tolchakov, in* The Tragedian in Spite of Himself

Above all, Chekhov used the vaudeville during this experimental period to explore, freely and energetically, the coexistence of the comedic and the tragic in his dramatic writing. It is through this experimentation that Chekhov found his mature voice as a dramatist in his later plays, which pemitted him to express his unique, tragicomedic vision of the absurdity of life.

The precious discoveries Chekhov made while writing his vaudevilles paved the way to many of the great moments of the later plays. Vanya with his roses in Act III of *Uncle Vanya,* Kulygin with his false beard and Andrey with his baby carriage in Act IV of *The Three Sisters,* Pishchik with his money and Trofimov with his galoshes in Act IV of *The Cherry Orchard* — these are only a few of the many exquisite tragicomedic moments of the absurd that are the leitmotifs of the later plays. They pass so fleetingly before our eyes, and yet they produce such a lasting effect. And with Chekhov — who as a mature artist became an impressionist, the gentle cumulative effect of these moments *is* the magic of the plays. And this magic is a result of Chekhov's earlier exploration of the absurd in the vaudevilles.

Chekhov's first few attempts at the short form were either wholly comedic, parodic, or wholly tragi-melodramatic. Although the texts do not survive, the titles of his earliest attempts at vaudeville-writing from 1876–1884 (from ages sixteen till twenty-four, when he graduated from medical school) — *Laugh It*

Off If You Can, Scythe Strikes Stone, Why the Hen Clucks, The Cleanshaven Secretary with the Pistol — suggest a lively, fully comedic vaudevillian tone. In 1885, Chekhov experimented with the wholly tragi-melodramatic tone in *On the High Road* (the first in this collection) — the only one of the short works that is entirely devoid of comedic elements. It brings to the stage the themes of poverty and the savagery of provincial Russia, themes that he treated in his short stories (*Peasants, In the Ravine, Misery, The Witch*, and others). With its tavern scenes and "low-life" characters, some feel that *On the High Road* reads more like Gorky *(The Lower Depths)* than like Chekhov. (After *On the High Road*, Chekhov never again wrote a play — either one-act or full-length — that was totally devoid of comedic elements.)

It is with *On the Harmful Effects of Tobacco* and *Swan Song* that we see the beginning of the coexistence of the comedy and tragedy within a given one-act play. With the portrayals of Nyukhin and Svetlovidov, we see the predecessors of the richly tragicomedic portrayals of Masha and Medvedenko *(The Seagull)*; Uncle Vanya; Chebutykin and Kulygin *(The Three Sisters)*; Gaev, Pishchik, and Varya *(The Cherry Orchard)*.

The fact that Chekhov wrote the first draft of *On the Harmful Effects of Tobacco* in 1886, and then rewrote it five times during his lifetime, is illuminating with respect to the development of Chekhov's *weltanschauung*. (It is the final version of 1902 that has been translated for this collection — Chekhov instructed Marks, the publisher of his collected works, to exclude any earlier drafts.) In each draft the tone darkens, the character becomes more desperate, and the elements of the absurd are intensified. There was clearly something critical to Chekhov in the characterization of Nyukhin and in the balance of the tragic and comedic — something that Chekhov was determined to refine and to resolve as the years passed. The final draft was written in 1902, when Chekhov's health had so deteriorated that his productivity diminished to one story a year (he had written dozens a year only fifteen years previously). The Moscow Art Theatre was insistent on a fourth play from Chekhov, and he had already been developing an idea for *The Cherry Orchard,* but in the fall of 1902, before he began writing what was to be his final full-length play, he returned to *On the Harmful Effects of Tobacco* to refine it yet once more. This revision was to be the second-to-last work of his life. The image of this remarkable writer, returning again to comedy as a source of final consolation as he faced the end of his life, is profounding moving.

What was there so crucial to Chekhov in *Tobacco* that required resolution? It was, I believe, the "alternating" pattern, as he put it in his letter to Polonsky, of the "serious" and the "trivial" that Chekhov sought to resolve. There was a balance that Chekhov was always striving to achieve — the balance between the comedic and the tragic elements that coexisted in his work. And yet, I believe his ultimate discovery, in the end, was that comedy and tragedy could *not* be blended, or balanced, but only alternated, equally or unequally — that is to say, "imbalanced" delicately, within a given work. For it is the alternation of the comedic and the tragic that is true to life. And finding the *way* in which to alternate these coexisting elements, in order to produce the effect he was seeking, to communicate his vision of life, was what made him, ultimately, a great artist.

Over the period of the five revisions, by making carefully selected deletions of extraneous humorous embellishments and digressions, by adding the tragic moment of Nyukhin's self-revelation to the audience, by expressing Nyukhin's longing to become an inanimate object and forget his existence altogether, Chekhov arrives closer to the effect he was so determined to achieve — a character whom we can both laugh at and cry with and *for,* an object of our disdain, our pity, and our compassion simultaneously.

But ultimately, and most importantly, Chekhov takes us one step further, beyond Gogol's laughter-through-tears, into a colder, more detached, more objective place. And that place is the true understanding of human nature and the human condition. In the end, we understand that there is nothing Nyukhin — or Svetlovidov — can, or will, do for himself. Nor can we do anything for him — or for ourselves. And so, as Dr. Chebutykhin says in *The Three Sisters*: it doesn't matter…

•   •   •

In his reminiscenes of Chekhov written in 1902, Gorky tells of how Chekhov, despite his ailing health, once launched into a passionate and indignant defense of the plight of the poor, unrewarded schoolteacher in provincial Russia:

> "A teacher must be a true artist, one who is deeply in love with his calling; but in our country he is a journeyman, ill-educated, a man who goes to the village to teach children as though he were going into exile. He is downtrodden, starving, crushed, terrorized by the fear of losing his daily bread. And yet he ought to be the first man in the village…no one should dare shout at him or humiliate him personally, as everyone does in our country…It is ridiculous to pay kopeks to the man who has to educate the people. It is intolerable that he should go around in rags, shiver with cold in damp and draughty schools, catch colds, and at about the age of thirty get laryngitis, rheumatism, or tuberculosis…We ought to be ashamed

of it! Our teacher, for eight or nine months in the year, lives like a recluse...he grows dull...All this is disgusting; it is the mockery of a man who is doing great and vitally important work...Do you know, whenever I see a teacher, I feel ashamed for him, for his timidity, for the fact that he is badly dressed...and it seems to me that I myself am to blame for the teacher's wretchedness...

...This Russia of ours is such an absurd, clumsy country."

Chekhov to Gorky, in Gorky, *A. P. Chekhov*

For those who laugh and cry at the schoolteachers Medvedenko and Kulygin in *The Seagull* and *The Three Sisters,* there is something even more hopeless and pathetic and funny about the prototype of all these Chekhovian characters — the miserable, would-be little teacher of a myriad of subjects who never gives the lecture on the harmfulness of tobacco to which he has been assigned by his wife. And anyway, as he tells us, he smokes...

With Chekhov, insights into the comedic and tragic in life are strongest when they are least anticipated. In *Swan Song*, for example, the drunken old spear-carrying has-been actor laments on his pathetic career and his fading into oblivion. And yet, when he breaks into inspired recitation of the great Shakespearean roles he has never played, accompanied by the even more ancient prompter, he experiences a moment of such complete freedom and exhilaration, as can only be found in plays with a happy ending. Similarly — in reverse — the hilarious contrast in *Tatyana Repina* between the Orthodox church service litany and the chaos and confusion in the congregation is undercut by a strange and unexpected coda to the play. As the priests are closing up the chapel for the evening, the church watchman remarks on how the priests' day is so filled with weddings, baptisms, burials, and over and over and over the cycle continues, and what does it all mean? What's the point? There is a strange and disturbing pause to the play's frantic pace, and we hear a silence echoing. "There's no point at all," the little watchman says again. The other priests, of course, have no further comment. Again, this is a truly Chekhovian moment — "Chekhovian" in the sense of the later, major plays.

There is something about the moment when Nyukhin tears off his tattered tailcoat and tramples on it with rage and joy in a single moment of freedom and pride and self-assertion that will pass and return no more — something emblematic of Chekhov's insight into human nature. The vaudevilles abound with such moments, such characters, such details — insights into the human condition, harbingers of the great plays to come. What Chekhov began for the fun of it — his canon of vaudevilles — proved to be a period of experimentation of the youthful dramatist, from which the voice of the mature one would emerge.

(Translator's note: The quotes from Chekhov's letters and from the reminiscences of his contemporaries have all been newly translated for this introduction.)

ON THE HIGH ROAD

A Dramatic Study in One Act

TIKHON YEVSTIGNEEV, proprietor of a tavern on the high road

SEMYON SERGEEVICH BORTSOV, a ruined landowner

MARYA YEGOROVNA, his wife

SAVVA, an old pilgrim

NAZAROVNA
YEFIMOVNA } devout pilgrims

FEDYA, an itinerant factory worker

YEGOR MERIK, a tramp

KUZMA, a vagabond

POSTMAN

A COACHMAN from the village of Bortsovka

Pilgrims, Herdsmen, Vagabonds, etc.

The action takes place in one of the southern Russian provinces.

On the High Road

The scene is TIKHON's tavern. To the right, a counter and shelves with bottles. Upstage, a door, leading to the exterior. A greasy red lantern hangs outside. The floor and benches by the wall are crowded with pilgrims and travelers. Many are sleeping in a sitting position, due to close quarters. It is the dead of night. As the curtain rises, thunder is heard, and a flash of lightning can be seen through the door.

TIKHON stands behind the counter. FEDYA is sprawled out on one of the benches, and softly plays the accordion. BORTSOV sits nearby, dressed in shabby summer clothing. SAVVA, NAZAROVNA, and YEFIMOVNA are settled on the floor near the benches.

YEFIMOVNA: *(To NAZAROVNA.)* Give the old man a little nudge, dearie! See if his soul's gone to heaven.

NAZAROVNA: *(Lifts the edge of SAVVA's coat, which has been covering his face.)* Brother dear, hey, you, good Christian! You alive or dead?

SAVVA: What d'ya mean, dead? I'm plenty alive, dearie. *(Raises himself up on his elbow.)* Cover up my legs, will you, y'old beggar! That's it. A little more on the right side. That's it, dearie. God bless you.

NAZAROVNA: *(Covering SAVVA's feet.)* Sleep, dearie.

SAVVA: How can I sleep? If only I had the patience to bear this torture, I wouldn't need to sleep. A sinner doesn't deserve peace. What's that noise, sister?

NAZAROVNA: God's sent us a storm. The wind is howling, and the rain's coming down in torrents. It's crashing on the rooftop and the windowpanes like pellets. Can you hear it? The floodgates of heaven are open.

Thunder.

Saints above, saints above…

FEDYA: Thundering, and booming, and crashing…on and on and on. There's no end to it! Ooooo…like the roar of the forest…Ooooo…like the howl of a dog…What a wind! *(Shivers.)* It's freezing! My clothes are drenched, I'd take 'em off and wring 'em out, but the door's wide open…*(Plays softly.)* My accordion's soaked, brothers, can't make much music, or I'd play you a concert, would make your head spin! Fantastic! How 'bout a quadrille, or a polka, say…or a Russian ballad, even…you name it, I play it. When I was a porter at the grand hotel, never made any money, but with the accordion, now that's where I shone. I can play guitar, too.

A VOICE FROM THE CORNER: A foolish man talks foolishness.

FEDYA: Well said by a fool.

Pause.

NAZAROVNA: *(To SAVVA.)* You should be lying in a warm place now, old fellow, and warming your poor old leg.

Pause.

Old fellow! Brother! *(Nudges SAVVA.)* Not about to die on us, then, are you?

FEDYA: You oughta have a shot of vodka, grandpa. Drink, and it'll put fire in your belly, do you wonders. Go on, drink!

NAZAROVNA: Quit showing off, young man! The old fellow's trying to give up his soul, confess all his sins, and you and your accordion keep playing away…Enough with that music! Shame on you!

FEDYA: Then why're *you* bothering him? As bad off as he is, you go on and on with your foolish woman's talk…And he's so saintly, he'd never talk back to you…Pretty pleased he'd listen to a fool like you, aren't 'cha?…Sleep on, grandpa, and don't you listen! Let her babble away, to hell with her. A woman's tongue is the devil's broom, it sweeps the wise and sly ones out of the house. To hell with her…*(Throws up his hands.)* You've gotten so thin, brother! It's terrible! All skin and bones! Like nothing alive! Are you really gonna die on us?

SAVVA: Why should I die? The Lord won't let me die before my time…I'm having a bit of a spell, that's all…I'll survive, God willing…The Holy Mother won't let me die in a strange land…I'll die at home…

FEDYA: Where's home? Far from here?

SAVVA: Vologda. I'm a humble citizen of Vologda…

FEDYA: Where's Vologda?

TIKHON: Other side of Moscow…In the province of…

FEDYA: Whoa…That's a long way off, old fellow! You came all this way on foot?

SAVVA: That's right, my boy, on foot. I've been to the Shrine of Tikhon, now I'm on my way to the Holy Mountains…And then, God willing, on to

Odessa…From there, they say, you can get a cheap passage to Jerusalem. Only twenty-one rubles, think of it…

FEDYA: Ever been to Moscow?

SAVVA: Have I ever! Five times!…

FEDYA: A decent town? *(Lights a cigarette.)* Is it worth a visit?

SAVVA: Plenty of shrines there, my boy…And wherever there's shrines, it's always worth a visit…

BORTSOV: *(Approaching the counter and TIKHON.)* Give me another drink! Please! For Christ's sake!

FEDYA: The main thing is, a town should be clean…If it's dusty — water it, if it's muddy, sweep it up. The houses should be tall…there should be a theatre, police…cabbies…I've lived in towns myself, I should know.

BORTSOV: Just one little glass…that's all. Come on…put it on credit! I'll pay you!

TIKHON: All right, that's enough.

BORTSOV: Please! I beg of you!

TIKHON: Get out of here!

BORTSOV: You don't understand me! Listen, you boor, get it into that thick peasant head of yours, if you have an ounce of brains, that is, it's not me that's asking for it, it's my gut, to put it in your language, you peasant, it's my gut that's asking for it! It's my sickness that's asking for it! Understand?

TIKHON: There's nothing to understand…Go away!

BORTSOV: Look, if I don't get a drink right now, see, if I don't satisfy this raging thirst, I'm going to do something terrible. God only knows what I might do! You've seen lots of drunks in your time, I imagine, you lowlife, don't tell me you don't know what they're like by now! They're sick! Chain 'em up, beat 'em up, knife 'em, even, as long as you give 'em their vodka! I humbly beg of you! I beseech you! I'm groveling! My God, how I'm groveling!

TIKHON: Show me the money, and you'll have your vodka.

BORTSOV: And where am I supposed to get money? I've spent it all on drink! All of it! So what am I going to give you? All I've got left is my overcoat, and I can't give you that…I don't have any clothes on underneath! How about a cap? *(Takes off his hat and offers it.)*

TIKHON: *(Examines the cap.)* Hm…There are caps, and then there are caps…This one's full of holes; it's like a sieve, this one…

FEDYA: *(Laughs.)* It's a gentleman's cap, that's what it is! You wear it to walk down the street and tip it to all the mam'selles. "How d'ya do! And how are you today!"

TIKHON: *(Gives the cap back to BORTSOV.)* I wouldn't take it even if you gave it to me. It's filthy.

BORTSOV: Don't want that? All right — in that case, put it on credit. Soon as I get back from town, I'll bring you your five kopek piece! I hope you choke on it! Do you hear me? Choke on it! I hope it sticks in your throat! *(Coughs.)* I despise you!

TIKHON: *(Bangs on the counter with his fist.)* Stop bothering me! Who are you, anyway? Some kind of operator? Why have you come here?

BORTSOV: I want a drink! No, wait — it's not *I* that wants it, it's my sickness that wants it! Do you see?

TIKHON: Don't try my patience here! Or else you'll be out in the cold, but quick!

BORTSOV: What can I do? *(Walks away from the counter.)* What can I do? *(Falls deep in thought.)*

YEFIMOVNA: It's the devil enticing you. You pay him no heed, sir. The evil one, he's whispering in your ear: "Drink! Drink!" So you just answer back: "No! No!" He'll leave you alone!

FEDYA: Your brain's pounding, isn't it…trum-trum-trum-trum…and your stomach's turning over and over, like! *(Laughs uproariously.)* You're an odd one, your honor. Go on, go to sleep! No point in flappin' 'round the tavern like a great big scarecrow! You won't find a kitchen garden in here!

BORTSOV: *(Maliciously.)* Shut up! No one asked you, jackass!

FEDYA: Hey, watch what you're saying, there! I know your kind! I seen a lot like you come along the high road! And as for me being a jackass, once I clap you one over the head, you'll howl louder than the wind! Jackass yourself! Scum!

Pause.

Swine!

NAZAROVNA: And meanwhile, the old fellow's praying and preparing his soul for God, while these fools are cursing and fighting…Shame on you!

FEDYA: Stop sniveling, y'old cabbage! When you're in a tavern, you live the tavern life. Get used to it!

BORTSOV: What's to become of me? What can I do? How can I make him understand? What more can I say? *(To TIKHON.)* My blood runs cold! Tikhon, old man! *(Weeps.)* Dear old Tikhon!

SAVVA: *(Moans.)* There's pain shooting up my leg…like a bullet of fire…Sister, please!

YEFIMOVNA: What is it, dearie?

SAVVA: Who's that crying?

YEFIMOVNA: It's the master.

SAVVA: Ask the master to shed a tear for me, too, that I might die in Vologda. Tearful prayers are answered.

BORTSOV: I'm not praying, old fellow! And these aren't tears, either! This is my blood! They've squeezed my soul dry and the blood's flowing out. *(Sits at SAVVA's feet.)* Blood! However, you wouldn't understand! No, old fellow, this is beyond your dim powers of comprehension. You people live in darkness!

SAVVA: And where are those who see the light?

BORTSOV: You can find them...They would understand!

SAVVA: Yes, they would, my son...The saints could see the light...They knew all kinds of sorrow...You needn't say a word, they'd understand...They'd look into your eyes, they'd understand...And with their compassion, your sorrows will vanish like magic!

FEDYA: And you've really seen the saints?

SAVVA: I have, my boy...There are all kinds of people on this earth. There are sinners, and there are servants of God.

BORTSOV: I don't understand anything...*(Gets up quickly.)* Talking should make sense, but nothing makes sense to me any more. Only instinct — thirst! *(Hurries up to the counter.)* Tikhon, take my coat? Do you hear me? *(Goes to remove his coat.)* My coat...

TIKHON: And what do you have underneath that coat? *(Looks under BORTSOV's coat.)* Your naked body? I'm not going to take it off, I won't... I won't have that sin on my soul.

Enter MERIK.

BORTSOV: Fine, I'll take it on mine! All right?

MERIK: *(Silently removes his coat, and is left wearing a long, tightfitting vest. In the belt around his waist, he carries an axe.)* For some, it's cold, but for the bear and homeless wanderer, it's hot as hell. I'm sweating sheets! *(Lays his axe on the floor, and removes his long vest.)* You drag your leg out of the mud, and you're drenched in sweat. And no sooner you got one leg out, than the other one gets stuck.

YEFIMOVNA: And so it goes...Is the rain letting up, my son?

MERIK: *(Glances at YEFIMOVNA.)* I don't talk to any old crones.

Pause.

BORTSOV: *(To TIKHON.)* I'll take this sin upon myself! Do you hear me, or don't you?

TIKHON: I don't want to hear anything! Leave me alone!

MERIK: So dark out...looks like the sky's been smeared with tar. Can't see the nose in front of you. The rain whips against your face, like you're in a blizzard...*(Gathers his clothes and axe in his arms.)*

FEDYA: For our friend, the thief, it's a great day. Even the beasts of prey are taking cover, but for you, it's a hoodlum's holiday.

MERIK: And who might be the author of those words?

FEDYA: Why don't you open your eyes and look...or maybe you can't see.

MERIK: I'll remember that...*(Goes up to TIKHON.)* Hey, you —with the ugly face! Hello, there! Or don't 'cha recognize me?

TIKHON: If I could remember every lousy drunk who traveled the high road, I'd need ten eyes in my head.

MERIK: Well, look again...

Pause.

TIKHON: Well, now, wait, I'll be...I do recognize you! By your eyes, I recognize you! *(Offers him his hand.)* Andrey Polikarpov?

MERIK: That's right, the former Andrey Polikarpov, and now, it appears to be Yegor Merik.

TIKHON: How did that happen?

MERIK: Whatever name God gives me, that's what I'm called. I've been Merik for a coupla months now...

The sound of thunder.

Rrrrrrr...Go on, roar all you want, you can't scare me! *(Looks around him.)* Got any wolfhounds around here?

TIKHON: Whaddya mean, wolfhounds? More likely to be gnats and mosquitoes...The people here are a real soft touch...You'd probably find a wolfhound sleeping in their featherbeds...*(Loudly.)* Attention, all true believers, watch your pockets, and your clothes, too, if you care about 'em! This is a dangerous man. He'll steal anything.

MERIK: All right, watch out for your money, then, but as for your clothes, I wouldn't touch 'em. Where would I wear 'em?

TIKHON: Where in hell are you off to?

MERIK: To the Kuban steppes.

TIKHON: You don't say!

FEDYA: Kuban? Really? *(Sits up.)* That's glorious country. The kind you only dream about, my friends! It's vast! They say there's every kind of bird and creature you can think of. The grass — my God! — it grows all year round, the people there are the salt of the earth, and the land — they've got so much, they don't know what to do with it! They say…now this, a soldier told me, who was passing through the other day…that the government gives the people almost three hundred acres per head. May God strike me dead with such good fortune!

MERIK: Good fortune…Fortune follows you, it walks behind you…You can't see it…If you had eyes in the back of your head, then you might see good fortune…It's all nonsense, anyway…*(Looks around at the benches and the people.)* This looks like a scene from the local jail…Hello there, scum-of-the-earth!

YEFIMOVNA: You have fury in your eyes!…The devil lives inside you, young man…Don't look at us.

MERIK: Hail to the poor and downtrodden!

YEFIMOVNA: Turn away! *(Nudges SAVVA.)* Savvushka, there's an evil man who's looking at us! He'll curse us, dearie. *(To MERIK.)* I say: Cast your eyes away from us, you viper!

SAVVA: He won't hurt you, dearie, he won't…God won't let him!

MERIK: Hail, true believers! *(Shrugs his shoulder.)* They're silent! You can't all be sleeping, you clods! Why're you so silent?

YEFIMOVNA: Cast your eyes away! And cast away the pride of Satan!

MERIK: Shut up, you old crone! What do you mean, pride of Satan? I was offering a kind word to cheer you in your miserable state! You're like flies all pinched together in the cold — I felt sorry for you, I was offering a kind word to help you in your time of need, and you just turn your ugly mugs away! Well, what the hell, then! I don't need this! *(Goes up to FEDYA.)* And what parts do you come from?

FEDYA: From these parts, from the Khamonevsky brickworks.

MERIK: Get up!

FEDYA: *(Raising himself up a bit.)* What?

MERIK: Get up! Get up, that's my place…

FEDYA: Oh, really…is that so?

MERIK: Yes. Go lie down on the floor!

FEDYA: Out of my way, you tramp…You don't scare me…

MERIK: He's a sharp one, isn't he…Listen, get lost, and shut up, too, will you? Or else you'll regret it, you fool!

TIKHON: *(To FEDYA.)* Don't start in with him, fellow! Let him have it, and to hell with him!

FEDYA: How dare you talk to me that way? He stares at me with those fishy eyes and thinks he can scare me, eh? *(Gathers his belongings in his arms, and makes a bed for himself on the floor.)* To hell with you. *(Lies down and covers his head.)*

MERIK: *(Makes a bed for himself on a bench.)* Well, it's obvious you've never seen a devil, if you think *I'm* one. That's not what a devil looks like. *(Lies down and places his hatchet along side of him.)* Go to sleep, little hachet, my sweet little friend...I'll cover up your handle for you.

TIKHON: Where did you get the hachet?

MERIK: Stole it...Stole it, and now I carry it everywhere with me, I'm stuck with it...sort of...pity to throw it away...don't know what else to do with it. It's like a wife you're sick of...Yes...*(Covers it up.)* No, devils aren't like me, my friend...

FEDYA: *(Sticks his head out from underneath the caftan.)* What are they like, then?

MERIK: They're like spirit...or air...Go on — breathe *(he exhales)*...they're like that. You can't even see 'em.

A VOICE FROM THE CORNER: If you're sitting under a plow, you can see 'em.

MERIK: No, you can't...That's an old wives' tale. Devils, demons, ghosts, you can't see any of 'em...The eye wasn't made to see everything...When I was small, I'd sneak out into the woods at night, to see all the wood demons... I'd call and I'd call for the spirits to come out, I wouldn't dare blink an eye, even...saw all kinds of creatures, but never saw a wood demon. Went to the graveyard at night in the churchyard, looking for ghosts — but that was an old wives' tale, too. Saw all kinds of wild beasts, but as for a spirit, you know, one who could frighten you — forget about it. The eye just can't see 'em...

A VOICE FROM THE CORNER: Don't say that, it can happen, the eye *can* see them...Once, in our village, a peasant was gutting a wild boar...He was pulling out the entrails, and out jumps one of 'em!

SAVVA: *(Raises himself up.)* Come on, now, lads, don't talk of the devil! It's a sin, fellows!

MERIK: Aha...old grey beard speaks! The skeleton speaks! *(Laughs.)* No need to go to the churchyard, we've got our own corpses crawling out the woodwork to admonish us...Sin, he says...You and your stupidity, who are you to talk "sin"! You people live in darkness, you live in ignorance...*(Lights up a pipe.)* My father was a peasant, he, too, tried to put the fear of God in us. One night, he stole a bag of apples from a priest, brought it to us, and said: "Listen, children, don't you go gobbling up these apples before the Sabbath, because that's a sin!"…You're just like him…You won't speak of the devil, but you'll behave like the devil himself…Take this old crow, for instance…*(Indicates YEFIMOVNA.)* She sees the devil in me, but she's probably sold her soul to the devil five times over, because she's a foolish woman.

YEFIMOVNA: Tfoo, tfoo, tfoo!…May the sign of the cross protect us! *(Covers her face with her hands.)* Savvushka!

TIKHON: Why are you trying to frighten us? Having a good time, is that it?

The door bangs from the wind.

Good Christ…Listen to that wind!

MERIK: *(Stretches.)* Ach, if only I could show my strength!

The door bangs from the wind.

I'd measure my strength to the wind's! The wind can't rip that door down, but I could tear this entire tavern up by its roots! *(Stands up and lies down again.)* I've had it!

NAZAROVNA: Say a prayer, you miserable man! Why can't you keep still?

YEFIMOVNA: Leave him alone, let the devil take him! He's casting the evil eye on us! *(To MERIK.)* Don't look at us, you demon! Look at those eyes, he looks like Satan saying his prayers!

SAVVA: Let him look, true believers! Say a prayer, and the evil eye can't touch you…

BORTSOV: No, I can't bear it! I can't bear it any longer! *(Goes up to the counter.)* Listen to me, Tikhon, for the last time, I beg of you…Just half a glass!

TIKHON: *(Shakes his head.)* Money!

BORTSOV: My God, I've already told you! I've lost it all! Where can I get any to give to you? And would it really ruin you, to give me a drop of vodka on credit? A glass of vodka costs you half a kopek, that's next to nothing, but it can deliver me from suffering! And how I suffer! I'm not just saying it, this is real suffering! Can't you understand?

TIKHON: Tell someone else about it, not me…Go on, beg all these Christians for it, let *them* give you charity if they want to, I only give bread to beggars.

BORTSOV: No, *you* take the poor peasants' money, I can't…forgive me! I don't have it in me to rob them! Not I! Understand? *(Bangs his fist on the counter.)* Not I!

Pause.

Hm…Wait a minute…. *(Turns to the pilgrims.)* I have an idea, brothers! Be charitable: make a donation of five kopeks! My insides are begging for it! I'm sick!

FEDYA: Look, you want charity, you sponger…How 'bout a glass of water?

BORTSOV: How I have humiliated myself! Humiliated myself! Never mind! I don't need anything! It was only a joke!

MERIK: You'll never get it from him, sir…Everyone knows he's too stingy… Wait, I think I have a five-piece here somewhere. We'll have a glass together…we'll share it…*(Rummages in his pockets.)* Damn…it's stuck in here somewhere…I heard it jingling in my pocket the other day…No, I don't have it…I have nothing, brother! Just your luck!

Pause.

BORTSOV: I've got to have a drink, or else I'll get violent, I might even kill myself…What can I do, my God! *(Looks out the door.)* Where can I go? Out into the darkness, into the void….

MERIK: Why don't you preach at him, pilgrims? And you, Tikhon, why don't you throw him out? He certainly hasn't paid for lodgings for the night. Go on, throw him out, by his neck! Ach, people are hard nowadays. There's no pity, no kindness…People are cruel! If they see a drowning man, they cry out to him: "Hurry up and drown, we don't have much time, we've got a day's work to do!" And as for throwing him a rope, don't even think about it…A rope costs money…

SAVVA: Don't judge me, my good fellow!

MERIK: Quiet, you old dog! You're a cruel lot! Fiends! Soulmongers! *(To TIKHON.)* Get over here and take off my boots! Come on!

TIKHON: Hah! He's losing it, isn't he! *(Laughs.)* A real terror, that's what you are!

MERIK: Get over here, I said! And make it fast!

Pause.

Do you hear me, or not? Am I talking to the walls? *(Gets up.)*

TIKHON: All right, all right…Calm down!

MERIK: I want you to take off my boots, you bloodsucker, the boots of a lowly vagabond!

TIKHON: Take it easy, will you! Have a drink!…Come on!

MERIK: What did I say I wanted, people? For him to treat me to a glass of vodka or for him to take off my boots? Didn't I make myself clear, didn't I say it right? *(To TIKHON.)* So you didn't catch what I said, is that it? Well, then, I'll just wait a little bit, until you catch it.

There is a stir among the pilgrims and travelers. They sit up, and look at TIKHON and MERIK. They wait in silent expectation.

TIKHON: Who in hell brought you here, the devil? *(Comes out from behind the counter.)* Thinks he's a gentleman, doesn't he? All right, why not, give 'em here! *(Removes MERIK's boots.)* The progeny of Cain...

MERIK: That's right. Now put them down, side by side...That's it...Now get away from me!

TIKHON: *(Having taken off the boots, returns to behind the counter.)* Think you're so smart, don't you? Just keep pulling stunts like that, and you'll see how fast you'll be flying out of this tavern! That's right! *(Goes up to BORTSOV.)* You again?

BORTSOV: Now look, I have something in gold I might give you. If you like, I can give it to you now...

TIKHON: Why are you trembling? Talk straight.

BORTSOV: It's a vile and loathesome thing on my part, but what else can I do? I've made up my mind to do a despicable deed, but then again I'm not in my right mind, am I...so any court would acquit me. Take it, but only on the condition that you return it to me when I get back from town. I give it to you before witnesses...Ladies and gentlemen, you are witnessing this! *(Takes out a gold medallion from under his shirt.)* Here it is...I should remove the picture, but I've nowhere else to put it: I'm wet all over!.... Go on, take it, the picture too! There's only one thing...please...don't touch the face with your finger...I beg of you...My dear man, I was rude to you just now...I acted foolishly, but forgive me, please and...don't touch it with your finger... And don't lay eyes on the face...*(Gives TIKHON the medallion.)*

TIKHON: *(Examines the medallion.)* A stolen watch.... All right, fine, go ahead, have a drink...*(Pours the vodka.)* Pour *that* down your throat...

BORTSOV: Don't touch it...that's all...*(Drinks slowly, with convulsive gulps.)*

TIKHON: *(Opens the medallion.)* Hm...*Bonjour, madame!* Where did you pick this up?

MERIK: Give it here! *(Gets up and goes to the counter.)* Lemme have a look at it!

TIKHON: *(Pushes his hand away.)* What do you think you're doing? You can look at it, but *I'm* holding it.

FEDYA: *(Stands up and goes to TIKHON.)* Lemme have a look at it, too!

The various pilgrims and vagabonds approach the counter from all sides and gather round.

MERIK: *(Firmly holds TIKHON's hand, which is holding the medallion, and silently observes the portrait.)*

Pause.

Lovely little devil, isn't she? She's some lady...

FEDYA: I'll say, she's a lady...Look at those cheeks, and those eyes...Move your fingers away, I can't see! She's got hair flowing down to her waist...She looks like she's alive, even! Like she's going to speak to us at any moment...

Pause.

MERIK: For the man who is weak, it's the road to ruin. Put this 'round your neck...*(waves his hand)* and you've had it!

KUZMA's voice is heard: "Whoaaa...Stop, you dumb creature!" Enter KUZMA.

KUZMA: "There stands a tavern on the way, And here it is that I must stay." You can pass your own father in broad daylight and never notice him, but you can spot a tavern in the black of night from miles and miles away. Out of my way, true believers! Hey, you, there! *(Bangs on the counter with a coin.)* A glass of real madeira! Look alive!

FEDYA: Hey, you're in a hell of a hurry, aren't you?

TIKHON: Watch it! Don't wave your arms around like that! You'll knock something over!

KUZMA: That's what arms are made for...waving. What are you so scared of, you chickens! A little drop of rain, and it's frightened you, poor things! *(Drinks.)*

YEFIMOVNA: Who wouldn't be frightened, my good fellow, traveling on a night like this. Nowadays, thank the Lord, there are plenty of villages and farms to shelter one from the storm, but not in the olden days, nothing even to pray for. You'd go as far as seventy miles without seeing a splinter of wood, let alone a village or farm. You'd have to spend the night out in the open...

KUZMA: And how long have you been toiling on this earth, old woman?

YEFIMOVNA: I'm in my seventies, dearie.

KUZMA: Seventies! You'll live to be a hundred. *(Looks at BORTSOV.)* Who's this the cat dragged in? *(Looks more closely at BORTSOV.)* Master!

BORTSOV recognizes KUZMA; embarrassed, he retreats into a corner and sits on a bench.

Semyon Sergeich! Is it really you? What are you doing in this godforsaken tavern? This is no place for you to be!

BORTSOV: Be quiet!

MERIK: *(To KUZMA.)* Who is this?

KUZMA: An unfortunate martyr! *(Nervously paces near the counter.)* And in a tavern, too, eh? Heaven help us! Ragged, disheveled! Dead drunk! This upsets me terribly, my friends…Terribly…*(Speaks to MERIK, in a half whisper.)* This is our master…the owner of our land, Semyon Sergeich Bortsov, Gentleman…You see what shape he's in? Almost unrecognizable, isn't he? That's what drink does to you…Hit me one! *(Drinks.)* I come from his village, from Bortsovka, you may have heard of it, it's about one hundred and thirty miles or so from here, in the Yergovsky district. We were his father's serfs… What a pity!

MERIK: Was he rich?

KUZMA: Plenty rich…

MERIK: What did he do — squander all his father's money?

KUZMA: No, it was fate, my good man…He was a gentleman, powerful, rich, sober…*(To TIKHON.)* No doubt you seen him yourself, driving past the tavern on his way into town. He had proper horses then, smart and sharp they were, and a fancy carriage — real first-class! He kept five troikas, my friend…Five years ago, I remember, he was crossing on the Mikishkinsky ferry, and instead of a five kopek piece he was handing out rubles. "I don't have time to wait for the change," he said…You see!

MERIK: Must have lost his mind, then.

KUZMA: No, he still seems to have his wits about him…It all came from weakness! And indulgence! And above all, my friends, from women…He fell in love, the poor man, with one of the local girls from the town, he imagined her the loveliest creature on earth…Well, maybe she wasn't, but *he* thought she was. Head-over-heels, he fell. She was of good stock, this girl…Not a libertine or anything like that…Capricious, she was, always twirling about and flashing her eyes! And laughing, always laughing! No sense, she had…The gentry like that kind — think they're real clever, while we peasants, we'd chase 'em out of the yard. Anyway…he fell in love, and it's so long, master! He starts carrying on with her, and one thing leads to another, he's getting sugar with his tea and so on…they're out boating all night, playing piano and all that…

BORTSOV: Don't tell them this, Kuzma! What's the use? What business is it of theirs, how I live?

KUZMA: Sorry, your honor, but I'm only telling them a little…There, that's all they're going to get from me...I told them that bit, because I was upset...Very upset! Hit me again! *(Drinks.)*

MERIK: *(In a half whisper.)* And did she love him?

KUZMA: *(In a half whisper, which gradually, little by little, becomes full-voiced.)* What's not to love? The master's not just anybody, you know...You'd love someone, too, who had thousands of acres of land, and sacks full of money...And respectable too, and dignified, and sober.... and tight with the authorities, just like I am with you right now...you know, on a hand-shaking basis...*(Takes MERIK's hand.)*..."Hello, good-bye, you're most welcome"...Well, one evening I was walking through the garden...and let me tell you, friend, what a garden it was! acres and acres of it.... I was walking along quietly, I look, and what do I see, but the master and her sitting on the bench together *(makes the sound of a kiss)* kissing. He kisses her once, and she, the snake, she kisses him twice...He takes her lily-white hand in his, and she blushes and snuggles up to him, closer and closer..."I love you, Senya," she says...and Senya, like a man in a trance, runs around from place to place, bragging about his happiness, weak-willed fellow that he is...Gives this one a ruble, and that one two...Even gave me a horse. Forgave everyone's debts, he was so overjoyed.

BORTSOV: Ach...Why are you telling us all this? These people here have no compassion...It's agony!

KUZMA: I'm only telling a bit of it, master! They're begging for it! Why not tell them a little bit? All right, all right, I won't, if it makes you angry...I won't...To hell with 'em...

The sound of the mail carrier's bells are heard.

FEDYA: Don't yell, speak softly...

KUZMA: I *am* speaking softly...He forbids me to tell it, so what can I do about it?...And besides, there's nothing more to tell. They got married — that's all...There's no more to it than that...Pour a glass for good old Kuzma, everybody's friend, will you! *(Drinks.)* I don't like getting drunk! Anyway, after the wedding ceremony, while all the guests were sitting down to supper, she up and drives off in the carriage...*(In a whisper.)* Went straight to her lover, the lawyer, in town...Eh? Whaddya think of that? That very moment! Killing her would be letting her off too easy, eh?

MERIK: *(Pensively.)* Yes...And then what happened?

KUZMA: He went crazy...As you can see, he went on a drinking spree, and now, they say, he's lost his mind...No, worse, he's just stark raving mad...Still, he loves her till this very day. Look at how he loves her! He's probably on his way into town now just to have a look at her...He looks, and then he goes home...

The mail carriage drives up to the tavern. Enter the POSTMAN; he orders a drink.

TIKHON: Mail's late!

The POSTMAN quietly pays and leaves. The carriage drives away, with the sound of the bells jingling.

A VOICE FROM THE CORNER: Fine weather for a mail robbery — it'd be a song.

MERIK: I've lived on this earth for thirty-five years, and I've never done a mail robbery.

Pause.

The coach is gone, it's too late now...too late...

KUZMA: You want to end up in Siberia, is that it?

MERIK: You don't always get caught...And anyway, if you do, so what! *(Abruptly.)* So then what happened?

KUZMA: To whom, to this poor unfortunate fellow?

MERIK: Who else?

KUZMA: The second thing, my friends, that brought him to rack and ruin was his brother-in-law, his sister's husband...He gets it into his head to back his brother-in-law with a bank loan...thirty thousand, to be exact...Well, this brother's not exactly "in law," as it turns out...plays it real cool, the swine...He takes the money, and doesn't feel obliged to pay it back...So the master here has gotta pay the whole thirty thousand. *(Sighs.)* A foolish man will even suffer flies for his foolishness. The wife has children with this lawyer-lover, the brother-in-law buys an estate near Poltava, and our friend here, like a fool, crawls from tavern to tavern, blubbering to every peasant in sight: "I've lost my faith, my friends! There's no one I can trust any more!" Weakness, that's what I call it! Every man has his grief, we all have the blood sucked out of us in life, but that doesn't mean we have to drink, does it? Take our local village elder, for example. His wife goes around with the schoolmaster in broad daylight, and wastes her husband's money on drink, while the elder goes around with a big smile on his face...He's gotten thin as a rail, though...

TIKHON: *(Sighs.)* It depends on how much strength God gives you...

KUZMA: True, God gives strength to some...How much, then, has he given to you? Eh? *(Pays up.)* Take my hard-earned money, go on! Good-bye, my friends! Good night, pleasant dreams! I'm off, it's time…Gotta fetch the midwife from the hospital for my mistress…Poor thing probably got tired of waiting, and her water broke…*(Hurries off.)*

TIKHON: *(After a pause.)* Hey, you! What's your name? Come have a drink, you poor unfortunate sinner, you! *(Pours.)*

BORTSOV: *(Approaches the counter hesitantly, and drinks.)* So now I owe you for two glasses.

TIKHON: Whaddya mean, "owe"? Forget about it! Drink up! Drown all your sorrows!

FEDYA: Have one on me too, master! Ach! *(Tosses a five-kopek piece on the counter.)* You die if you drink, you die if you don't! Without vodka, you can do all right, but with vodka, my God, you're free and easy! With vodka, grief isn't grief anymore…Cheers!

BORTSOV: Foo! This stuff is strong!

MERIK: Give it here! *(Takes the medallion from TIKHON and studies the portrait.)* Hm…So she ran away on her wedding day…What kind of a woman is that?

A VOICE FROM THE CORNER: Pour him another glass, Tisha. This one's on me!

MERIK: *(Bangs the locket on the floor.)* Curse her! *(Quickly returns to his place and lies down, face toward the wall.)*

Lightning.

BORTSOV: What's this? What's going on here? *(Picks up the locket.)* How dare you, you swine? You have no right! *(Whimpering.)* Do you want me to kill you? Yes? Peasant! Boor!

TIKHON: Now, now, master, don't be angry…It isn't glass, it's not shattered…Have another drink, and get some rest…*(Pours.)* I've listened to all your talk, and the tavern should've been closed long ago. *(Goes and locks the outer door.)*

BORTSOV: *(Drinks.)* How dare he? What a fool! *(To MERIK.)* Do you understand, you're an idiot! A jackass!

SAVVA: Fellows! Kind friends! Don't use such language! What good does it do? Let everyone sleep!

TIKHON: Go on, now, lie down…That's enough! *(Goes behind the counter and locks the cash drawer.)* Time for sleep!

FEDYA: Yes, time for sleep! *(Lies down.)* Pleasant dreams, lads!

MERIK: *(Stands and spreads his sheepskin coat on the bench.)* Go on, master, lie down!

TIKHON: And where are *you* going to lie down?

MERIK: Wherever…on the floor, even…*(Lays his caftan on the floor.)* I don't care. *(Places the axe next to him.)* It'd be torture for him to sleep on the floor…Him being used to silk and soft bedding, and all…

TIKHON: *(To BORTSOV.)* Go to sleep, your honor! And it's enough with that portrait — don't look at it any more! *(Extinguishes candle.)* Forget about her!

BORTSOV: *(Reeling.)* Where can I lie down?

TIKHON: In the tramp's place! Didn't you hear, he wants you to have it, after all!

BORTSOV: *(Approaches the place that has been given to him.)* I'm…ah…drunk…What is this? I'm supposed to lie down here? Eh?

TIKHON: Yes, there, don't be afraid, lie down…*(Stretches out on the counter.)*

BORTSOV: *(Lies down.)* I'm…drunk…My head is spinning…*(Opens the locket.)* Have you got a candle?

Pause.

You're a funny one, Masha…You look at me from the frame and you laugh at me…*(Laughs.)* I'm a drunk! How can you laugh at a drunk! But "never mind," as the man in the play says…you love the poor lush!

FEDYA: Listen to the wind howl! Eerie, isn't it!

BORTSOV: *(Laughs.)* You're something, aren't you…See how you whirl? I can't even catch you!

MERIK: He's delirious. Can't take his eyes off that portrait. *(Laughs.)* It's crazy! Smart men have dreamed up all sorts of inventions and medicines, but what about a cure for the love of a woman…They try to cure every other disease, but how come they don't know that men suffer more from women than from illness…Women…they're crafty, cunning, cruel, and senseless…Mothers torment daughters-in-law, daughters-in-law torture their husbands…There's no end to it…

TIKHON: Women have led him around by the nose for so long, that he doesn't know whether he's coming or going.

MERIK: I'm not the only one…Ever since the world began, men have been lamenting this…Not without reason are women and the devil mentioned in the same breath in songs and in fairy tales…Not without reason! It's more truth than not…

Pause.

The master may make a fool of himself, but meanwhile why did I have to scorn my own mother and father? Why did I become a tramp? Was I crazy?

FEDYA: Women?

MERIK: Same story as the master's…I fell under a spell, I was bewitched, delirious…Day and night I was on fire, but the time would come when my eyes were open…It wasn't love, it was delusion…

FEDYA: And what did you do to her?

MERIK: None of your business…

Pause.

Think I killed her, is that it? My arms are too short for that…No, I didn't kill her, I felt sorry for her, is more like it…"Live and be well, be happy," I told her…"Only don't ever let me set eyes on you again, I wish I'd never met you, you viper!"

Knock at the door.

TIKHON: Who the devil is that?…Who's there?

Knock.

Who's knocking? *(Stands and goes to the door.)* Who's knocking? Move along, we're locked up for the night!

A VOICE FROM BEHIND THE DOOR: Let me in, Tikhon, have mercy! A carriage spring is broken! Help me, please, for pity's sake! I only want a little rope to tie it with, and then I'll be on my way…

TIKHON: Who is it?

A VOICE FROM BEHIND THE DOOR: A lady is traveling from town to Varsonofyevo…Only three miles left to go…Help me, please, for pity's sake!

TIKHON: Go, tell the mistress, if you give me ten rubles, you'll have your rope and your spring will be fixed…

A VOICE FROM BEHIND THE DOOR: Are you out of your mind? Ten rubles! You're mad as a dog, that's what you are! You like to see people suffer!

TIKHON: Whatever you say…If you don't want it and you don't need it, well then…

A VOICE FROM BEHIND THE DOOR: All right, all right, wait a minute…

Pause.

The mistress said: all right.

TIKHON: Be my guest, then! *(Opens the door and lets the COACHMAN in.)*

COACHMAN: Hello, true believers! All right then, let me have that rope. Hurry it up! So who's going to come help me, fellas? You'll be rewarded for your pains!

TIKHON: Never mind them…Let 'em sleep it off, we'll manage it between us.

COACHMAN: Whew, I'm beat! It's cold and muddy, and I'm soaking wet…Oh, by the way, my good man…you don't happen to have a free room, where the mistress can warm herself for a while? The carriage is tilted, it's impossible to sit in it…

TIKHON: Oh, so now she wants a room? She can warm herself in here if she's cold…We'll make room for her. *(Goes up to BORTSOV and makes a place next to him.)* Get up, get up! You can camp out on the floor for an hour or so, while the mistress warms up. *(To BORTSOV.)* Get up, your honor! Sit over here! *(BORTSOV stands up.)* Here's a place for you.

The COACHMAN exits.

FEDYA: So now we got company! What fool's luck brought *her* here! Now we won't get a wink of sleep before dawn!

TIKHON: Pity I didn't ask for fifteen rubles…She would have paid it…*(Stands before the door, waiting.)* Listen folks, behave yourselves, now…And watch your language…

Enter MARYA YEGOROVNA, followed by the COACHMAN.

TIKHON: *(Bows.)* Welcome, dear lady, to our humble dwelling. It's a place fit for peasants and cockroaches. But never mind, don't be squeamish. Make yourself at home!

MARYA YEGOROVNA: I can't see a thing in here…Where should I go?

TIKHON: Right this way, most noble lady! *(Leads her over to a place next to BORTSOV.)* Right this way, please! *(Blows on the seat.)* We have no separate rooms here, forgive me, but don't you worry, dear lady. These are good and gentle people…

MARYA YEGOROVNA: *(Sits down right next to BORTSOV.)* It's terribly stuffy in here! At least let's open the door!

TIKHON: Yes, Madam! *(Runs and opens the door wide.)*

MERIK: Everyone'll be frozen stiff, but she has to have the door open wide! *(Gets up and slams the door.)* Who does she think she is, anyway? *(Lies down.)*

TIKHON: Forgive us, gracious lady, he's a fool…the village idiot, so to speak…But don't be frightened, he won't harm you…Only forgive me, madame, I can't agree to ten rubles…Fifteen, if you would be so kind…

MARYA YEGOROVNA: Fine, only hurry up!…

TIKHON: Right away…We'll do it immediately…*(Takes rope out from under the bench.)* Right away…

Pause.

BORTSOV: *(Looks at MARYA YEGOROVNA.)* Marie...Masha...

MARYA YEGOROVNA: *(Looks at BORTSOV.)* What is it?

BORTSOV: Marie...Is it you? Where have you come from?

> *MARYA YEGOROVNA, recognizing BORTSOV, cries out and rushes to the middle of the tavern. BORTSOV follows after her.*

Marie, It is I...I! *(Laughs wildly.)* My wife! Marie! But where am I? Give me some light, people!

MARYA YEGOROVNA: Get away from me! You're lying, it's not you! It's impossible! *(Covers her face with her hands.)* It's a lie, this is nonsense!

BORTSOV: Your voice, your movements...Marie, it is I! You see...I'm not... drunk, any more...It's just that my head keeps going round...My God! Wait, wait...I simply can't understand it! *(Cries out.)* My wife! *(Falls at her feet and sobs.)*

> *A group gathers round the couple.*

MARYA YEGOROVNA: Get away from me! *(To the COACHMAN.)* Denis, let's go! I can't stay here any longer!

MERIK: *(Jumps up and stares intently at her face.)* The portrait! *(Seizes her arm.)* She's one and the same! It's her! Hey, people! It's the master's wife!

MARYA YEGOROVNA: Get away from me, you boor! *(Tries to free her arm.)* Denis, don't just stand there! *(COACHMAN and TIKHON rush to her and seize MERIK by the arm.)* This is a den of thieves! Let go of my arm! I'm not afraid!...Get away from me!

MERIK: Wait a minute, then I'll let you go...Just let me have a word with you...Just one word, so that you might understand...Wait...*(Turns to TIKHON and THE COACHMAN.)* Let me go, you louts, take your hands off me! I'm not letting her go, until I say what I'm going to say! Just wait a minute. *(Bangs his forehead with his fist.)* God, how stupid can you get! Now I can't think of what I wanted to say!

MARYA YEGOROVNA: *(Pulls her arm away.)* Get away from me! You're drunk...Let's go, Denis. *(Starts toward the door.)*

MERIK: *(Blocks her way.)* Look at him, just look at him! Give him at least one kind word. For God's sake!

MARYA YEGOROVNA: Get this lunatic away from me.

MERIK: Then curse you, and may you rot in hell! *(Brandishes the axe.)*

> *There is a terrible commotion. Everyone jumps up noisily. There are shouts of horror. SAVVA places himself in between MERIK and MARYA YEGOROVNA...THE COACHMAN shoves MERIK aside violently, and*

carries his mistress out of the tavern. After this, all stand as if rooted to the ground. There is a prolonged pause.

BORTSOV: *(Clutches at the air.)* Marie…Where are you, Marie?

NAZAROVNA: My God, my God…My heart can't take it, you murderers! What an accursed night!

MERIK: *(Lowering his hand that is holding the axe.)* Did I kill her, or not?…

TIKHON: Thank God you got out of this alive…

MERIK: I didn't kill her, so then…*(Staggers over to his place.)* Then it's not my fate to die from a stolen axe…*(Sinks into his place and sobs.)* O anguish! My accursed anguish! Have pity upon me, true believers!

Curtain.

1885

On the Harmful Effects of Tobacco

A Monologue in One Act

IVAN IVANOVICH NYUKHIN, his wife's husband, she being the proprietress of a music conservatory and boarding school for young ladies.

The scene takes place on the dais of an auditorium in a provincial club.

On the Harmful Effects of Tobacco

Enter NYUKHIN, wearing long side-whiskers, with no moustache, and an old, threadbare tailcoat. He strides in majestically, bows, and adjusts his waistcoat.

NYUKHIN: Ladies, and, in a manner of speaking, gentlemen. *(Combs his whiskers.)* It has been suggested to my wife that I deliver a public lecture here today for charitable purposes. Well, why not? If I'm supposed to lecture, I'll lecture. It's all the same to me, really. I mean, I'm not a professor, well of course I'm not, in fact, I have no academic degree of any kind, but, nevertheless, and be that as it may, I have worked these past thirty years, worked without cease, I might very well add, to the detriment of my own health and so on and so forth, worked on issues of purest science, reflecting upon them, even writing scholarly articles on them from time to time, if you can imagine, well not exactly scholarly, but, if you'll pardon the expression, sort of scholarly, so to speak. Incidentally, I wrote a very extensive article recently, entitled: "Certain insects and their adverse effects." My daughters liked it very much, particularly the part about the bedbugs, but then I reread it and tore it to pieces. Because it's all the same in the end, really, you know, whether you write articles or not, you just can't get by without insect powder. We've even got bedbugs in the piano… I have chosen, as it were, for the topic of today's lecture: the harmful effects of tobacco on humans. Now I myself am a smoker, but my wife has instructed me to talk about the harmfulness of tobacco today, and so, as they say, that's that. If it's tobacco, then it's tobacco — really, I couldn't care less, but I do ask you, distinguished ladies and gentlemen, to try to take my lecture today as seriously as you possibly can, or else I shall suffer the consequences. And whosoever is put off by pure scientific discourse, then by all means, he or she is absolutely free to leave. *(Adjusts his waistcoat.)* I would, however, specifically like to call to attention any doctors who might be present, who might glean from my lecture some particularly useful information, inasmuch as tobacco, apart from its harmful effects, also has practical medical application. For example, if we were to place a fly into a snuffbox, then it would most likely die from a nervous disorder. Tobacco is considered, for the most part, to be a plant…When I give a lecture, I find that my right eye tends to twitch, so please, pay no attention to it, it's because I'm nervous. I'm a very nervous person, generally speaking, and my eye started twitching on the thirteenth of September, 1889, the very same day upon which my wife gave birth, so to speak, to our fourth daughter, Varvara. All my daughters were born on the thirteenth day of the month. However *(looks at his watch)* in view of the shortage of time, let us not stray from the subject of our lecture. At this time I should call to your attention that my wife runs both a music conservatory and a private boarding school, well, not exactly a boarding school, but something along those lines. Confidentially, my wife is fond of complaining about financial difficulties, but she's got money stashed away, forty or fifty thousand rubles, to be exact, while I haven't got a kopek to my name, not one single kopek — oh well, what's the use in talking about it! I manage the housekeeping department in the boarding school. I buy the supplies, supervise the servants, keep the accounts, stitch the copy books, get rid of the bedbugs, walk my wife's dog, catch the mice…Last evening, it was my responsibility to provide the cook with flour and oil, because we were having blinis. Well, today, to make a long story short, after the blinis were already made, my wife came into the kitchen to inform us that three of the pupils would not be eating blinis, because they had swollen glands. And, so it seems, we found ourselves with an overabundance of blinis. What were we supposed to do with them? At first, my wife ordered me to store them in the cellar, but she thought for a moment, and then she said: "Oh, go eat them yourself, dummy." That's what she calls me when she's in a bad mood: dummy. Or viper. Or Satan. Where did she get "Satan" from? She's always in a bad mood. Anyway, what happened was, I swallowed them whole, the blinis, swallowed them without chewing them, even, I was so hungry. I'm always hungry. Yesterday, for example, she wouldn't give me any dinner. "What's the point in feeding you, dummy?" However *(glances at his watch)* we're digressing again, we're off the subject. As I was saying…You'd much rather be listening to a love song right now, wouldn't you, or a symphony, or an aria…*(Bursts into song.)* "We will never blink an eye, when we hear the battle cry!" I never can remember where that comes from…By the way, I forgot to tell you that, in my wife's music conservatory, in addition to managing the housekeeping, I also have the responsibility of teaching mathematics, physics, chemistry, geography, history, musical theory, literature, etcetera etcetera. For dancing, singing, and drawing lessons my wife charges extra, although I am the dancing and singing instructor as well. Our music conservatory is located on Five Dogs Lane, Number 13.

That's why I've been so unlucky in life, in all likelihood, because we live at House Number 13. And my daughters were all born on the thirteenth day of the month, and our house has thirteen windows...Oh, what's the use of talking about it! My wife is available by appointment, at our home, any time of day, and brochures can be obtained, if you wish, from the porter at the door, thirty kopeks a copy. *(Takes some brochures from his pocket.)* I happen to have a supply on me for distribution, if anyone's interested. Thirty kopeks each! Anyone want one? *(Pause.)* No one? How about twenty kopeks! *(Pause.)* Too bad. That's right, house number thirteen! Nothing has worked out for me in life, I've gotten older, and duller...Here I am, delivering a lecture to you, with a great big smile on my face, but deep down inside I want to scream at the top of my lungs, I want to fly away to the ends of the earth. I want to weep...and I've no one to tell my troubles to...What about my daughters, you say...Well, what about them? When I try to talk to them, they only laugh in my face...My wife has seven daughters...No, sorry, six...*(Quickly.)* Seven! The eldest one, Anna, is twenty-seven, and the youngest is seventeen. Ladies and gentlemen! *(Glances around.)* I'm so unhappy, I've become a fool, a nobody, and yet, really and truly, you see standing before you the most fortunate of fathers. Really and truly. And that's as it should be, what more can I say. If only you knew! I've been married to my wife for thirty-three years, and I can safely say that these have been the best years of my life, well, maybe not exactly the best, but something along those lines. They have flown by, in a word, like one happy moment, so to speak, and curse them all, curse them. *(Glances around.)* Anyway, she still hasn't arrived, she's not here yet, so I can say whatever I like...I'm terribly frightened...I'm frightened whenever she looks at me. What was I saying? Oh yes: My daughters are taking a long time getting themselves married, probably because they're shy, and also because they never get to meet any men. My wife doesn't like giving parties, she never invites anyone over for dinner, she's such a miserable, miserly, hellish sort of woman, and so no one ever comes to visit us, but...I'll let you in on a secret...*(Comes down to the footlights.)* My daughters can be found on all major holidays at their aunt's, Natalya Semyonovna's, you know, the one who suffers from rheumatism and goes around wearing this horrendous yellow dress with the black spots that looks like it has cockroaches crawling all over it. Go and visit, they'll even feed you. And if my wife isn't there, you might even...you know...*(Makes a gesture of drinking.)* I should tell you, by the way, it only takes one glass and away I go, and oh, do I I feel good inside, so good, and at the same time so sad, I can't tell you how sad I feel then, I start thinking of when I was young, and then suddenly for some reason I feel like running away, oh, if only you knew how much I wanted to run away!

(Passionately.) To run, to throw everything to the winds and just run, without once looking back…and where? It doesn't matter where…if only to run from this vulgar, rotten, worthless, good-for-nothing life, which has made an old man of me, a pitiful, pathetic old fool, a wretched old idiot, to run from this stupid, petty, shallow, miserable, miserable, miserable miser, to run from my wife, who has tortured me for thirty-three years, to run from the conservatory, from the kitchen, from my wife's money, from all the stupidity and vulgarity… and stop somewhere far far away, out in a field somewhere, and stand there like a tree, or a telegraph pole, or a scarecrow, under the wide-open sky, and gaze all night at the silent moon shining above, and forget, forget…Oh, how I wish never again to remember, never!…How I long to tear off this wretched old coat, the coat I was married in thirty-three years ago…*(tears off coat)* the coat in which I give my never-ending lectures for charitable purposes…Take that! *(Throws coat on ground and tramples on it.)* And that! I'm old, and poor, and pathetic, like this shabby old waistcoat with its threadbare seams…*(Indicates the back.)* I don't want anything! I'm above all this! Once upon a time I was young, and brilliant, I went to the university, I had dreams, I was a human being… And now, now I want nothing! Nothing, only leave me in peace…leave me in peace! *(Glances around, puts on his coat.)* There's my wife, she's waiting out there in the wings…She's come at last, and she's waiting for me…*(Looks at his watch.)* We're out of time…If she asks you, then please, I beg of you, tell her that the lecture did take place…that the dummy — that is to say, me, that *I* conducted myself with complete decorum. *(Looks around, clears his throat.)* She's looking this way… *(Raises his voice.)* And thus, in conclusion, based on the evidence presented here today, as I have proven, that tobacco is a terribly poisonous substance, it therefore follows that you should not smoke under any circumstances, and I venture to say, furthermore, that I hope that my lecture "On the Harmful Effects of Tobacco" has been of benefit to you, to whatever extent. There. I've said it. And now I feel much better. "Dixi et animam levavi!" *(Bows and exits majestically.)*

1886–1902

SWAN SONG

(Calchas)

A Dramatic Study in One Act

VASILY VASILYICH SVETLOVIDOV, a comic actor, sixty-eight years
   of age

NIKITA IVANICH, an elderly prompter

The action takes place on the stage of a provincial theatre, at night, after a performance.

Swan Song

The empty stage of a second-rate provincial theatre. On the right, a row of unpainted, roughly constructed doors, leading to the dressing rooms; on the left and upstage, assorted rubbish. In the middle of the stage, an overturned stool. Nighttime. It is dark.

SVETLOVIDOV, in the costume of Calchas, with a candle in his hand, enters from the dressing room, laughing.

SVETLOVIDOV: Well, well, well, what do you know? What-do-you-know! That's a fine kettle of fish! That's a fine how-do-you-do! Fell asleep in the dressing room, didn't I? Show's over, theatre's empty, everyone's gone home, and I'm left behind, snoring away, like an old saw. You old relic, you! You old fossil! Had one too many, dropped off without knowing it, didn't you? You old mummy! *(Calls out.)* Yegorka! Yegorka, damn you! Petrushka! Out cold, the devils...curse 'em! Yegorka! *(Takes a stool, sits on it and places the candle on the floor.)* Silence...Only an echo...that's all... Yegorka and Petrushka...three rubles apiece they got from me today...for their diligence...won't find them around here any more, not even with bloodhounds...gone, probably locked the theatre up behind them, too, the miserable wretches...*(Shakes his head.)* Drunk! Ugh! A benefit performance, thank you very much, and all that wine and beer they poured down my throat tonight...good God! I'm completely hung over, I've got twelve tongues rolling around in my mouth...Disgusting...

Pause.

Stupid, isn't it...The old fool — drunk again, and in the name of what... Ugh! Good God!...My back aches, my head aches, I feel feverish all over... but in my soul, it's cold and dark, like a cave. All right, so ruin your health, who cares, but at least take pity on your old age, Vasilyich, you fool...

Pause.

Old age...Go on, play your games, put on the mask, play the fool...your life's over...sixty-eight years old and you've had it! Too late!...You've drained the bottle, there's nothing left...only the dregs...So...Too bad, Vasyusha...that's the way it goes...Like it or not, time to rehearse the part of the corpse...Old mother death waiting for her cue...*(Looks around.)*... Do you know, I've been on the stage for forty-five years now, and it's the first time I've ever seen an empty theatre at night...Yes, the very first time...Strange, isn't it...*(Goes to the footlights.)* Can't see a goddamn thing...Wait... prompter's booth...reserved box...conductor's stand...and beyond? Darkness! A black hole, a yawning grave, where death itself is lurking!... Brrrr!...it's cold! A draft from the hall, cold, like an empty chimney, ghosts drifting down the the aisles...sends chills up your spine!... *(Calls out.)* Yegorka! Petrushka! Where are you, devils? Good God, why do I curse so much! Stop it! Stop this swearing! Stop this drinking — you're too old...time to die...At sixty-eight years of age, respectable people, they get up, they go to church, they prepare themselves for death, and you... Good God! Just look at you! Profanity, debauchery, buffoonery...You're not fit to be seen! Got to get dressed...Terrifying! Could have sat here all night...could have died of fright...*(Goes toward his dressing room.)*

At the same time, from the farthest dressing room door upstage, NIKITA IVANICH appears in a white dressing gown.

SVETLOVIDOV: *(Sees NIKITA IVANICH, screams with fright and staggers backwards.)* Who's there? Omigod! Who is it? Who are you?

NIKITA IVANICH: It is I, sir!

SVETLOVIDOV: Who are you?

NIKITA IVANICH: *(Slowly approaching him.)* It is I, sir, the prompter, sir, Nikita Ivanich...Vasily Vasilyich, it is I, sir, really and truly!

SVETLOVIDOV: *(Sinks down onto the stool with exhaustion, breathing heavily and trembling all over.)* Omigod! Who?...Is it you, Nikitushka, really? Why...why are you here?

NIKITA IVANICH: I've been sleeping in the dressing rooms, sir...only, I beg of you, sir, don't tell Aleksey Fomich...I have nowhere else to spend the night, sir, as God is my witness...

SVETLOVIDOV: You, Nikitushka...My God, my God! Sixteen curtain calls, three bouquets, God only knows what else, everyone in ecstasy, and not one living, breathing soul to wake up a poor, drunken old man and take him home...I am an old man, Nikitushka...I'm sixty-eight years old...I'm sick! My poor, weak soul is withering away...*(Takes the prompter's hands and weeps.)* Don't leave me, Nikitushka...I'm old, sick, feeble...should have been dead long ago...It's terrible! Terrible!...

NIKITA IVANICH: *(Tenderly and respectfully.)* Vasily Vasilyich, time to go home, sir!

SVETLOVIDOV: I'm not going! I have no place to go home to — none, none, none!

NIKITA IVANICH: Heavens! Forgotten where we live, now, have we!

SVETLOVIDOV: I won't go there, I won't! I'm alone…I have no one, Nikitushka, no one, no family, no wife, no children…I'm alone, like the wind in the field…I'll die, and no one will remember me…How terrible it is to be alone…No one to warm me, comfort me, put me to bed when I'm drunk…Whom do I belong to? Who needs me? Who loves me? No one loves me, Nikitushka!

NIKITA IVANICH: *(Through tears.)* The public loves you, Vasily Vasilyich!

SVETLOVIDOV: The public went home, they went to bed, they've forgotten their clown! No, no one needs me, no one loves me…I have no wife, no children…

NIKITA IVANICH: Nonsense! What are you grieving about…

SVETLOVIDOV: I am a human being, I'm alive, I have blood coursing through my veins, not water. I'm a gentleman, if you please, Nikitushka, I'm from good stock…Before I fell into this black hole, I served in our military, in the artillery unit…How young I was, then, how bold, handsome, daring, passionate! My God, where has it all gone? And what an actor I was, then, Nikitushka, wasn't I? *(Having risen to his feet, leans on the prompter's arm.)* Where has it all gone to, where is it, that time? My God! And now I look into this hole — and I remember everything, everything! This hole has swallowed up forty-five years of my life, and what a life it was, Nikitushka! I look into this hole now and I see its every feature, as clear as the nose on your face. The joys of youth, the fire, the passion, the love of women! Women, Nikitushka!

NIKITA IVANICH: Time for you to go to bed, Vasily Vasilyich!

SVETLOVIDOV: When I was a young actor, when I was just starting out, in the heat of it all, I remember — a woman in the audience fell in love with me, with my stage persona…Elegant, shapely, like a poplar tree, young, innocent, pure, fiery as the summer dawn! A glance from her blue eyes, a flash of her dazzling smile, and night itself could not maintain its darkness. Ocean breakers beat the rocky shores, but waves of her golden curls might have crushed cliffs, melted icebergs, snowdrifts! I remember I stood before her once, just as I stand before you now…So lovely was she, lovelier than ever before, and the look that she gave me that day I take with me to my grave…Such softness, sweet soulfulness, the velvet of youth, the brilliance of it! Thrilled, ecstatic, I fell on my knees before her, and asked for her hand…*(Continues in a hushed voice.)* And she…she said: leave the stage! Leave-the-stage!…Do you hear me? All well and good to fall in love with an actor, but to marry one — never! I remember, I had a performance that night…A crude, clownish role…So, I played it, and felt my eyes opening right then and there…And then I saw that nothing is sacred about our art, that it's all deceit, delirium, and that I — I am but a slave, an idle plaything, a fool, a buffoon! How well I understood the public then! From that time on I never believed the applause, the bouquets, the wreaths, the rapturous raves…Yes, Nikitushka! They applaud me, buy my photograph for a ruble, but I'm an outcast to them — I'm scum, a public prostitute! They seek me out for their vanity, but would they lower themselves to let me marry their sisters, their daughters?…No, I don't trust them! *(Sinks down on the stool.)* Not one bit!

NIKITA IVANICH: You're not yourself, Vasily Vasilyich! You're frightening me, really…Come home, now, for heaven's sake!

SVETLOVIDOV: And that day, I began to see the light…And how dearly that vision cost me, Nikitushka! After that little incident…after the lady in question…I wandered, aimlessly, I lost my reason for living, for looking to the future…I played the fools, the buffoons, I clowned, I caroused, and yet what an artist I was, what talent! I buried that talent, I vulgarized it, I lost my voice, my inspiration…The yawning black hole has swallowed me alive! I didn't feel it before, but today, for the first time…I woke up, looked around, and there lay sixty-eight years behind me. And now I see it — old age! My song is sung! *(Sobs.)* My song is sung!

NIKITA IVANICH: Vasily Vasilyich! My dear, sweet fellow…There, there, you mustn't, you mustn't! Good heavens! *(Calls out.)* Petrushka! Yegorka!

SVETLOVIDOV: What talent I had! What power! You can't imagine, what delivery! What feeling and grace, what spirit, in this breast! *(Beats his chest.)* Overpowering! Hey, listen to this, old fellow…wait, let me catch my breath…here's something from *King Lear*…Picture it — black sky, torrents, thunder —- rrrrrrrr!…lightning —- zzzhhhhh! streaking through the sky, and then:

"Blow, winds, and crack your cheeks. Rage, blow!
You cataracts and hurricanoes, spout
Till you have drenched our steeples, drowned the cocks.
You sulph'rous and thought-executing fires,
Vaunt-couriers of oak-cleaving thunderbolts,
Singe my white head. And thou, all-shaking thunder,

Strike flat the thick rotundity o' th' world,
Crack Nature's molds, all germains spill at at once,
That makes ingrateful man."

(Impatiently.) Quickly — the Fool's lines! (Stamps his foot.) Give me the Fool's lines! Quickly! I'm running out of time.

NIKITA IVANICH: (In the role of "The Fool".) "O Nuncle, court holy-water in a dry house is better than this rain water out o' door. Good Nuncle, in; ask thy daughters' blessing. Here's a night pities neither wise man nor fools."

SVETLOVIDOV: "Rumble thy bellyful. Spit, fire. Spout, rain!
Nor rain, wind, thunder, fire are my daughters.
I tax not you, you elements, with unkindness.
I never gave you kingdom, call'd you children."

Power! Talent! Artistry! Something else...something else...from the old days...(bursts into joyous laughter)...let's have some *Hamlet!* I'll begin... How does it go? Oh, yes...(Playing "Hamlet".)

"O, the recorders. Let me see one. To withdraw with you — why do you go about to recover the wind of me, as if you would drive me into a toil?"

NIKITA IVANICH: (As "Guildenstern".) O my lord, if my duty be too bold, my love is too unmannerly."

SVETLOVIDOV: "I do not well understand that. Will you play upon this pipe?"

NIKITA IVANICH: "My lord, I cannot."

SVETLOVIDOV: "I pray you."

NIKITA IVANICH: "Believe me, I cannot."

SVETLOVIDOV: "I do beseech you."

NIKITA IVANICH: "I know no touch of it, my lord."

SVETLOVIDOV: "It is as easy as lying. Govern these ventages with your fingers and thumb, give it breath with your mouth, and it will discourse most eloquent music. Look you, these are the stops."

NIKITA IVANICH: "But these cannot I command to any utt'rance of harmony. I have not the skill."

SVETLOVIDOV: "Why, look you now, how unworthy a thing you make of me! You would play upon me, you would seem to know my stops, you would pluck out the heart of my mystery, you would sound me from my lowest note to the top of my compass; and there is much music, excellent voice, in this little organ, yet cannot you make it speak. 'Sblood, do you think I am easier to be played on than a pipe? Call me what instrument you will, though you can fret me, you cannot play upon me." *(Laughs and applauds.)*

Bravo! Encore! Bravo! Old age be damned! There is no old age, it's all nonsense, rubbish! The fountain of youth gushes through my veins — strength, freshness, life! Where there is talent, Nikitushka, there is no old age! Have I gone crazy, Nikitushka? Have I gone mad? Wait, I'm coming to my senses...Oh, my God, oh, heavens above! Just listen to this, what delicacy, what subtlety...what music! Hush!...Ssshhhh!

"A quiet night in the Ukraine,
With sparkling stars, translucent sky;
A gentle drowsiness remains,
A subtle stillness — just a sigh
Of breeze-kissed branches trembling there
On silvery poplar —"

A sound of doors opening.

What's that?

NIKITA IVANICH: It must be Petrushka and Yegorka...What talent, Vasily Vasilyich, what talent!

SVETLOVIDOV: *(Calls out, in the direction of the sound.)* In here, wretches! *(To NIKITA IVANICH.)* Let's go and get dressed...There is no old age, it's all rubbish, nonsense...*(Laughs merrily.)* Why are you crying? My poor old fool, what's all this sniveling? We can't have that! We can't have that! Come on, old fellow, now, what's that face for? What's it for, eh? Come on, come on...*(Embraces him, through tears.)* No need to cry...Where there is art, where there is talent, there's no old age, no loneliness, no illness...and death itself is a just a detail...*(Weeps.)* No, Nikitushka, you're right, our song is sung...What talent do I have!? I'm a squeezed out lemon, an icicle, a rusty old nail, and you...you're just a prompter, an old theatre rat...Let's go, then!

They start to exit.

What talent do I have? I'm a spear-carrier, Nikitushka, the last of Fortinbras's retinue...and a tad too old for that, too...Yes...Do remember the lines from *Othello,* Nikitushka?

"O, now forever
Farewell the tranquil mind! farewell content!
Farewell the plumed troop, and the big wars
That make ambition virtue! O, farewell!
Farewell the neighing steed and the shrill trump,
The spirit-stirring drum, th'ear-piercing fife,
The royal banner, and all quality,
Pride, pomp, and circumstance of glorious war!
And O you mortal engines whose rude throats
Th' immortal Jove's dread clamors counterfeit,
Farewell! Othello's occupation's gone!"

NIKITA IVANICH: What talent! What talent!
SVETLOVIDOV: And what about:

"A horse…my kingdom for a horse…"

Reciting, he exits with NIKITA IVANICH.

The curtain lowers slowly.

1887

THE BEAR

A Farce in One Act

DEDICATED TO N. N. SOLOVTSOV

CAST OF CHARACTERS

YELENA IVANOVNA POPOVA, a lovely little widow with dimples, also a landowner

GRIGORY STEPANOVICH SMIRNOV, a landowner in his prime

LUKA, Popova's elderly servant

The drawing room of POPOVA's country estate.

The Bear

POPOVA and LUKA. POPOVA is in a state of deep mourning; her eyes are fixed on a photograph.

LUKA: It's not right, mistress…You're wasting away…Cook and parlor maid have gone berry-picking, rejoicing in the out-of-doors, taking in the pure, fresh air, every living creature is happy, even the cat knows how to take her pleasure in life, she's out chasing after the little birds, while here you sit inside, all day long, like a nun in a convent, you take no pleasure in life at all. Yes indeed, and that's the truth! Just think of it, a year has gone by since you've been out of the house!…

POPOVA: And never shall I go out again, ever!…Why should I? My life is over. He lies in his grave, and I'm buried between these four walls…We've both died.

LUKA: Listen to you! My ears shouldn't hear such things, truly. Nikolai Mikhailovich died, and what can we do, it's all God's will, may his soul rest in peace…You've mourned him, and now enough's enough, don't overdo it. You can't weep and wail over him forever. Now I had a wife once too, in my time, she died…And what did I do? I grieved, I cried over her for a month, and that was it, I wasn't going to weep forever, and anyway the old lady wasn't worth it. *(Sighs.)* You've forgotten all your neighbors…You don't visit them, you don't invite them here…We live like spiders, forgive me for saying so — we never see the light of day. The mice have eaten all the provisions…And it's not as if there weren't any proper people around…why, the district is full of gentlemen…There's a regiment over in Riblova, and those officers are as handsome as they can be! Not a Friday night goes by there isn't a ball, and every day the brass band plays…Ah, mistress! Dear mistress! You're young and pretty as peaches and cream, why don't you just live to your heart's content…Beauty doesn't last forever! Wait ten years till you show yourself off to the officers, and it will be too late.

POPOVA: *(Emphatically.)* I ask you never to speak of this to me again! You know very well, since Nikolai Mikhailovich died, that life has lost all meaning to me. It seems to you that I'm alive, but seems is all it is! I've made a vow never to shed my widow's weeds and never to see the light of day, not until I reach the grave…Do you hear me? Let his spirit see how much I love him…Yes, I know, it's no secret to you, he often was mean to me, and cruel and…even unfaithful, but I shall remain true to him unto the grave, I'll prove to him that I am capable of love. And there, from the beyond, he'll see me for the woman I truly was…

LUKA: Better to take a stroll around the garden than say such things, better to have Toby or Giant harnessed up and call upon your neighbors…

POPOVA: Ach!…*(She weeps.)*

LUKA: Mistress!…Matushka! What's this? For God's sake!

POPOVA: He loved Toby so! He always rode Toby — to the Korchagins, to the Vlasovs, everywhere. How beautifully he rode! How gracefully! How powerfully he pulled upon those reins! Remember? Toby, Toby! Tell them to give him an extra handful of oats today!

LUKA: Yes, mistress!

The doorbell rings sharply.

POPOVA: *(Shudders.)* Who's there? Tell them I am receiving no one.

LUKA: Yes, mistress! *(Exits.)*

POPOVA: *(Alone. Gazes at the photograph.)* You'll see, *cher Nicolas,* how I'm able to love and to forgive…While this poor heart still beats, so shall I love you. *(Laughs through her tears.)* And aren't you ashamed of yourself? Here am I, the dutiful little wife, I've shut myself away under lock and key, I'll be faithful to you unto the grave, while you…aren't you ashamed, you cur? You deceived me, betrayed me, you made scenes, you left me alone for weeks at a time…

Enter LUKA.

LUKA: *(Anxiously.)* Mistress, someone is inquiring after you. He wishes to see you…

POPOVA: But haven't you told him that I am receiving no one since the day of my husband's death?

LUKA: I told him, but he doesn't want to listen, he says that he is here on urgent business.

POPOVA: I am re-cei-ving no one!

LUKA: I told him that, but…the devil, he just kept on swearing and barged right in…he's already in the dining room…

POPOVA: *(Irritated.)* Very well, show him in…What boorishness!
Exit LUKA.

These people! What do they want from me? Why do they disturb my peace? *(Sighs.)* No, it's all very clear, really, I'll just have to take myself off to a nunnery…*(Deep in thought.)* Yes, to a nunnery…

Enter LUKA and SMIRNOV.

SMIRNOV: *(To LUKA.)* Idiot, you know what your problem is? You talk too much…Jackass! *(Seeing POPOVA, with decorum.)* Allow me, madam, to introduce myself: Grigory Stepanovich Smirnov, retired artillery lieutenant and landowner! I am obliged to disturb you on highly urgent business…

POPOVA: *(Without extending her hand.)* And what may I do for you?

SMIRNOV: Your late husband, with whom I had the honor of being acquainted, left behind him two outstanding debts to me personally, totalling one thousand two hundred rubles. And since tomorrow I am faced with a mortgage payment myself, I'd be much obliged, madam, if you would pay me the money you owe me today.

POPOVA: One thousand two hundred…But why was my husband in debt to you?

SMIRNOV: He used to buy oats from me.

POPOVA: *(Sighing, to LUKA.)* Oh, that's right, Luka, don't forget to tell them to give Toby an extra handful of oats.

Exit LUKA.

(To SMIRNOV.) If Nikolai Mikhailovich owed you money, then of course, it goes without saying, I shall pay you; but forgive me, please, I don't have the money to do so today. My steward returns the day after tomorrow, and I shall tell him to pay you what you are owed, but until that time I cannot oblige you…In addition to which, it is seven months ago today that my poor husband died, and I am in no mood to concern myself with monetary matters.

SMIRNOV: And I am in no mood to go bankrupt. If I don't pay the interest on the mortgage tomorrow, they'll seize my estate!

POPOVA: You'll get your money the day after tomorrow.

SMIRNOV: I don't need my money the day after tomorrow, I need it today.

POPOVA: Forgive me, but I simply cannot pay you today.

SMIRNOV: And I cannot wait till the day after tomorrow.

POPOVA: But what can I do if I just don't have it today!

SMIRNOV: So therefore, you cannot pay me?

POPOVA: I cannot…

SMIRNOV: Hm!…And this is your last word?

POPOVA: Yes, my last word.

SMIRNOV: Your last word? Positively?

POPOVA: Positively.

SMIRNOV: Well, I most humbly thank you. I shall remember this. *(Shrugs his shoulders.)* And they expect me to be calm, cool, and collected about it! On the way over here, I met the tax collector, and he asks me: "Why are you always so angry, Grigory Stepanovich?" Well excuse me, please, why shouldn't I be angry? I'm in dire need of money…I set out yesterday morning, long before dawn, I visited all my debtors, and not one of them paid what he owed me! I'm dead as a dog, I spent the night god knows where — in some tavern next to a vodka barrel — and finally I come out here, almost fifty miles from home, I expect to get paid, and what do I get: "I'm not in the mood!" Why shouldn't I be angry?

POPOVA: I believe that I made it quite clear: When my steward comes back from town, you'll get your money.

SMIRNOV: I haven't come to see your steward, I've come to see you! What in hell, you should pardon the expression, do I care about your steward?

POPOVA: Forgive me, dear sir, but I am unaccustomed to such strange expressions, and to such a tone of voice. I shall listen to you no longer. *(Rushes out.)*

SMIRNOV: *(Alone.)* Well, excu-u-use me! Not in the mood…Her husband died seven months ago! And what about me? Do I have to pay my interest or don't I? I ask you: Do I or don't I? All right, your husband died, you're not in the mood, whatever…your steward's gone off somewhere, curse him, so what am I supposed to do? Flee from my creditors in an hot air balloon? Take a flying leap and bash my head against a wall? I go and call on Gruzdev — and nobody's home. Yaroshevich is in hiding. I have a knock-down-drag-out fight with Kuritzyn and almost hurl him out a window, Mazutov has cholera, and this one is "not in the mood." Not one of these swine will pay me. And all because I've spoiled them, I'm a "Milquetoast," a sniveler, a soft touch! I'm too easy on them! But just you wait! You will remember me! I will not be trifled with, confound it! I'll stand my ground — I'll stay here here until she pays up, that's what I'll do! Brrrr!…I'm in a rage today, a real rage! I'm shaking with fury, I can't even breathe…My God, I feel positively faint! *(Cries out.)* Hey, you!

Enter LUKA.

LUKA: And what may I do for you, sir?

SMIRNOV: Water, give me water...or kvass!

Exit LUKA.

I mean, what sort of sense does it make, now I ask you! A man is badly in need of money, he's ready to hang himself, and she won't pay up, because, you see, she's in no condition to discuss financial matters!...That's the feminine mind for you! Crinoline logic, is what I call it! And that's why I don't like talking to women, never have, never will. I'd rather sit on a barrel of gunpowder than talk to a woman. Brrr!...That dress of hers, the sight of it makes my flesh creep. The mere glimpse of a woman gives me cramps in my legs. Makes me want to cry "help!"

Enter LUKA.

LUKA: *(Gives him water.)* The mistress is ill, she's not receiving.
SMIRNOV: Get out of here!

Exit LUKA.

"She's ill, she's not receiving!" Fine, don't...I'll stay here, that's what I'll do, I'll sit here till she gives me my money. She can be sick for a week, and I'll sit here for a week...She can be sick for a year, and I'll sit here for a year...I'll have what is mine, madam! Neither widow's weeds nor dimpled cheeks will fool me...We know all about those dimples! *(Shouts through the window.)* Semyon, unharness those horses! We're not leaving so fast! I plan to stay here for a while! Tell them in the stables to give the horses oats! And look, you swine, you've got the left trace horse all tangled up in the reins again! *(Mimics.)* Never mind?...I'll give you "never mind!" *(Goes away from the window.)* I feel terrible...the heat is unbearable, nobody's paying me, I haven't slept all night, and now the one in the widow's weeds isn't in the mood...My head aches...Vodka, that's what I need. Why not? *(Shouts.)* Hey, you!

Enter LUKA.

LUKA: And what may I do for you, sir?
SMIRNOV: Bring me a glass of vodka!

Exit LUKA.

Ugh! *(Sits down and looks himself over.)* Well, I must look a sight! Dusty, dirty, unwashed, uncombed, mud on my boots, straw on my waistcoat...I'm afraid the little lady took me for a highwayman. *(Yawns.)* It's not polite to appear in the drawing room in such attire, but so what, the hell with it…I'm not a guest here, I'm a creditor, there's no dress code for cred-itors…

LUKA: *(Enters and serves the vodka.)* I see you're making yourself right at home here, sir…

SMIRNOV: *(Angrily.)* What?

LUKA: I…I…never mind, I only meant…

SMIRNOV: Who do you think you're talking to?! Be quiet!

LUKA: *(Aside.)* Swooped down upon us, hasn't he, the demon…sent by Satan himself…

Exit LUKA.

SMIRNOV: A rage, I'm in a rage! I'm so angry, I could blow up the entire world…I feel faint…*(Cries out.)* Hey, you!

Enter POPOVA.

POPOVA: *(Her eyes lowered.)* My dear sir, in my deepest of solitudes I have grown unaccustomed to the sound of the human voice, and I cannot bear shouting. I beg you, I beseech you in all earnestness, do not disturb my peace!

SMIRNOV: Pay me my money, and I'll go away.

POPOVA: I have already told you in the Russian language: I have no money available today; wait until the day after tomorrow.

SMIRNOV: And I also have the honor to reply to you in the Russian language: I do not need my money the day after tomorrow, I need it today. If you do not pay me today, tomorrow I shall be forced to hang myself.

POPOVA: But what can I do, if I have no money! This is positively strange!

SMIRNOV: So you're not going to pay me now? Is that it?

POPOVA: I cannot…

SMIRNOV: In that case I shall remain here, and wait until I get it…*(Sits.)* The day after tomorrow you'll pay me? Fine! I'll sit here till the day after tomor-row. Just like this…*(Leaps up.)* I ask you: Do I have to pay the interest tomorrow or don't I?…Or do you think I'm only joking?

POPOVA: Sir, I ask you not to shout! This is not a stable.

SMIRNOV: I'm not asking you about stables, I'm asking you this: Do I have to pay the interest tomorrow or don't I?

POPOVA: You don't know how to conduct yourself in female company!

SMIRNOV: Oh no no no, I most certainly *do* know how to conduct myself in female company!

POPOVA: Oh no, you don't! You're a coarse, uneducated man! Proper people don't talk like that in the company of ladies!

SMIRNOV: I mean, this is amazing! How do you expect me to talk to you? In French, or what? *(Fuming, he lisps.) Madame, je vous prie*...how happy I am that you haven't paid me my money yet...Oh, *pardon,* I've disturbed you! Lovely weather we're having today! And how charming you look all in black! *(Bows and scrapes.)*

POPOVA: Coarse and not very clever.

SMIRNOV: *(Mimicking.)* Coarse and not very clever! And I don't know how to conduct myself in female company! My dear lady, I have seen more women in my time than you've seen sparrows! Three duels I have fought over women, I've spurned a dozen women, nine more have spurned me! Yes, indeed! Oh, there were times when I played the fool, when I whispered sweet nothings, uttered honeyed words, showered pearls of flattery, when I simpered and swooned...I loved, I suffered, I sighed at the moon, I pined, languished, wasted away, I blew hot and cold...I loved madly, passionately, every which way, heaven help me, I chattered like a magpie about emancipation, I squandered half my soul on the tender passion, and now, thank you very much, but no thank you! You beguile me no longer! Enough! *(Sings.)* "Ochi chornye, ochi strastnye," dark eyes, passionate eyes, crimson lips, dimpled cheeks, moonlit nights, tender whispers, timid sighs — for all this, madam, I wouldn't give a copper kopek! Present company excluded, of course, but all other women, great and small, they're hypocrites, phonies, gossips, scandalmongers, haters, slanderers, liars to the marrow of their bones, they're petty, fussy, ruthless, they're absolutely illogical, and as for what they've got upstairs, *(strikes his forehead)* well, forgive me for saying so, but a sparrow could outdo a philosopher if the philosopher's wearing a skirt! Just look at one of those poetic creatures: a haze of muslin, an elixir of essence, a veritable goddess, but look deeper into her soul, and what do you see: your everyday common crocodile! *(He seizes the back of a chair; it splinters and breaks.)* And do you know what's so outrageous? What do you think this crocodile imagines is her *chef d'oeuvre,* her privilege, her sacred domain? The human heart! Curse me, hang me upside down by my heels, if a woman can love anyone more than a lapdog!...In love, she only can simper and snivel! While the man suffers and sacrifices, she shows her love by swirling her train and holding on tighter to his nose. You have the extreme misfortune of being a woman, you must know from personal experience all about feminine nature. Tell me the truth — have you ever in your life seen a woman who is capable of being honest, faithful and true? You haven't! The only honest and true ones are old maids and freaks! You'd sooner see a horned cat or a white woodcock than you would a faithful woman!

POPOVA: So then who, in your opinion, if you'll permit me to inquire, is faithful and true in love? Surely not a man!

SMIRNOV: Yes indeed, a man it is!

POPOVA: A man! *(With a malicious laugh.)* A man, faithful and true in love! Tell me about it! That's news to me! *(Passionately.)* What right have you to say that? A man, faithful and true in love! Now that we're on the subject, then let me inform you, for your information, that of all the men I've ever known or shall know, the noblest among them was my late husband...I loved him passionately, with all of my being, as only a young and progressive-minded woman can love; I gave him my youth, my happiness, my life, my fortune, I lived and breathed for him, I worshipped the ground he walked on, like a heathen...and what happened? This noblest of men has shamelessly betrayed me at every opportunity! After his death I found drawers full of love letters in his desk, and while he was alive — I shudder to remember it — he would leave me alone for weeks at a time, he would chase other woman right under my nose, he was unfaithful to me, he squandered my money, he laughed at my feelings...And in spite of it all, I loved him and remained true to him...And what's more, he died, and I still remain faithful and true to him. I've buried myself forever between these four walls, I shall wear these widow's weeds unto my grave...

SMIRNOV: *(With a contemptuous laugh.)* Widow's weeds!...I don't understand, what do you take me for, anyway? As if I didn't know why you walk around in this get-up and bury yourself alive! Oh, please! It's so alluring, so poetic! Some young officer happens to wander past the estate, or some crackpot poet, say, and he looks up at the window and he thinks: "There dwells the mysterious Tamara, our dark lady of Lermontov, who out of love for a man has enterred herself twixt these four walls!" We all know that story!

POPOVA: *(Incensed.)* What! How dare you say such things to me?

SMIRNOV: You've buried yourself alive, and yet you haven't forgotten to powder your nose!

POPOVA: How dare you speak to me in such a manner!

SMIRNOV: Will you stop shouting at me, please, I'm not your steward! And let's call things by their proper names here, shall we? I am not a woman, I'm accustomed to speaking my mind plainly! So will you kindly stop shouting!

POPOVA: I'm not shouting, you're shouting! And you can kindly leave me in peace!

SMIRNOV: Pay me my money, and I'll go away.

POPOVA: I am not giving you any money!

SMIRNOV: Oh yes you will, give it to me!

POPOVA: You're not getting a single kopek, that'll serve you right! So you can kindly leave me in peace!

SMIRNOV: I do not have the pleasure of being either your husband or your fiancé, so let's not make a scene here, thank you very much. *(Sits down.)* I don't like it.

POPOVA: *(Choking with rage.)* So you've taken a seat?

SMIRNOV: Yes, I have.

POPOVA: I am asking you to go away!

SMIRNOV: Give me my money...*(Aside.)* What a rage I'm in! What a rage!

POPOVA: I have no desire to converse with insolent individuals! Will you kindly get out of here!

Pause.

So are you going? Yes or no?

SMIRNOV: No.

POPOVA: No?

SMIRNOV: No.

POPOVA: Very well, then! *(Rings.)*

Enter LUKA.

POPOVA: Luka, please show this gentleman out!

LUKA: *(Goes up to SMIRNOV.)* Sir, please, if you're told to go, then go! And let's not have any discussion about it...

SMIRNOV: *(Jumping up.)* Will you shut up! Who do you think you're talking to? I'll make a salad out of you!

LUKA: *(Clutching his heart.)* Oh good heavens!...Saints above!...*(Collapses into an armchair.)* I feel faint! I feel faint! I can't breathe!

POPOVA: Where is Dasha? Dasha! *(Shouts.)* Dasha! Pelegea! Dasha! *(Rings the bell.)*

LUKA: Ach! They're all out picking berries...There's no one home...I feel faint! Water!

POPOVA: Will you please get out of here!

SMIRNOV: Would you mind putting it more politely?

POPOVA: *(Clenching her fists and stamping her feet.)* Peasant! Boor! Bear! Lout! Monster!

SMIRNOV: What? What did you say?

POPOVA: I said you're a bear, a monster!

SMIRNOV: *(Advances toward her.)* Excuse me, but what right do you have to insult me in this way?

POPOVA: That's right, I'm insulting you…so what? You think I'm afraid of you? Is that it?

SMIRNOV: And you think that just because you're a woman, you have the right to insult me with impunity? Is that what you think? I challenge you to a duel!

LUKA: Oh good heavens!…Saints above!…Water!

SMIRNOV: Bring out the pistols!

POPOVA: Just because you can clench your fists and bellow like a bull, you think I'm afraid of you? Eh? You boor!

SMIRNOV: A duel! I will not tolerate an insult! Never mind that you're a member of the weaker sex!

POPOVA: *(Trying to outshout him.)* Bear! Bear! Bear!

SMIRNOV: Why is it only men who must pay for their insults! The dark ages are over! You want equality, you'll get equality, goddammit! Choose your weapons!

POPOVA: You want a duel? You've got a duel! Be my guest!

SMIRNOV: This very minute!

POPOVA: This very minute! My husband left a pair of pistols…I'll bring them right away…*(Rushes out and stops for a moment.)* What a pleasure it will be to blow your brains out! Damn you to hell! *(Exits.)*

SMIRNOV: I'll wing her like a chicken! I'm no sissy, no simpering, sentimental little puppy, there's no such thing as the weaker sex, not as far as I'm concerned, there isn't!

LUKA: Dear sir!…*(Gets on his knees.)* Have mercy on me, pity an old man, go away from here! First you frighten me to death, and now you're getting ready to fight a duel!

SMIRNOV: *(Not hearing him.)* A duel, now there's equality, there's emancipation for you! Parity of the sexes! I'll shoot her out of principle! But what sort of woman is this? *(Mimics.)* "Damn you to hell…I'll blow your brains out…" What sort of woman? Her face was flushed, her eyes were shining…She rose to the challenge! I swear, I've never seen such a woman before in my entire life…

LUKA: Go away, sir! And I'll pray for you for the rest of my days!

SMIRNOV: Now this is what a woman is! This I understand! A real woman! This is not a whiner, this is not a wimp, this is a fireball, a rocket, this is gunpowder! A shame to have to kill her, though!

LUKA: *(Weeping.)* Sir...dear sir, go away!

SMIRNOV: I positively like her! Positively! Yes, she's got dimples, and I like her anyway! Forget the debt...I'm not even angry any more...What an astonishing woman!

Enter POPOVA with the pistols.

POPOVA: Here they are, the pistols...But before we fight, if you don't mind, please, show me how to shoot...I've never held a pistol before in my life.

LUKA: Heavenly father, have mercy upon us...I'll go and get the gardener and the coachman...Why has this calamity befallen us?...*(Exits.)*

SMIRNOV: *(Looking the pistols over.)* All right, now, you see, there are several different types of pistols...There's a special Mortimer percussion cap dueling pistol, for example. But what you've got here is a Smith and Wesson revolver, triple action with extractor, central firing mechanism... Marvelous firing pistols!...Cost you at least ninety rubles a pair...So, you hold the revolver like this...*(Aside.)* Those eyes, those eyes! The woman is on fire!

POPOVA: Like this?

SMIRNOV: That's right, like this...Next, you cock the pistol...then you aim...Head back just a little bit! Extend your arm "so"...Like that, right... Next, you squeeze this little gadget with your finger — and that's all there is to it...Only remember this golden rule: Don't get excited, and don't be in a rush to take aim...Try to keep your arm steady.

POPOVA: Very good...It's awkward shooting indoors, let's go outside.

SMIRNOV: Fine, let's go. Only I warn you, I shall shoot in the air.

POPOVA: This is the last straw! Why?

SMIRNOV: Because...Because...That's my business, why!

POPOVA: So, you're afraid, are you? Really? Ah ha-a-a-a! No, sir, you can't get out of this one! Follow me, please! I won't have satisfaction until I put a hole in your head...that head which I so deeply despise! Afraid, eh?

SMIRNOV: Yes, I'm afraid.

POPOVA: Liar! Why don't you want to fight?

SMIRNOV: Because...because...I think I've taken a liking to you.

POPOVA: *(With a malicious smile.)* Taken a liking to me! He dares to say he's taken a liking to me! *(Shows him the door.)* After you!

SMIRNOV: *(Quietly lays down the pistol, takes his cap, and starts to go; he stops at the door, and they stare at each other silently for half a minute; then he speaks, as he approaches POPOVA uncertainly.)* Listen…Are you still angry with me?…I'm pretty angry myself, you know, but, please try to understand…how shall I put it…The fact of the matter is, you see, let me put it this way…*(Shouts.)* For Christ's sake, is it my fault that I've taken a liking to you? *(Seizes a chair by its back; the chair cracks and breaks.)* Fragile furniture you've got here, goddammit! I like you! Understand? I…I almost love you!

POPOVA: Get away from me — I hate you!

SMIRNOV: My God, what a woman! I've never seen anything like it in my life! I'm lost! Undone! I'm caught like a mouse in a mousetrap!

POPOVA: Stand back or I'll shoot!

SMIRNOV: Shoot! You have no idea what bliss it would bring me to perish under the gaze of those glorious eyes, to perish from the pistol once held in those tiny velvet hands…I've lost my mind! Decide once and for all, because once I pass through that door, we shall never ever see each other again! Decide…I'm a landowner, a respectable man, I have an income of ten thousand rubles a year…I'm a great shot…I've got a sizeable stable…Will you be my wife?

POPOVA: *(Indignant, brandishing the pistol.)* Choose your weapons! A duel!

SMIRNOV: I've gone mad…I don't know what I'm doing any more…*(Shouts.)* Hey, you, water!

POPOVA: *(Shouting.)* A duel!

SMIRNOV: I've gone mad, I'm in love, like a schoolboy, like a fool! *(Seizes her hand, she shrieks in pain.)* I love you! *(Gets down on his knees.)* I love you, as I've never loved before! A dozen women I have spurned, nine more have spurned me, but none have I loved, as I love you…I've lost all my strength, I'm melting, I'm limp…I'm down on my knees like a fool, I offer you my hand…The shame of it, the ignominy! For five years I've scorned love, I made myself a vow, and now suddenly I'm struck down, by a bolt from the blue. I offer you my hand. Yes or no? You don't want it? Fine! Forget it! *(Gets up and hurries to the door.)*

POPOVA: Wait…

SMIRNOV: *(Stops.)* What?

POPOVA: Nothing, go away…No, wait…Never mind, go away, go away! I hate you! But no…Don't go! Ach, if only you knew, what a rage I'm in, what a rage! *(Throws the pistol on the chair.)* My fingers are swollen from holding that loathesome thing…*(Rips her handkerchief to shreds with rage.)* Well, what are you waiting for? Get out of here!

SMIRNOV: Farewell.

POPOVA: Yes, yes, go away!…*(Shouts.)* Where do you think you're going? Wait a minute…No, forget it, get out of here. Oh, what a rage I'm in! Don't come near me, don't come near me!

SMIRNOV: *(Approaching her.)* I make myself sick! I've fallen in love, like a schoolboy, I've gotten down on my knees…I make my own flesh creep… *(Roughly.)* I love you! I really needed this! Tomorrow, the interest is due, it's mowing time, and now on top of it all, you…*(Takes her by the waist.)* I shall never forgive myself…

POPOVA: Get away from me! Get your hands off me! I…I hate you! Let's d-d-duel!

A prolonged kiss.

Enter LUKA with an axe, a GARDENER with a rake, a COACHMAN with a pitchfork, and WORKMEN with staves.

LUKA: *(Upon seeing the couple kissing.)* Saints above!

Pause.

POPOVA: *(Eyes averted.)* Luka, tell them in the stables that there will be no oats for Toby today, none at all.

Curtain.

1888

THE PROPOSAL

A Farce in One Act

CAST OF CHARACTERS

STEPAN STEPANOVICH CHUBUKOV, landowner

NATALYA STEPANOVNA, his daughter, twenty-five years of age

IVAN VASILYEVICH LOMOV, a neighbor of CHUBUKOV, a healthy, rather portly landowner, but somewhat of a hypochondriac

The action takes place on CHUBUKOV's estate.

The Proposal

The drawing room of CHUBUKOV's house.

Enter LOMOV, in tails and white gloves. CHUBUKOV goes to greet him.

CHUBUKOV: Why look who's here, my dear dear fellow! Ivan Vasilyevich! I'm so delighted! *(Shakes his hand.)* Such a surprise, my dear dear man, yes, indeed…And how are you?

LOMOV: Very well, thank you. And permit me to inquire, how are you?

CHUBUKOV: Not bad, not bad at all, my angel, thank you for asking, etcetera etcetera. Sit down, sit down, I beg of you…Mustn't forget one's neighbors, my dear fellow, no indeed. But my dear man, why so formal? Tails and gloves, etcetera etcetera. Planning on going somewhere?

LOMOV: No, only to visit you, my esteemed Stepan Stepanich.

CHUBUKOV: But why the tails, my dear boy? You look like it's New Year's eve!

LOMOV: Well, you see, here's the thing. *(Takes his arm.)* I have come to see you, my esteemed Stepan Stepanich, to trouble you with a certain request. On more than one occasion I have had the honor of turning to you for your help, and you have always been, well, what can I say…forgive me, I'm a bit agitated. I'll just have a drink of water, my esteemed Stepan Stepanich. *(Drinks water.)*

CHUBUKOV: *(Aside.)* He's come to ask for money! Well, I'm not giving him any! *(To LOMOV.)* What's up, my dear friend?

LOMOV: Well, you see, my esteemed Stepanich…sorry, my Stepan Esteem'dich…what I mean is, I'm terribly agitated, as you can plainly see… In a word, you and you alone can help me, although, of course, I don't deserve it…I have no right, no right at all to rely upon your assistance…

CHUBUKOV: Oh, will you please stop beating around the bush, my dear man? I mean, really! Tell me this instant! What is it?

LOMOV: Yes, this instant…right away. The fact of the matter is, that I have come here today to ask for the hand of your daughter, Natalya Stepanovna.

CHUBUKOV: *(Ecstatically.)* My dearest fellow! Ivan Vasilyevich! Would you kindly repeat that — I didn't quite hear you!

LOMOV: I have the honor of asking…

CHUBUKOV: *(Interrupting him.)* My dear dear fellow…I'm so very happy, etcetera etcetera…Yes, indeed, and so on and so on. *(Embraces and kisses him.)* I've waited for this moment for so long. It has been my fondest dream. *(Sheds tears.)* I have always loved you, dear boy, like my own son. May God bless you, and may you live happily ever after, etcetera etcetera… I have longed for this day…What am I doing, standing around like a blockhead for? I'm dumbfounded, simply dumbfounded with joy! With all my heart, I wish you…all sorts of things…I'll go call Natasha, and so on and so on.

LOMOV: *(Deeply moved.)* My esteemed Stepan Stepanich, do you think I can count on her acceptance?

CHUBUKOV: A handsome young man like you — what's not to accept? She'll curl up like a kitten, etcetera etcetera…Be right back! *(Exits.)*

LOMOV: *(Alone.)* It's cold…I'm trembling, like a schoolboy before an exam. Act now…that's the main thing. He who hesitates is lost: Wait around for true love, for ideal love, and you'll never get married…Brrrrr!…It's cold… Natalya Stepanovna is an excellent housekeeper, she's not bad looking, she's educated…what more could I want? Only now I'm so agitated I've got ringing in my ears. *(Takes a drink of water.)* Anyway, I can't *not* get married…I mean, first of all, I'm already thirty-five years old — I'm at the critical age, so to speak. Second of all, I've got to settle down, lead an orderly life…I've got heart trouble, constant palpitations, I get agitated easily, I'm always worked up about something or other…Look, right now, how my lips are trembling and my right eyelid is twitching…But the worst thing is, trying to get some sleep. No sooner to I get into bed and start to fall asleep, when all of a sudden I get this pain in my left side, and — whoosh! — it goes right to my shoulder and then to my head…I leap up, like some sort of madman, I walk around for a bit, and then I lie down again, but no sooner do I start to fall asleep, when suddenly — whoosh!— there it is again! I mean, if it happens once, it happens twenty times…

Enter NATALYA STEPANOVNA.

NATALYA STEPANOVNA: Well, look who's here! You! Papa said: "Go inside — there's a merchant come to collect his goods." Hello, Ivan Vasilyevich!

LOMOV: Hello, esteemed Natalya Stepanovna!

NATALYA STEPANOVNA: Excuse my apron, I look like a mess…We're shelling peas for drying. Why haven't you come to visit in so long? Sit down…

They sit.

NATALYA STEPANOVNA: Would you like something to eat?

LOMOV: No, thank you, I've already eaten.

NATALYA STEPANOVNA: Do smoke, if you want to…Here…matches… The weather's wonderful, but it rained so hard yesterday that the workers haven't been able to do a thing all day. How much haying have you gotten done? Imagine, I got so carried away, I mowed our entire meadow, but now I'm sorry I did it, I'm afraid it's all going to rot. I should have waited. Oh, well. So look at you, all dressed up in tails! Aren't you something! Where are you going, to a ball? Not bad, not bad at all…No really, what are you all dressed up for?

LOMOV: *(Agitated.)* Well, you see, my esteemed Natalya Stepanovna…it's like this…The fact of the matter is, I've decided to ask you to…actually, to listen to what I'm going to say to you…Now, of course, it may come as a surprise to you, and indeed it might offend you, but I…*(Aside.)* It's freezing in here!

NATALYA STEPANOVNA: What's up?

Pause.

Well?

LOMOV: I'll try to make it brief. As you know, my esteemed Natalya Stepanovna, I have long had the honor of knowing your family, ever since my childhood, in fact. My late aunt and her husband, from whom, as you may well know, I have inherited my land, have always held your father and your dear departed mother in the highest esteem. The Lomovs and the Chubukovs have always been on the most friendly, why you might even say, affectionate terms. Moreover, as you may well know, my land actually borders on yours. And furthermore, as you may also recall, my Oxen Meadows actually adjoin your birch groves.

NATALYA STEPANOVNA: Sorry, but I'm going to interrupt you. You just said "*my* Oxen Meadows"…But surely they're not yours?

LOMOV: Well of course they're mine.

NATALYA STEPANOVNA: What do you mean? Oxen Meadows are ours, not yours!

LOMOV: I beg your pardon, my esteemed Natalya Stepanovna, they're mine.

NATALYA STEPANOVNA: Well, that's news to me. And how did it come to pass, that they happen to be yours?

LOMOV: What do you mean, "how did it come to pass?" I'm talking about Oxen Meadows, you know, the land that's wedged in between your birch groves and Burnt Swamp.

NATALYA STEPANOVNA: Right, right…They're ours.

LOMOV: No, I believe you are mistaken, my esteemed Natalya Stepanovna — they're mine.

NATALYA STEPANOVNA: Oh, come on, Ivan Vasilyevich! Since when have they been yours?

LOMOV: Since when? Since as long as I can remember, they've always been ours.

NATALYA STEPANOVNA: Excuse me, but now you've really gone too far!

LOMOV: It's all in the records, my esteemed Natalya Stepanovna. The owner-ship of Oxen Meadows was once under dispute, it's true; but now every-one knows that they're mine. There's no disputing that any more. And as I am sure you are aware, my late aunt's grandmother granted those Meadows to your father's grandfather indefinitely, for use by the peasants free of charge, in return for baking her bricks. Your father's grandfather's peasants made good use of those meadows free of charge for forty years, and had come to consider them as theirs. But then, when the new land registry was published…

NATALYA STEPANOVNA: What are you talking about, it isn't like that at all! My grandfather and great-grandfather considered that their land extended all the way to Burnt Swamp — meaning, that Oxen Meadows belonged to us. What's there to quarrel about? — I don't understand it. I mean, really, it's very annoying!

LOMOV: I'll show you the papers, Natalya Stepanovna!

NATALYA STEPANOVNA: No, really, you're just kidding me, you're only jok-ing, right…It's all some kind of a game! We've owned that land for thirty years and now suddenly we're being told that it's no longer ours! Ivan Vasilyevich, forgive me, please, but I cannot believe my own ears…I mean, it's hardly worth arguing about these Meadows. They're not more than a dozen acres or so, and they're worth only three hundred rubles, but it's the injustice of it all that upsets me. Say whatever you like, but injustice I can-not bear.

LOMOV: Listen to me, I beg of you! Your father's grandfather's peasants, as I have already had the honor of telling you, baked bricks for my late aunt's grandmother. My late aunt's grandmother, wishing to return the favor…

NATALYA STEPANOVNA: Grandfather, grandmother, dead aunt…I don't know what you're talking about! The Meadows are ours, and that's all there is to it.

LOMOV: They're mine!

NATALYA STEPANOVNA: They're ours! You can stand here arguing for two days, you can put on fifteen pairs of tails, they'll still be ours, ours, ours!…I have no desire to take what's yours, and by the same token, I do not intend to lose what's mine…So say whatever you like.

LOMOV: I do not need these Oxen Meadows, Natalya Stepanovna, but it's the principle of the thing. If you want them, then by all means, I shall give them to you.

NATALYA STEPANOVNA: Well if you want to put it that way, then *I* can very well give them to *you,* because they're *mine!* All this is really very very strange, to say the least, Ivan Vasilyevich! Up until now we've thought of you as a good neighbor, as a friend, we even lent you our threshing machine last year, which meant, it just so happens, that we had to finish threshing in November, and now you treat us as if we were gypsies! Trying to give me my own land! Sorry, but that is not a very neighborly thing to do! In my opinion, it's downright impertinent, if you really want to know…

LOMOV: So now you're telling me that, in your opinion, I'm stealing your land, is that what you're telling me? My dear dear madam, never in my entire life have I ever stolen anyone else's land, and I shall never allow anyone to accuse me of such a thing…*(Hurries over to the carafe, and drinks some water.)* Oxen Meadows are mine!

NATALYA STEPANOVNA: That's a lie! They're ours!

LOMOV: They're mine!

NATALYA STEPANOVNA: A lie! I can prove it! Today I shall send my mowers out to work these meadows!

LOMOV: What did you say?

NATALYA STEPANOVNA: I shall have my mowers on that land today!

LOMOV: And I'll throw them out by their necks!

NATALYA STEPANOVNA: You wouldn't dare!

LOMOV: *(Clutches at his heart.)* Oxen Meadows are mine! Understand? Mine!

NATALYA STEPANOVNA: Stop shouting, please! You can shout yourself blue in the face in your own house, if you want to, but here I must ask you to control yourself!

LOMOV: My dear lady, if I weren't having absolutely agonizing palpitations right now, if my veins weren't popping right out of my head, than I would be talking very differently to you! *(Shouts.)* Oxen Meadows are mine!

NATALYA STEPANOVNA: Ours!

LOMOV: Mine!

NATALYA STEPANOVNA: Ours!

LOMOV: Ours!

Enter CHUBUKOV.

CHUBUKOV: What's going on here? What's all this shouting about?

NATALYA STEPANOVNA: Papa, tell this gentleman, will you, please: to whom do Oxen Meadows belong — to us or to him?

CHUBUKOV: *(To LOMOV.)* My dear sweet fellow, they're ours!

LOMOV: For goodness's sake, Stepan Stepanich, how do they come to be yours? At least *you* be reasonable, please! My late aunt's grandmother gave the Meadows to your grandfather's peasants for temporary use, free of charge, for a certain period of time only. The peasants made use of that land for forty years, they regarded it as their own, but then when the new land registry was published...

CHUBUKOV: Permit me to say, my precious man...You're forgetting the fact that these peasants didn't pay your grandmother and so on and so on for the very reason that the Meadows were under disputed ownership, etcetera etcetera...And anyway, every dog in the district knows that those Meadows are ours, yes, indeed. It's obvious you haven't looked at the land registry!

LOMOV: And I can prove it to you that they're mine!

CHUBUKOV: You can prove nothing of the kind, my darling fellow!

LOMOV: Oh yes I can!

CHUBUKOV: My dear sweet fellow, why are you shouting? Shouting proves absolutely nothing, no, indeed. I'm not after anything that is yours and by the same token I don't intend to give up what is mine. Why should I? If it comes to that, my dear dear fellow, if you really intend to dispute the ownership of the Meadows etcetera etcetera, why then I'd sooner give it to the peasants than to you. So there!

LOMOV: I don't understand! What right have you to give away someone else's property?

CHUBUKOV: That's my business, whether I have the right to or not. And by the way, young man, I am not accustomed to being spoken to in that tone of voice, no, indeed, I'm not. I'm twice as old as you are, young man, and I must ask you to speak to me with civility, and so on and so on.

LOMOV: Oh no you don't, you're making a fool of me, you're laughing at me! You say that my land belongs to you — and then you have the nerve to ask me to calm down and speak civilly to you! Good neighbors don't behave that way, Stepan Stepanich! And anyway, you're not a neighbor, you're a landsnatcher!

CHUBUKOV: What? What did you say?

NATALYA STEPANOVNA: Papa, send the men out right away to mow Oxen Meadows!

CHUBUKOV: *(To LOMOV.)* What did you say, sir?

NATALYA STEPANOVNA: Oxen Meadows are ours, and I will not give them up, I won't, I won't!

LOMOV: We'll see about that! I'll prove it in court that they're mine.

CHUBUKOV: In court? So you just might go to court, sir, and so on and so on! Is that what you just might do! Really! I know your kind, indeed, I do, you've been waiting for this, the chance to go to court, etcetera etcetera... You troublemaker, you! You come from a whole line of rabblerousers! The whole lot of you!

LOMOV: I must ask you not to insult my family. Everyone in the Lomov family is an honest man, we've never had anyone who's been tried for embezzling, no, not like your uncle!

CHUBUKOV: But you've had plenty in the Lomov family who've been certified lunatics!

NATALYA STEPANOVNA: All of you! All of you! All of you!

CHUBUKOV: Your uncle was a drunk, and as for your other aunt, Nastasya Mikhailovna, yes indeed, the younger one, she ran off with an architect, etcetera etcetera...

LOMOV: And your mother was a hunchback. *(Clutches at his heart.)* There's a pain in my side...My head is pounding...Good heavens!...Water!...

CHUBUKOV: And your father was a gambler and a glutton.

NATALYA STEPANOVNA: And your aunt is the greatest gossip in the district!

LOMOV: My left leg is paralyzed...You conniver, you...Ach, my heart!...And it's no secret around here that you help fix the elections...I'm seeing stars... Where is my hat?

NATALYA STEPANOVNA: Lowlife! Cheat! Villain!

CHUBUKOV: And you're a spiteful, two-faced schemer, yes indeed! That's what you are!

LOMOV: My hat, here it is...My heart...Where am I going? Where's the door? Ach!...I think I'm dying...My foot isn't working...*(Walks toward the door.)*

CHUBUKOV: *(Following after him.)* And may you never set foot in this house again! Ever!

NATALYA STEPANOVNA: Go on, take us to court! Then we'll see!

Exit LOMOV, staggering.

CHUBUKOV: To hell with him! *(Walks about the stage in agitation.)*

NATALYA STEPANOVNA: Did you ever meet such a scoundrel! And that's what they call "a good neighbor!"

CHUBUKOV: The miserable swindler! The scarecrow!

NATALYA STEPANOVNA: The monster! He takes your land, and then he has the nerve to curse at you.

CHUBUKOV: And this nightmare, this — this aberration, has the audacity to make a proposal to you, etcetera etcetera! Can you imagine? A proposal!

NATALYA STEPANOVNA: What proposal?

CHUBUKOV: What do you mean, "what proposal?" He came to make a proposal to you.

NATALYA STEPANOVNA: A proposal? To me? Why didn't you say so before?

CHUBUKOV: And all stuffed up in a pair of tails! The sausage! The mushroom!

NATALYA STEPANOVNA: A proposal? To me? Ach! *(Collapses into the armchair and moans.)* Bring him back! Bring him back! Ach! Bring him back!

CHUBUKOV: Who? Bring who back?

NATALYA STEPANOVNA: Hurry, hurry! I'm fainting! Bring him back! *(Hysterics.)*

CHUBUKOV: What's going on here? What's the matter with you? *(Grasps his head in his hands.)* Oh, what a wretched creature am I! I shall shoot myself! Hang myself! I'm exhausted!

NATALYA STEPANOVNA: I'm dying! Bring him back!

CHUBUKOV: All right, all right! Stop howling! *(Runs offstage.)*

NATALYA STEPANOVNA: *(Alone, moaning.)* What have we done? Bring him back! Bring him back!

CHUBUKOV: *(Runs in.)* He's coming, he's coming, damn him! Ugh! You talk to him, I have no desire to, no indeed, I don't...

NATALYA STEPANOVNA: *(Moans.)* Bring him back!

CHUBUKOV: *(Shouting.)* He's coming, I tell you. "O, what a trial it is, dear Lord, to be the father of a full-grown daughter!" I shall kill myself! I shall absolutely positively kill myself! We've cursed the man, we've disgraced him, we've thrown him out, all this is your doing...yours!

NATALYA STEPANOVNA: No, yours!

CHUBUKOV: I am to blame, of course!

LOMOV appears at the door.

Go speak to him yourself! *(Exits.)*

LOMOV: *(Enters, exhausted.)* Terrible palpitations...My foot's gone numb... there's a pain in my side...

NATALYA STEPANOVNA. Forgive me, Ivan Vasilyevich, I think we overreacted...Now I remember: Oxen Meadows are yours, actually.

LOMOV: My heart is pounding, terribly...*My* Meadows...I'm seeing stars...in both eyes...

NATALYA STEPANOVNA: They're your Meadows, yours…Sit down…

They sit.

We made a mistake.

LOMOV: It's the principle of the thing…It's not the land that matters, it's the principle…

NATALYA STEPANOVNA: Yes, yes, of course, the principle…Let's talk about something else.

LOMOV: Moreover, I have proof. My aunt's grandmother gave your father's grandfather's peasants…

NATALYA STEPANOVNA: Enough, enough with all this…*(Aside.)* I don't know, how should I bring it up?…*(To LOMOV.)* Are you planning to go hunting soon?

LOMOV: For grouse, yes, most esteemed Natalya Stepanovna, after the harvest, I hope. Oh, have you heard? Imagine, what a misfortune has befallen me! My dog, Spotter, whom of course you may remember, has gone lame.

NATALYA STEPANOVNA: What a pity! How come?

LOMOV: Don't know…He probably twisted his leg, or else another dog bit him…*(Sighs.)* The best dog I ever had, never mind how much I paid for him! I bought him from Mironov — actually paid one hundred and twenty-five rubles.

NATALYA STEPANOVNA: Too much, Ivan Vasilyevich, too much!

LOMOV: Actually, I thought it was quite cheap. He's a marvelous dog.

NATALYA STEPANOVNA: Papa paid seventy-five rubles for his Sprinter, and Sprinter's better than your Spotter any old day.

LOMOV: Sprinter better than Spotter? What are you saying! *(Laughs.)* Sprinter better than Spotter!

NATALYA STEPANOVNA: Well, of course, he's better! Sprinter is young, it's true, he's not yet fully grown, but on points and on pedigree there isn't a better dog in the district, why Volchanetsky can't even match him.

LOMOV: Forgive me, Natalya Stepanovna, but truly you've forgotten, he's got an overbite, and dogs with an overbite never make good hunters.

NATALYA STEPANOVNA: Overbite? That's the first I've heard of it!

LOMOV: I assure you, his lower jaw is shorter than his upper one.

NATALYA STEPANOVNA: Have you measured it?

LOMOV: Yes, I have, I have measured it. He's good enough for pointing, of course, but when it comes to retrieving…

NATALYA STEPANOVNA: First of all, our Sprinter is a pedigree, a borzoi, he's the son of Harness and Chisel, whereas you'll never find a pedigree for that spotted mongrel of yours…And anyway, he's old and ugly as death…

LOMOV: All right, he's old, but I wouldn't swap him for five of your Sprinters…Am I really hearing this? Spotter's a dog, but Sprinter…I mean, it's ridiculous even to argue about it…Dogs like your Sprinter are as common as…as dogs. Every hunter has one. If you'd paid a quarter of that price, the former owner was lucky.

NATALYA STEPANOVNA: You seemed to be possessed by the demon of contradiction today, Ivan Vasilyevich. First you got it into your head that the Meadows were yours, now you're saying that Spotter is better than Sprinter. I don't like it when a man doesn't say what he really thinks. You know very well that Sprinter is a hundred times better than…than your stupid Spotter. Why do you say the opposite?

LOMOV: I see, Natalya Stepanovna, that either you think I'm blind or else I'm a fool. Face it, your Sprinter has an overbite.

NATALYA STEPANOVNA: That's a lie!

LOMOV: Overbite!

NATALYA STEPANOVNA: *(Shouts.)* Lie!

LOMOV: Why are you shouting, madam?

NATALYA STEPANOVNA: Why are you talking nonsense? Really, it's shocking! Your Spotter should be put to sleep already, and you're comparing him with Sprinter!

LOMOV: Forgive me, I cannot continue this discussion. I've having palpitations.

NATALYA STEPANOVNA: Well, you know what they say about hunters: It's the ones who argue the most, that know the least.

LOMOV: I beg of you, madam, be quiet…I'm having a heart attack…*(Shouts.)* Be quiet!

NATALYA STEPANOVNA: I shall not be quiet, not until you admit that Sprinter is one hundred times better than your Spotter!

LOMOV: One hundred times worse! I hope he dies, your Sprinter! My head…my eyes…my shoulder…

NATALYA STEPANOVNA: Well, there's no need for your stupid Spotter to die, because he's dead already!

LOMOV: *(Weeps.)* Be quiet! I'm having heart failure!!

NATALYA STEPANOVNA: I shall *not* be quiet!

Enter CHUBUKOV.

CHUBUKOV: *Now* what's going on?

NATALYA STEPANOVNA: Papa, tell the truth, honestly: Which dog is better — our Sprinter or his Spotter?

LOMOV: Stepan Stepanovich, I beseech you, tell me only one thing: Does your dog Sprinter have an overbite or doesn't he? Yes or no?

CHUBUKOV: And what if he does? So what! There isn't a better dog in the district, etcetera etcetera.

LOMOV: But truly, isn't my Spotter better? Honestly!

CHUBUKOV: Don't get excited, my precious man...Permit me to explain...Your Sprinter has his good features, indeed he does...He's a pedigree, sure-footed, strong-flanked, and so on and so on. But this dog, if you really must know, my lovely fellow, has two fundamental flaws: He's old, and he's got a short muzzle.

LOMOV: Excuse me, I've having palpitations...Let's look at the facts...I beg to remind you, that in Marusky's Meadows, my Spotter was running neck and neck with the Count's Springer, while your Sprinter was running a good two-thirds of a mile behind.

CHUBUKOV: He was behind, because the Count's huntsman was whipping him, that's why he was behind.

LOMOV: Yes, and why! Because all the other dogs were chasing the foxes, while your Sprinter was running after sheep!

CHUBUKOV: That's a lie!... My dear dear man, I've got a very bad temper, indeed I have, and I beg of you, let's cut this conversation short. The Count's huntsman whipped him, simply because everyone's jealous of everyone else's dog...Yes! Everyone hates everyone else! And you, my dear sir, are not above it all, either! Yes, indeed, the moment you notice that somebody else's dog is better than your Spotter, right away you start in with this, that, the other thing, and so on and so on...You see, I remember everything!

LOMOV: And I remember everything, too!

CHUBUKOV: *(Mimics him.)* I remember everything, too...What? What do you remember?

LOMOV: Palpitations...My foot's paralyzed...I can't bear it any more.

NATALYA STEPANOVNA: *(Mimics him.)* Palpitations...What kind of a hunter are you, anyway? You should be home, lying on top of the stove squashing cockroaches, not out hunting foxes! Palpitations...

CHUBUKOV: That's right. What kind of a hunter are you, anyway? You should be sitting home with your palpitations, not chasing around in a saddle. It's fine to go out hunting and all that, but all you want to do is go out and argue with your neighbors and bother their dogs, etcetera etcetera.

I've got a very bad temper, so let us quit this conversation, shall we? Hunter "my foot"; I'll say you're no hunter!

LOMOV: And you call yourself a hunter? You only go out hunting so you can fawn all over the Count, and plot and scheme...My heart!...Schemer!

CHUBUKOV: What did you say? I, a schemer? *(Shouts.)* Be quiet!

LOMOV: Schemer!

CHUBUKOV: Crybaby! Puppy dog!

LOMOV: You old rat! You Jesuit!

CHUBUKOV: Be quiet; or else I'll shoot you down like a partridge! Blabbermouth!

LOMOV: Everyone in the world knows that — ach! my heart! — that your wife, may her soul rest in peace, used to beat you...My foot...my head...I see stars...I'm fainting, I'm fainting!...

CHUBUKOV: And your housekeeper has you tied to her apron strings!

LOMOV: You see, you see, you see...my heart's exploding! My shoulder's falling off...Where's my shoulder?...I'm dying! *(Collapses into the armchair.)* Get a doctor! *(Faints.)*

CHUBUKOV: Crybaby! Infant! Blabbermouth! I feel faint! *(Drinks water.)* Faint!

NATALYA STEPANOVNA: What kind of a hunter are you, anyway? You can't even sit on a horse! *(To CHUBUKOV.)* Papa! What's the matter with him? Papa! Look, Papa! *(Screams.)* Ivan Vasilyevich! He's dead!

CHUBUKOV: I feel faint!...I can't breathe!...Air, give me air!

NATALYA STEPANOVNA: He's dead! *(Tugs at LOMOV's sleeve.)* Ivan Vasilyich! Ivan Vasilyich! What have we done! He's dead! *(Collapses into the armchair.)* A doctor, get a doctor! *(Hysterics.)*

CHUBUKOV: Ach!...What's going on? What's the matter with you?

NATALYA STEPANOVNA: *(Moans.)* He's dead!...dead!

CHUBUKOV: Who's dead? *(Looks at LOMOV.)* He really *is* dead. Good heavens! Water! A doctor! *(Puts a glass to LOMOV's lips.)* Drink!...No, he's not drinking...That means he's dead, and so on and so on...Oh misfortune! Why haven't I put a bullet through my brain! Why haven't I put an end to it all! What am I waiting for? Give me a knife! Give me a pistol!

LOMOV stirs.

I think he's coming 'round!...Here, drink this water!...That's it...

LOMOV: Stars...mist...Where am I?

CHUBUKOV: Please, just marry her as soon as possible — and get it over with! She accepts! *(Joins LOMOV's hand with NATALYA STEPANOVNA's.)* She accepts, and so on and so on. My blessings, etcetera etcetera. Only now, leave me in peace!

LOMOV: Eh? What? *(Gets up.)* Who?

CHUBUKOV: She accepts! So? Kiss each other…and to hell with you both!

NATALYA STEPANOVNA: *(Moans.)* He's alive… Yes, yes, I accept…

CHUBUKOV: Kiss!

LOMOV: Eh? Who? *(Kisses NATALYA STEPANOVNA.)* Delighted, I'm sure… Excuse me, what's going on? Ach, yes, now I understand…My heart…I see stars…I'm so happy, Natalya Stepanovna…*(Kisses her hand.)* My foot was paralyzed…

NATALYA STEPANOVNA: I'm…I'm happy too…

CHUBUKOV: That's a load off my shoulders…Ugh!

NATALYA STEPANOVNA: Anyway…let's get it straight: Spotter is a worse dog than Sprinter.

LOMOV: No, he's not!

NATALYA STEPANOVNA: Yes, he is!

CHUBUKOV: And so, the beginnings of marital bliss! Champagne!

LOMOV: Is not!

NATALYA STEPANOVNA: Is too! Is too! Is too!

CHUBUKOV: *(Attempting to shout them down.)* Champagne! Champagne!

Curtain.

1888

Tatyana Repina

A Drama in One Act

DEDICATED TO A. S. SUVORIN

CAST OF CHARACTERS

OLENINA, the bride

SABININ, the bridegroom

KOTELNIKOV, a best man

VOLGIN, a young officer; also a best man

STUDENT, brother of the bride; also attendant to the bride

AN ASSISTANT PUBLIC PROSECUTOR, attendant to the bride

MATVEEV, leader of the local theatre troupe

KOKOSHKIN
KOKOSHKINA
PATRONNIKOV   } wedding guests
SONNENSTEIN
A YOUNG LADY

FATHER IVAN, a cathedral archpriest; seventy years of age

FATHER NIKOLAI and FATHER ALEKSEY, young priests

DEACON

SEXTON

KUZMA, the church caretaker

WOMAN IN BLACK

Actors and Actresses

The scene takes place in the cathedral.

Tatyana Repina

It is seven o'clock in the evening. The scene takes place in the cathedral. All the chandeliers and votive candles are burning. The holy gates to the altar are open. Two choirs are singing: the bishop's choir and the cathedral choir. The church is filled with people. It is crowded and stuffy. A wedding is taking place. SABININ and OLENINA are getting married. The best men are KOTEL-NIKOV and VOLGIN, an officer; the bride is attended by her brother, a STU-DENT, and the ASSISTANT PUBLIC PROSECUTOR. The entire local intelligentsia is present. The guests are dressed elaborately. Presiding over the marriage ceremony are FATHER IVAN, in faded priest's headgear; FATHER NIKOLAI, in a skullcap, revealing a head of tousled hair; and FATHER ALEKSEY, who is very young and wears dark glasses. Behind them, to the right of FATHER IVAN, stands a tall, gaunt DEACON holding a book. Also included in the congregation is the local theatrical troupe, with its leader, MATVEEV.

IVAN: Remember them, O Lord our God, and the parents who have nurtured them; for the prayers of parents make firm the foundations of houses. Remember, O Lord our God, thy servants the groomsman and the bridesmaid of the bridal pair, who are come together in this joy. Remember, O Lord our God, thy servant, Pyotr, and thy handmaid, Vera, and bless them. Grant them of the fruit of the womb, fair offspring, concord of soul and of body: exalt them like the cedars of Lebanon, like a luxuriant vine. Give them seed in number like unto the full ears of grain; that, having sufficiency in all things, they may abound in every work that is good and acceptable unto thee. And let them behold their children's children, like a newly planted olive-orchard, round about their table; that, obtaining favor in the sight, they may shine like the stars of heaven, in thee, our God. For unto thee are due all glory, honor, and worship, to the Father, who is from everlasting, and to the Son, and to thy Life-giving Spirit, now and forever, and unto ages of ages.
BISHOP'S CHOIR: *(Singing.)* Amen.

PATRONNIKOV: God, it's stuffy in here! What kind of decoration is that around your neck, David Solomonovich?

SONNENSTEIN: It's Belgian. Why are there so many people here? Who let them all in? Ugh! It's like a Russian bathhouse!

PATRONNIKOV: We have the wretched police to thank for that.

DEACON: Let us pray to the Lord!

CATHEDRAL CHOIR: *(Sings.)* Lord, have mercy!

FATHER NIKOLAI: *(Reads.)* O holy God, who didst create man out of the dust, and didst fashion his wife out of his rib, and didst join her unto him as a helpmeet; for it seemed pleasing to thy majesty that man should not dwell alone upon earth; do thou, the same Lord, stretch out now also thy hand from thy holy dwelling-place, and conjoin this thy servant, Pyotr, and this thy handmaid, Vera; for by thee is the husband united unto the wife. Unite them in one mind, wed them into one flesh, granting unto them of the fruit of the womb and procreation of fair offspring. For thine is the majesty, and thine are the kingdom, and the power, and the glory, of the Father, and of the Son, and of the Holy Spirit, now and forever, and unto ages of ages.

CATHEDRAL CHOIR: *(Sings.)* Amen.

YOUNG LADY: *(To SONNENSTEIN.)* They're going to put the wedding crowns on. Oh, look, look!

FATHER IVAN: *(Takes the crowns from the lectern and turns to face SABININ.)* The servant of God, Pyotr, is crowned unto the handmaid of God, Vera, in the name of the Father, and of the Son, and of the Holy Spirit, amen. *(Gives the crown to KOTELNIKOV.)*

VOICES IN THE CONGREGATION: — The best man is the same height as the groom. He's not really all that attractive. Who is he? — Oh, that's Kotelnikov. That officer isn't very attractive, either. — Ladies and gentlemen, will you please let the ladies pass! — Madame, you're not permitted to go through here.

FATHER IVAN: *(Turning to OLENINA.)* The handmaiden of God, Vera, is crowned unto the servant of God, Pyotr, in the name of the Father, and of the Son, and of the Holy Spirit. *(Gives the crown to the STUDENT.)*

KOTELNIKOV: These crowns are heavy. My hand feels numb already.

VOLGIN: Never mind, it'll be my turn to hold it soon. Who smells of patchouli, that's what I'd like to know!

ASSISTANT PROSECUTOR: It's Kotelnikov.

KOTELNIKOV: Liar!

VOLGIN: Shhhhh!

FATHER IVAN: O Lord our God, crown them with glory and honor! O Lord God, crown them with glory and honor! O Lord our God, crown them with glory and honor!

KOKOSHKINA: *(To her husband.)* How lovely Vera looks today! I've been admiring her. And she's not even a bit nervous, either.

KOKOSHKIN: She's used to it. It's her second wedding, isn't it?

KOKOSHKINA: Yes, you're right. *(Sighs.)* I wish her happiness…She's a good-hearted girl.

SEXTON: *(Coming into the center of the church.)* The Prokimenon, Tone VIII. Thou has set upon their heads crowns of precious stones; they asked life of thee, and thou gavest it them.

BISHOP'S CHOIR: *(Sings.)* Thou hast set upon their heads…

PATRONNIKOV: I feel like having a smoke.

SEXTON: A reading from Paul, the Apostle.

DEACON: Let us attend!

SEXTON: *(In a low bass.)* Brethren, give thanks always for all things unto God and the Father, in the name of our Lord, Jesus Christ; submitting yourselves one to another in the fear of God. Wives, submit yourselves unto your own husbands, as unto the Lord, for the husband is the head of the wife, even as Christ is the head of the church, and he is the Savior of the body. Therefore as the church submits unto Christ, so shall wives submit to their husbands in everything…

SABININ: *(To KOTELNIKOV.)* You're squishing my head with that crown…

KOTELNIKOV: What do you mean? I'm holding it at least three inches above your head.

SABININ: I'm telling you, you're squishing my head!

SEXTON: Husbands, love your wives, even as Christ also loved the church, and gave himself for it; that he might sanctify and cleanse it with the washing of water by the word, that he might present it to himself a glorious church, not having spot or wrinkle, or any such thing; but that it should be holy and without blemish.

VOLGIN: He's got a good bass voice…*(To KOTELNIKOV.)* Do you want me to hold it?

KOTELNIKOV: I'm not getting tired yet.

SEXTON: So ought men to love their wives, as their own bodies. He that loveth his wife loveth himself. For no man ever yet hated his own flesh; but nourisheth and cherisheth it, even as the Lord the church: for we are members of his body, of his flesh, and of his bones. For this cause shall a man leave his father and mother…

SABININ: Hold that crown higher. It's squishing my head.

KOTELNIKOV: Nonsense!

SEXTON:…and shall be joined unto his wife, and they two shall be one flesh…

KOKOSHKIN: The governor's here.

KOKOSHKINA: Where do you see him?

KOKOSHKIN: There, standing near the choir on the right, next to Altukhov. He's here incognito.

KOKOSHKINA: I see him, I see him. He's talking to Mashenka Ganzen. He's mad about her.

SEXTON: This is a great mystery, but I speak concerning Christ and the church. Nevertheless, let every one of you in particular so love his wife even as himself: and the wife see that she obey her husband!!

CATHEDRAL CHOIR: *(Sings.)* Hallelujah, hallelujah, hallelujah…

VOICES IN THE CONGREGATION: — Did you hear that, Natalya Sergeevna! The wife must obey her husband. — Leave me alone.

Laughter.

— Shhhh! Ladies and gentlemen, for shame!

SEXTON: Wisdom, O believers! Let us listen to the Holy Gospel!

FATHER IVAN: Peace be with you all!

BISHOP'S CHOIR: *(Sings.)* And with thy spirit.

VOICES IN THE CONGREGATION: — The Apostles, the Gospel…it takes forever! It's time they gave us a break. — I can't even breathe. I'm getting out of here. — You won't be able to. Wait, it'll be over soon.

FATHER IVAN: The Lesson from the holy Gospel according to John!

SEXTON: Let us attend!

FATHER IVAN: *(Removes his priest's headgear.)* At that time, there was a marriage in Cana of Galilee; and the mother of Jesus was there. And both Jesus was called, and his disciples, to the marriage. And when they wanted wine, the mother of Jesus saith unto him, They have no wine. Jesus saith unto her, Woman, what have I to do with thee? mine hour is not yet come…

SABININ: *(To KOTELNIKOV.)* Will it be over soon?

KOTELNIKOV: I'm not sure. I don't know this part. Probably.

VOLGIN: There's still the procession.

FATHER IVAN: His mother saith unto the servants, Whatsoever he saith unto you, do it. And there were set there six water-pots of stone, after the manner of the purifying of the Jews, containing two or three firkins apiece. Jesus saith unto them, Fill the water-pots with water. And they filled them up to the brim. And he saith unto them, Draw out now, and bear unto the governor of the feast…

A moan is heard.

VOLGIN: *Qu'est-ce que c'est?* Has somebody been trampled?
A VOICE IN THE CONGREGATION: "Shhhhh!" "Quiet!"

A moan.

FATHER IVAN:…And they bare it. When the ruler of the feast had tasted the water that was made wine, and knew not whence it was (but the servants who drew the water knew), the governor of the feast called the bridegroom, and saith unto him…
SABININ: *(To KOTELNIKOV.)* Who made that moaning sound just now?
KOTELNIKOV: *(Peers out into the congregation.)* There's something moving out there…Some woman in black…She must have fainted…They're leading her out…
SABININ: *(Peers out.)* Hold the crown a little higher…
FATHER IVAN: …Every man at the beginning doth set forth good wine; and when men have well drunk, then that which is worse: but thou hast kept the good wine until now. This beginning of miracles did Jesus in Cana of Galilee, and manifested forth his glory; and his disciples believed on him.
A VOICE IN THE CONGREGATION: — I don't know why they allow hysterical women in here!
BISHOP'S CHOIR: Glory to thee, O Lord, glory to thee!
PATRONNIKOV: Stop humming like a bumblebee, David Solomonovich. And don't stand with your back to the altar. It's just not done.
SONNENSTEIN: It's the young lady who's humming like a bumblebee, not me…hee, hee, hee!
SEXTON: Let us all say, with all our soul and with all our mind let us say…
CATHEDRAL CHOIR: *(Sings.)* Lord, have mercy.
SEXTON: O Lord Almighty, the God of our fathers, we beseech thee: hearken, and have mercy.
VOICES IN THE CONGREGATION: —Shh! Quiet! — But somebody's pushing me!
CHOIR: *(Sings.)* Lord, have mercy.
VOICES IN THE CONGREGATION: — Quiet! Shhhh! — Who just fainted?
SEXTON: Have mercy upon us according to thy infinite kindness, we beseech thee: hearken, and have mercy.
CHOIR: *(Sings.)* Lord, have mercy.

SEXTON: Let us also pray for his Most Pious and Devout Autocratic Great Sovereign, Aleksandr Aleksandrovich, Emperor of All Russia, for his power, victory, well-being, peace, health, and salvation. May our Lord God hasten to aid him in all things and to subdue all his enemies and foes beneath his feet.

CHOIR: *(Sings three times.)* Lord, have mercy.

A moan. Movement in the congregation.

KOKOSHKINA: What's that? *(To the woman standing next to her.)* This is intolerable, my dear. Why can't they leave the doors open, or something…You could die from the heat!

VOICES IN THE CONGREGATION: — They're trying to get her out of here, but she doesn't want to go. — Who is she? — Shhh!

SEXTON: Let us also pray for his Consort, the most Pious and Devout Sovereign, the Empress Marya Fyodorovna…

CHOIR: *(Sings.)* Lord, have mercy!

SEXTON: Let us also pray for his Heir and Successor, the Faithful Holy Sovereign, the Tsarevich and Grand Duke Nikolai Aleksandrovich, and for the entire reigning family.

CHOIR: *(Sings.)* Lord, have mercy!

SABININ: O my God…

OLENINA: What is it?

SEXTON: Let us also pray for his Most Holy Governing Synod and for our most reverend Feofile, Bishop of So-and-so and Such-and-such, and for all our brothers in Christ.

CHOIR: *(Sings.)* Lord, have mercy.

VOICES IN THE CONGREGATION: — Yesterday someone else took poison in the Hotel Europe…it was a lady. — Yes, they say it was the wife of some doctor. — Do you happen to know why?

SEXTON: Let us also pray for all their Christ-loving army…

CHOIR: *(Sings.)* Lord, have mercy.

VOLGIN: It sounds as if somebody's crying…This congregation is behaving disgracefully.

SEXTON: Let us also pray for all our brethren, our priests, our monks, and for all our brothers in Christ.

CHOIR: *(Sings.)* Lord, have mercy.

MATVEEV: The singers sound good today.

COMEDIAN: If only we could have singers like those, Zakhar Ilyich!

MATVEEV: You don't ask for much, do you, mug-face!

Laughter.

Shhh!

SEXTON: Furthermore we pray for mercy, life, peace, health, salvation and visitation for the servants of God, Pyotr and Vera.

CHOIR: *(Sings.)* Lord, have mercy.

SEXTON: Let us also pray for the blessed…

A VOICE IN THE CONGREGATION: That's right, some doctor's wife…in the hotel…

SEXTON: …and for the most holy of the Orthodox Patriarchs of eternal memory…

VOICES IN THE CONGREGATION: — This is the fourth instance of someone pulling a "Tatyana Repina" and poisoning herself. Explain these poisonings to me, old man, will you? — Hysteria. What else? — Are they imitating one another, do you think, or what?

SEXTON: …and the Pious and Devout Tsars and Tsarinas, and the keepers of this Holy Temple, and all the fathers and brothers whose souls now rest in the Lord…

VOICES IN THE CONGREGATION: — Suicide is contagious… — The number of psychopaths keeps multiplying. It's horrifying! — Quiet! And stop moving around so much!

SEXTON: …Christian souls here and everywhere.

A VOICE IN THE CONGREGATION: Stop shouting, please.

Moan.

CHOIR: *(Sings.)* Lord, have mercy!

VOICES IN THE CONGREGATION: — Tatyana Repina's death has poisoned the atmosphere. All our young ladies have been infected, and they're all going crazy with revenge. — Even in the church, the air is poisoned. Can't you feel the tension?

SEXTON: And let us also pray for those whose work has born fruit and perpetrated good, those who are toiling, those who singing and those who are standing in this holy and sanctified temple, awaiting the greatness and bounty of thy mercy…

CHOIR: *(Sings.)* Lord, have mercy.

FATHER IVAN: For thou art a merciful God, who lovest mankind, and unto thee do we ascribe glory, to the Father, and to the Son, and to the Holy Spirit, now and forever, and unto ages of ages.

CHOIR: *(Sings.)* Amen.

SABININ: Kotelnikov!

KOTELNIKOV: What?

SABININ: Nothing…O my God…Tatyana Petrovna is here…She's here…

KOTELNIKOV: You're out of your mind!

SABININ: The woman in black…it is she. I recognize her…I saw her…

KOTELNIKOV: There's no resemblance whatsoever…They're both brunette, that's all.

SEXTON: Let us offer prayer unto the Lord!

KOTELNIKOV: Stop whispering, it's improper. People are looking at you…

SABININ: For the love of God…I can hardly stand. It is she.

A moan.

CHOIR: Lord, have mercy.

VOICES IN THE CONGREGATION: — Quiet! Shhh! Hey, you people, who's pushing from behind? Shhh! — They've taken her behind that column… — There's no escaping from women here…They all should stay at home!

SOMEONE: *(Shouts.)* Quiet!

FATHER IVAN: *(Reads.)* O Lord our God, who in thy saving providence didst vouchsafe by thy presence in Cana of Galilee…*(Looks out at the congregation.)* Now, people, really, I must say…*(Reads.)*…to declare marriage honorable by thy presence…*(Raises his voice.)* I must ask you to be quieter. You're interfering with the completion of the sacrament! Stop walking around the church, stop talking and making so much noise, just stand quietly and pray to God. That's right. You must have the fear of God in you. *(Reads.)* O Lord our God, who in thy saving providence didst vouchsafe by thy presence in Cana of Galilee to declare marriage honorable: do thou the same Lord, now also maintain in peace and concord thy servants, Pyotr and Vera, whom it hath pleased thee to join together. Cause their marriage to be honorable. Preserve their bed blameless. Mercifully grant that they may live together in purity; and enable them to attain to a ripe old age, walking in thy commandments with a pure heart. For thou art our God, the God whose property it is to show mercy and to save, and unto thee do we ascribe glory, to the Father, and to the Son, and to the Holy Spirit, now and forever, and unto ages of ages.

BISHOP'S CHOIR: *(Sings.)* Amen.

SABININ: *(To KOTELNIKOV.)* Go tell the police not to admit anyone else into the church…

KOTELNIKOV: Why bother? There's no room, anyway. The church is packed. And be quiet…stop whispering.

SABININ: She is here...Tatyana is here.

KOTELNIKOV: You're raving...come on! She's lying in her grave.

SEXTON: Help us, save us, have mercy upon us, and keep us, O God, by thy grace!

CHOIR: *(Sings.)* Lord, have mercy.

SEXTON: A day all-perfect, holy, peaceful and sinless, let us beseech of the Lord.

CATHEDRAL CHOIR: *(Sings.)* Grant it, O Lord!

SEXTON: An Angel of Peace, the faithful guide and guardian both of our souls and bodies, let us beseech of the Lord.

CATHEDRAL CHOIR: *(Sings.)* Grant it, O Lord!

VOICES IN THE CONGREGATION: Will this deacon ever be finished...First it's "Lord, have mercy," then it's "Grant it, O Lord." — I'm tired of standing up.

SEXTON: The forgiveness and remission of our sins and transgressions, let us beseech of the Lord.

CHOIR: *(Sings.)* Grant it, O Lord!

SEXTON: All things which are good and profitable to our souls, and peace to the world, let us beseech of the Lord.

A VOICE IN THE CONGREGATION: — Again they're making noise! Come on, people!

CHOIR: *(Sings.)* Grant it, O Lord!

OLENINA: Pyotr, you're trembling and gasping for breath...What's happening? Are you going to faint?

SABININ: The woman in black...It is she...We are all to blame.

OLENINA: What woman?

A moan.

SABININ: It's Tatyana Repina who is moaning...Give me strength, give me strength...And Kotelnikov is pressing the crown down on my head...Never mind, never mind...

SEXTON: That we may pass the remainder of our life in peace and penitence, let us beseech of the Lord.

CHOIR: Grant it, O Lord.

KOKOSHKIN: Vera's as pale as death. Why, just look at her, I believe she's got tears in her eyes. And him...look at him!

KOKOSHKINA: I told her that everyone would behave badly! I don't understand, why she decided to get married here. She should have gotten married in a country church.

SEXTON: A Christian ending to our life, painless, blameless, peaceful; and a good defense before the dread Judgment Seat of Christ, let us beseech of the Lord.

CHOIR: *(Sings.)* Grant it, O Lord!

KOKOSHKINA: We should ask Father Ivan to hurry up. She looks awful.

VOLGIN: Please, let me have a turn! *(Changes places with KOTELNIKOV.)*

SEXTON: The unity of the faith, and the communion of the Holy Spirit let us beseech of the Lord: and let us commend ourselves, and each other, and all our life unto Christ our God.

CHOIR: *(Sings.)* To thee, O Lord!

SABININ: Hold on, Vera, just like I am...You can do it!...That's right...And the service is almost over, anyway. We'll leave right away...It is she...

VOLGIN: Shhh!

FATHER IVAN: And vouchsafe, O Lord, that boldly and without condemnation, we may dare to call upon thee, God, the heavenly Father, and to say:

CHOIR: *(Sings.)* Our father, which art in heaven, Hallowed be thy Name, thy kingdom come...

MATVEEV: *(To the actors.)* Move over, fellows, I want to kneel... *(Gets down on his knees and bows to the ground.)* Thy will be done, on earth as it is in heaven. Give us this day our daily bread and forgive us our trespasses...

CATHERDRAL CHOIR:...thy will be done...as it is in heaven...in heaven... our daily bread...daily...!

MATVEEV: Remember, O Lord, thy departed handmaiden Tatyana and forgive her her sins, intentional and unintentional, and also forgive us and have mercy upon us... *(Stands up.)* God, it's hot!

CATHEDRAL CHOIR:... give us this day and forgive...and forgive us our trespasses...as we forgive those who trespass against us...us...

A VOICE IN THE CONGREGATION: This music is going on forever!

CATHEDRAL CHOIR:...and lead us not...not...not! into temptation, but deliver us from eeeee-vil!

KOTELNIKOV: *(To the ASSISTANT PROSECUTOR.)* Our groom has been stung by something! Look how he's trembling!

ASSISTANT PROSECUTOR: What's the matter with him?

KOTELNIKOV: The woman in black, the one's who was having hysterics, he thought she was Tatyana. He's hallucinating.

FATHER IVAN: For thine is the kingdom, and the power, and the glory, of the Father, and of the Son, and of the Holy Spirit, now and forever, and unto ages of ages.

CHOIR: Amen.

ASSISTANT PROSECUTOR: Watch that he doesn't do something strange.

KOTELNIKOV: No, he'll hold himself together. He's not the type!

ASSISTANT PROSECUTOR: Yes, he's having a rough time.

FATHER IVAN: Peace be with you all.

CHOIR: And with thy spirit.

SEXTON: Bow your heads unto the Lord.

CHOIR: To thee, O Lord!

VOICES IN THE CONGREGATION: — I think the procession's about to start. Shhh! — Have they had an inquest on the doctor's wife? — Not yet. They say that her husband left her. Just like Sabinin left Tatyana Repina! It's true, isn't it? — Ye-es...— I remember Repina's inquest...

SEXTON: Let us pray to the Lord.

CHOIR: Lord, have mercy!

FATHER IVAN: *(Reads.)* O God, who has created all things by thy might, and confirmest the universe, and adornest the crown of all things which thou hast made: bless now, with thy spiritual blessing, this common cup, which thou dost give to those who are now united for a community of marriage. For blessed is thy Name, and glorified is thy kingdom, of the Father, and of the Son, and of the Holy Spirit, now and forever, and unto ages of ages. *(Gives SABININ and OLENINA wine to drink.)*

CHOIR: Amen.

ASSISTANT PROSECUTOR: Be careful that he doesn't faint.

KOTELNIKOV: He's as strong as an ox. He'll hold himself together.

VOICES IN THE CONGREGATION: — All right, everyone, don't wander away, let's all go out together. Has anyone seen Zipunov around? — He's here. We've got to stand around the carriage and whistle for five minutes.

FATHER IVAN: Give me your hands, please. *(Ties SABININ and OLENINA's hands together with a handkerchief.)* Is this too tight?

ASSISTANT PROSECUTOR: *(To the STUDENT.)* Give me the crown, young man — you can carry the bridal train.

CATHEDRAL CHOIR: *(Sings.)* Rejoice, O Isaiah! A Virgin is with child...

FATHER IVAN walks around the lectern followed by the bridal couple and their attendants.

A VOICE IN THE CONGREGATION: The student got tangled in her train.

CATHEDRAL CHOIR:...and shall bear a Son, Emmanuel, both God and man; and Orient is his name...

SABININ: *(To VOLGIN.)* Is it over yet?

VOLGIN: Not yet.

CATHEDRAL CHOIR:...whom magnifying, we call the Virgin blessed.

FATHER IVAN walks around the lectern a second time.

CATHEDRAL CHOIR: *(Sings.)* O holy martyrs, who fought nobly and now are crowned: entreat ye the Lord to have mercy upon our souls.

FATHER IVAN: *(Walks around the lectern for a third time and joins in the singing.)*...our so-o-uls...

SABININ: My God, this service is endless.

CATHEDRAL CHOIR: *(Sings.)* Glory to thee, O Christ-God, the Apostles' boast, the Martyrs' joy, whose preaching was the consubstantial Trinity.

AN OFFICIAL IN THE CONGREGATION: *(To KOTELNIKOV.)* Warn Sabinin that the students and the schoolboys will be whistling at him in the street.

KOTELNIKOV: Thank you. *(To the ASSISTANT PROSECUTOR.)* My God, this is going on forever! Will this service ever end! *(Wipes his face with a handkerchief.)*

ASSISTANT PROSECUTOR: Your hands are trembling...What a bunch of sissies you are.

KOTELNIKOV: I can't get Tatyana Repina out of my head. I keep hearing Sabinin singing, and her crying.

FATHER IVAN: *(Takes the crown from VOLGIN; to SABININ.)* Be thou exalted, O Bridegroom, like unto Abraham; and be thou blessed, like unto Isaac; and do thou multiply like unto Jacob, walking in peace, and keeping the commandments of God in righteousness.

A YOUNG ACTOR: What beautiful words falling upon scoundrels' ears!

MATVEEV: It's the same God for one and all.

FATHER IVAN: *(Taking the crown from the ASSISTANT PROSECUTOR; to OLENINA.)* And thou, O Bride, be thou exalted like unto Sarah; and exult thou, like unto Rebecca; and do thou multiply, like unto Rachel: and rejoice thou in thy husband, fulfilling the conditions of the law: for so is it well-pleasing unto God.

There is a great rush to the exit.

VOICES IN THE CONGREGATION: — Quiet, everyone! It's not over yet! — Shhh! Stop pushing!

SEXTON: Let us pray to the Lord!

CHOIR: Lord, have mercy.

FATHER ALEXEY: *(Reads, having taken off his dark glasses.)* O God, our God, who didst come to Cana of Galilee, and didst bless there the marriage feast;

bless, also, these thy servants, who through thy good providence are now united together in wedlock. Bless their goings out and their comings in: replenish their life with good things; receive their crowns into thy kingdom, preserving them spotless, blameless, and without reproach, unto ages of ages.

CHOIR: *(Sings.)* Amen.

OLENINA: *(To her brother, the STUDENT.)* Tell them to get me a chair. I feel faint.

STUDENT: It will be over any minute now. *(To the ASSISTANT PROSECUTOR.)* Vera feels faint!

ASSISTANT PROSECUTOR: Vera Aleksandrovna, it's almost over! Any minute now...Be patient, my darling!

OLENINA: *(To her brother, the STUDENT.)* Pyotr didn't hear me...It's like he's in a trance...My God, my God...*(To SABININ.)* Pyotr!

FATHER IVAN: Peace be with you all!

CHOIR: And with thy spirit!

SEXTON: Bow your heads unto the Lord!

FATHER IVAN: *(To SABININ and OLENINA.)* May the Father, and the Son and the Holy Spirit, the all-holy, consubstantial and life-giving Trinity, one Godhead, and one Kingdom, bless you; and grant unto you length of days, fair offspring, prosperity of life, and faith; and fill with abundance of all earthly good things! And make you worthy to obtain the blessings of the promise, through the prayers of the holy Birth-giver of God, and of all the Saints, amen! *(To OLENINA, with a smile.)* Kiss your husband.

VOLGIN: *(To SABININ.)* Don't just stand there! Kiss each other!

The bride and groom kiss.

FATHER IVAN: Congratulations! And may God grant...

KOKOSHKINA: *(Goes up to OLENINA.)* My darling...I'm so happy! Congratulations!

KOTELNIKOV: *(To SABININ.)* Congratulations, you did it...You can relax now, the ordeal is over...

SEXTON: Wisdom!

Congratulations.

CHOIR: *(Sings.)* More honorable than the Cherubim, and beyond compare more glorious than the Seraphim, thou who without defilement barest God the Word, true Birth-giver of God, we magnify thee. Bless us in the name of the Lord, Fa-a-ther!

The crowd pours out of the church; KUZMA extinguishes the candles.

FATHER IVAN: May he who by his presence at the marriage feast in Cana of Galilee did declare marriage to be an honorable estate, Christ our true God; through the prayers of his all-holy Mother; of the holy, glorious and all-laudable Apostles; of the holy, God-crowned Kings and Saints equal-to-the-Apostles Konstantin and Yelena; of the holy Great Martyr, Prokopia, and of all the Saints: have mercy upon you and save you; forasmuch as he is good, and loveth mankind!

CHOIR: Amen. Lord, have mercy, Lord, have mercy, Lo-rd, have mer-r-r-cy!

LADIES: *(To OLENINA.)* Congratulations, darling!…May you live to be a hundred…*(Kisses.)*

SONNENSTEIN: Madame Sabinin, you — how shall I put it? — as they say, in the Russian language…

CATHEDRAL CHOIR: Long, lo-o-ong li-fe! Long life…

SABININ: *Pardon*, Vera! *(Takes KOTELNIKOV by the hand and quickly leads him aside; trembling and gasping for breath.)* Let's go to the cemetery immediately!

KOTELNIKOV: Are you out of your mind! It's nighttime already! What are you going to do there?

SABININ: For God's sake, please, let's go! I beg of you…

KOTELNIKOV: You should be going home with your bride! You're crazy!

SABININ: I don't give a damn about anything anymore, to hell with it all! I'm — I'm going! We've got to hold a requiem…I'm going mad…I almost died…Ach, Kotelnikov, Kotelnikov!

KOTELNIKOV: Come on, let's go…*(Leads him to his bride.)*

A minute later a piercing whistle is heard coming from the street. Little by little, the crowd exits from the church. Only the SEXTON and KUZMA remain.

KUZMA: *(Extinguishes the chandeliers.)* The place was packed…

SEXTON: Yes…Quite a lavish wedding. *(Puts on his fur coat.)* These people really know how to live.

KUZMA: And all this for what?…For nothing.

SEXTON: What?

KUZMA: This wedding, I mean…Every day we marry 'em, we baptize 'em, and we bury 'em, and what sense does it all make…

SEXTON: And what exactly would you propose?

KUZMA: Nothing, I guess…It's just that there's no point to it. They sing, they burn incense, they recite, and meanwhile God doesn't hear any of it. Forty years I've worked here, and God has never listened once, not one single time…Where God *is,* exactly, I just don't know…There's no point to it.

SEXTON: Mm…I suppose you're right…*(Puts on his galoshes.)* It's just a lot of hocus pocus — makes your head spin. *(Walks off, his galoshes squeaking.)* Good-bye! *(Exits.)*

KUZMA: *(Alone.)* Today we buried one of the local gentlemen, we just performed a wedding, and tomorrow morning there'll be a christening. And there's no end to it. Who needs it? Nobody…You see? There's no point to it at all.

A moan is heard. FATHER IVAN and FATHER ALEKSEY, looking shaggy-haired and disheveled and wearing dark glasses, emerge from behind the altar.

FATHER IVAN: I'll bet he got a sizeable dowry, too…

FATHER ALEKSEY: I'll say…

FATHER IVAN: What a life, what a life! I, too, courted a young lady once, I married her, I even received a dowry, but now all that's forgotten in the general scheme of things. *(Shouts.)* Kuzma, why did you put out all the candles? I'm going to fall on my face in the darkness.

KUZMA: But I thought you'd already gone.

FATHER IVAN: So, Father Aleksey? Shall we have a cup of tea at my place?

FATHER ALEKSEY: No, thank you very much, Father. I don't have the time. I have another report to write.

FATHER IVAN: Whatever you say.

A WOMAN IN BLACK appears from behind the column. She is reeling as she walks.

WOMAN IN BLACK: Who's there? Take me away…take me away…

FATHER IVAN: What's going on here? Who's this? *(Frightened.)* What's the matter, my dear?

FATHER ALEKSEY: O Lord, forgive us, sinners that we are…

WOMAN IN BLACK: Take me away…Take me away…*(Moans.)* I'm the sister of Ivanov, the military officer…his sister.

FATHER IVAN: Why are you here?

WOMAN IN BLACK: I've poisoned myself…out of hatred…He has destroyed me…So why should he be happy? My God…*(Screams.)* Save me, save me! *(Sinks to the floor.)* Everyone should take poison, everyone! There is no justice…

FATHER ALEKSEY: *(In horror.)* What blasphemy! My God, what blasphemy!

WOMAN IN BLACK: Everyone should take poison…out of hatred…*(Moans and rolls on the floor.)* She lies in her grave, and he...An offense unto woman is an offense unto God...A woman has been destroyed...

FATHER ALEKSEY: What a blasphemy against religion! *(Throws up his hands.)* What a blasphemy against life!

WOMAN IN BLACK: *(Tears at her clothing and screams.)* Save me! Save me! Save me!...

CURTAIN

...and the rest I leave to the imagination of A. S. Suvorin...

1889

THE TRAGEDIAN IN SPITE OF HIMSELF

(a scene from "dacha" life)

A Farce in One Act

CAST OF CHARACTERS

IVAN IVANOVICH TOLCHAKOV, a family man

ALEKSEY ALEKSEEVICH MURASHKIN, his friend

The action takes place in St. Petersburg, in MURASHKIN's apartment.

The Tragedian
in Spite of Himself

MURASHKIN's study. Comfortable furniture. MURASHKIN sits behind a writing desk. Enter TOLCHAKOV, carrying a glass lamp globe, a child's bicycle, three hatboxes, a large bundle of clothes, a shopping bag filled with beer and many other smaller packages. Glassy-eyed, he collapses from exhaustion on the sofa.

MURASHKIN: Hello, Ivan Ivanich! So glad to see you! Where have you been?

TOLCHAKOV: *(Breathes heavily.)* My dear, dear fellow…Will you do me a favor…I beg of you…lend me your revolver till tomorrow. Be a good friend!

MURASHKIN: What do you want with a revolver?

TOLCHAKOV: I need one…O God!…Water!…Give me some water, quickly!…I need one…I have to travel through the woods at night, I have to be prepared…for anything. Lend me one, please!

MURASHKIN: You're lying, Ivan Ivanich! What the devil are you doing in the woods at night? Up to something, aren't you? And by the look of you, I can tell that it's no good! What's the matter? Are you going to faint?

TOLCHAKOV: Wait, let me catch my breath…Oh my goodness. I'm dead as a dog. My head — my whole body aches, I feel like I've been made into shashlik. I can't stand it any more. Be a good friend, don't ask me any questions…just lend me the revolver! I beg of you!

MURASHKIN: Enough! Ivan Ivanich, this is cowardice! You're a family man, and a civil servant! Shame on you!

TOLCHAKOV: What do you mean, a family man? I'm a martyr! A human sacrifice! A beast of burden, a slave, scum, the lowest of the low, who skulks around in this world instead of departing into the next, where I belong! I'm a "Milquetoast," a dummy, an imbecile! Why am I alive, I ask you? Why? *(Leaps up.)* Go on, tell me, what do I have to live for? Why this endless cycle of moral and physical torture? Yes, I can understand martyrdom to an ideal — but martyrdom to nonsense, to petticoats and lampshades, no, thank you very much! No, no, no! I've had enough! Enough!

MURASHKIN: Stop shouting, the neighbors will hear you!

TOLCHAKOV: Let them, what do I care! If you won't give me a revolver, someone else will, I'm not long for this world anyway! That's for certain!

MURASHKIN: Wait, you've just pulled off one of my buttons. Calm down, will you? I still don't understand what's so wrong with your life.

TOLCHAKOV: What's wrong? You're asking me: What's wrong? All right, all right, I'll tell you, what's wrong! I'll tell you, and then, perhaps, I'll get it off my chest. Sit down. Now, listen…Oh, my God, I can't catch even my breath!…Take today, for example. Yes, in fact, *take* today, please, you can have it! As you know, from ten till four I'm toiling away in the office. It's stifling and stuffy, there are flies everywhere — in short, my friend, it's utter chaos. My secretary's on vacation, my colleague's on his honeymoon, and all the office rank and file are frenzied from their summer homes, their love affairs, and amateur theatricals. Everyone's worn out, spent, exhausted, and you can't get a decent day's labor out of any of them…The Secretary's work is being handled by a fellow who is both deaf in the left ear *and* in love; our clients are crazed, they're rushing around in a terrible hurry, they're angry, they're threatening — and it's such pandemonium that it makes you want to scream. All hell has broken loose, and it's a total mess. And the work itself is sheer torture; it's the same thing, over and over again, inquiries, memoranda, inquiries, memoranda, — it's monotonous as the waves on the ocean. Your eyes are about to pop out of your head, almost. Give me some water, would you?…You leave the office defeated, exhausted, ready for a nice hot meal and bed, but no! — remember? — your family is on vacation at their dacha in the country — and you're a slave, a peon, a dishrag, an errand-boy, and you'd better shape up, you Milquetoast, you, you've got errands to do. There's a charming little custom among the dachniks where we're staying: If a husband travels into town for the day, then not only his wife, but any little nobody in the community is entitled to stick him with a thousand little errands. My wife commands me to stop in at the dressmaker's and scold her for cutting the bodice too wide and the shoulders too narrow on a dress; Sonichka needs a pair of shoes exchanged, my sister-in-law wants a sample cut of crimson silk and seven feet of ribbon…Wait a minute, I'll read you the list right now. *(Takes a piece of note paper from his pocket and reads it.)* One globe for the lamp; one pound ham sausage; five kopeks' worth of cloves and cinnamon; castor oil for Misha; ten pounds of granulated sugar; to bring from home: one copper bowl and mortar for sugar; carbolic acid, insect powder, ten kopeks' worth of face powder; twenty bottles of beer; vinegar, and a size eighty-two corset for Mademoiselle Chanceau...oh! and don't forget to bring Misha's fall coat and galoshes. So much for the list of family orders. Now on to the list of orders from beloved acquaintances and neighbors, curse every single one of them. Tomorrow at the Vlasin's they're celebrating Volodya's name day, so I have to buy a bicycle for him; Colonel Vikhrin's wife is expecting, so I've got to keep calling on the midwife every day to invite her to come. And so on and so on and so on. Five more lists I've got in my pocket, and my handerchief is all in knots. So, old man, in between leaving work and catching the train, you run around all over town like a dog with your tongue hanging out — you run and you run and you curse your fate. From the clothing store to the chemist's, from the chemist's to the dressmaker's, from the dressmaker's to the sausage maker's, then back again to the chemist's. Meanwhile, you trip over your own feet, you lose your money, in the third shop you forget to pay up, so they start chasing after you and causing a scandal, in the fourth place you tread all over a lady's skirt...and ugh! You get so wound up from such goings on that you grind your teeth all night, your bones ache, and you dream of crocodiles. And so, you've completed your errands, everything's been bought, so now how are you going to pack all this rigamarole up? How, for example, can you pack a copper mortar and pestle together with a glass lamp globe? Or carbolic acid with tea? How can you wrap up beer bottles with a goddam bicycle? It's a Herculean task, a Chinese puzzle, it's mind-boggling! You wrack your brain, you use all your wiles and arts, and in the end, no matter what, you end up breaking something or smashing something or spilling something anyway, and at the station and in the train compartment you find yourself standing bowlegged, arms outstretched, with some kind of bundle tucked under your chin, and shopping bags, cardboard boxes, and all other kinds of nonsense slung all over you. And the train starts moving, and the people start throwing all your things around, since you've put all your bundles on everybody's seats. And they start shouting, and calling for the conductor, and threatening to throw you off the train, and what are you supposed to do? So you stand there, blinking like a broken-down donkey. And now listen to what happens next. You finally arrive at your dacha. Oh, to have a lovely little drink, after all these noble deeds, a nice hot meal, and then fall fast asleep — right? — but no, it's not meant to be. Your dear wife has been on the lookout for you. You've hardly tasted your soup, when she sinks her claws into you with "wouldn't you just love to go to some amateur performance or other, or go to the dancing club?" How can you refuse? You are your wife's husband, and the word "husband," translated into "dacha" language, means a dumb silent beast upon whom you can load all kinds of baggage and make it come and go whenever you like, without worry of interference by the society for the prevention of cruelty to animals. So you go and gawk at *A Scandal in a Noble Family* or some other ridiculous play, you applaud on cue whenever your wife tells you, and meantime you're getting weaker and weaker and weaker by the minute, any moment now you think you're going to have a stroke. And at the club you watch the dancing and make sure that your wife has enough partners, and if there aren't enough gentlemen to go around, why then you just have to get up and dance the quadrille yourself. So you end up dancing with some Krivulya Ivanovna or other, you smile like a fool, and meanwhile you're thinking: "How long, O Lord, how long?" You arrive home after midnight from the theatre or some ball like a corpse, you're more dead than alive, it's hopeless. But then finally the end is in sight: You take off your clothes and at last you're in bed. Wonderful! — you can close your eyes and go to sleep now…And it's all so lovely, and poetic, and warm and cozy — isn't it? — the children aren't screaming away in the next room, the wife isn't there, your conscience is clear — what more can you want? So you drift off — and all of a sudden you hear: dzzzz!…Mosquitos! *(Jumps up.)* Mosquitos, curse them, damn them to hell, mosquitos! *(Shakes his fists.)* Mosquitos! An anathema! Worse than Egyptian torture, worse than the Spanish Inquisition! Dzzzz! they say, so sadly, so apologetically, as if they were asking your forgiveness, and meanwhile, the little villains bite you and you're scratching for hours after. You smoke, and you swat at them, and you cover up your head — but there's no escape, none! And in the end you say to hell with it, you give up, you're the sacrificial lamb: Go ahead, you say, eat me, you little devils! But no sooner does the feast begin, when a new Egyptian torture presents itself: Your wife is singing arias in the drawing room with her tenor friends. They sleep all day, and spend their nights practicing for amateur recitals. O my God! Tenors — what torture, no amount of mosquitos can equal them. *(Sings.)* "Don't say, that our youth has been wasted…" "Again, before you I stand, enchanted…" O ignoble villains! They wear you out! And so as to deafen their voices, you devise this little trick: You tap with your finger right here on your temple next to your ear. So there you are, tapping away for about four hours, until they go away. Ach, give me more water, please, my friend…I can't go on…And so, having slept not a wink, you get up at six o'clock — and off you go to the station to catch your train. You run and you run, afraid of missing it, and meanwhile, it's muddy and misty and cold, brrr! And you arrive in town, and you do the whole song and dance all over again! And so it goes, my friend. My life is absolutely terrible, I'm telling you, I wouldn't wish it on my own worst enemy. Do you understand — it makes me sick! I have shortness of breath, heartburn, anxiety attacks, indigestion, dizziness…I've become psychopathic, believe me…*(Looks around.)* Now this is just between us…I think I should consult a psychiatrist. I think I'm possessed, my friend…by demons. You see, in moments of deepest despair and frustration, when the mosquitos are biting and the tenors are singing, suddenly everything goes dark before your eyes, and you jump up and you start running around the house like a madman screaming: "Blood! I want blood! Blood!" And at the same time, you feel like plunging a knife into someone or bashing his head with a chair. And this is what dacha life drives you to! And you receive not even one ounce of sympathy or compassion, no, this is the way it's supposed to be. People even laugh at you. But don't you understand, I'm a living organism, I'm alive, aren't I? I want to live! This isn't a vaudeville, it's a tragedy! Listen, if you won't give me a revolver, at least show some me some sympathy!

MURASHKIN: I feel for you, I really do.

TOLCHAKOV: I know, I can see how much feeling you have…Good-bye, I have to pick up herring, and some sausages…oh, and tooth powder, too, and then it's off to the station.

MURASHKIN: Whereabouts is your dacha?

TOLCHAKOV: On Death Creek.

MURASHKIN: *(Joyfully.)* Really? Listen, you don't happen to know another summer resident there named Olga Pavlovna Feinberg, do you?

TOLCHAKOV: Yes, I do. She's an acquaintance of ours.

MURASHKIN: You're joking! What a coincidence! By the way, it would be so nice if you…

TOLCHAKOV: If I what?

MURASHKIN: My dear, dear fellow, may I trouble you for one small favor? Be a good friend! Promise me you'll do this for me!

TOLCHAKOV: Do what?

MURASHKIN: Not out of obligation, out of friendship! I beseech you, dear friend. First of all, give my regards to Olga Pavlovna and tell her that I'm alive and well, and that I kiss her pretty little hand. Secondly, there's a little something I want you to take to her. She's entrusted me to buy her a sewing machine, and there's no one to deliver it…Take it to her, would you, dear fellow? And by the way, while you're at it, you might as well take

her this birdcage too, with a canary…only be careful, the door's broken…
Why are you looking at me like that?

TOLCHAKOV: Sewing machine…canary cage…goldfinches, chaffinches…

MURASHKIN: Ivan Ivanovich, what's the matter with you? Why are you turning purple?

TOLCHAKOV: *(Stamps his feet.)* Give me the machine! Where is the birdcage? Now *you* climb on my back, too! Eat me up alive! Tear me to pieces! Go on, finish me off! *(Clenches his fists.)* Blood! I want blood! Blood!

MURASHKIN: You've gone mad!

TOLCHAKOV: *(Advancing on him.)* I want blood! Blood!

MURASHKIN: *(Horrified.)* He's gone mad! *(Shouts.)* Petrushka! Marya! Where are you? Someone, save me!

TOLCHAKOV: *(Chasing him around the room.)* Blood! I want blood! I'm thirsty! Blood!

Curtain.

1889

THE WEDDING

A Play in One Act

CAST OF CHARACTERS

YEVDOKIM ZAKHAROVICH ZHIGALOV, retired collegiate registrar

NASTASYA TIMOFEEVNA, his wife

DASHENKA, their daughter

EPAMINOND MAKSIMOVICH APLOMBOV, her fiancé

FYODOR YAKOVLEVICH REVUNOV-KARAULOV, retired captain
of the Imperial Russian navy

ANDREY ANDREEVICH NYUNIN, insurance agent

ANNA MARTYNOVNA ZMEYUKINA, midwife, wearing a bright
crimson dress; aged thirty

IVAN MIKHAILOVICH YAT, a telegraph clerk

KHARLAMPY SPIRIDONOVICH DYMBA, a Greek confectioner

DMITRY STEPANOVICH MOZGOVOY, a sailor in the Volunteer
Fleet

THE BEST MAN

Members of the wedding party, young gentlemen, servants, etc.

The action takes place in the reception room of a second-class restaurant.

The Wedding

A brightly lit reception room. A large table, set for supper. Servants in tails bustle about the table. Offstage, a band plays the last figure of a quadrille.

ZMEYUKINA, YAT, and the BEST MAN cross the stage.

ZMEYUKINA: No, no, no!

YAT: *(Pursuing her.)* Have pity on me! Please!

ZMEYUKINA: No, no, no!

BEST MAN: *(Chasing after them.)* Wait, you two! You can't do that! Where are you going? Why not dance? *Grand-rond, si'l vous plaît!*

They exit.

Enter NASTASYA TIMOFEEVNA and APLOMBOV.

NASTASYA TIMOFEEVNA: Will you please stop talking?! You're driving me crazy! Why don't you try dancing instead?

APLOMBOV: No, I will *not* take a "spin" on the dance floor! Who am I anyway, Spinoza? I'm an upright individual, a pillar of propriety, I derive no pleasure from idle amusements. And this is *not* about dancing. I mean really, *maman*, forgive me, but some things you do have me mystified. You daughter's dowry, for example: In addition to the customary household items, you promised me two lottery tickets. Where are they?

NASTASYA TIMOFEEVNA: I've got a headache…Must be the weather… There's a thaw coming on!

APLOMBOV: Don't try to change the subject. Today I found out that you pawned those tickets. Excuse me, *maman*, but that's simply dishonest. And I say this without an ounce of self-interest — I don't need your tickets, really, I don't, it's the principle of the thing, and I will not be made a fool of. I've made your daughter very happy, and if you don't give me those tickets back today, I'll eat her for breakfast, that's what I'll do! I am a man of my word!

NASTASYA TIMOFEEVNA: *(Examining the table and counting the place settings.)* One, two, three, four, five…

SERVANT: The chef asks how you wish the ice cream to be served: with rum, with madeira, or just as it is?

APLOMBOV: With rum. And tell the proprietor there's not enough wine. He should bring out some Haut Sauterne. *(To NASTASYA TIMOFEEVNA.)* As part of our prenuptial agreement, you promised to invite a general to supper, too. So where is he, I'd like to know?

NASTASYA TIMOFEEVNA: It's not my fault, dear.

APLOMBOV: Whose is it, then?

NASTASYA TIMOFEEVNA: Andrey Andreich's…Last night he came and promised to bring us a genuine general. *(Sighs.)* He probably couldn't find one, or else he would have brought him…What do you think we are, anyway, cheap? There is nothing we wouldn't do for our beloved daughter. She wants a general, she gets a general…

APLOMBOV: And another thing…Everyone, including you, *maman*, knows that this telegraph clerk, Mr. Yat, was making advances to Dashenka before I proposed to her. Why did you have to invite him? Didn't you know it would be awkward for me?

NASTASYA TIMOFEEVNA: Oh, please — what's your name again? — Epaminond Maksimich, you haven't been married twenty-four hours, and already you're torturing Dashenka and me to death with your talking. What will it be like a year from now? You're a bore, really you are, a bore.

APLOMBOV: Oh, so you don't like hearing the truth, is that it? Aha! I knew it! Just act honorably. That's all I ask of you: act honorably!

Couples pass the hall from one door through another, dancing the grand-rond. THE BEST MAN and DASHENKA are the lead couple, YAT and ZMEYUKINA bring up the rear. The last couple falls behind and remains in the hall.

ZHIGALOV and DYMBA enter and go to the table.

BEST MAN: *(Shouts.)* Promenade! Messieurs, promenade! *(Offstage.)* Promenade!

The couples exit.

YAT: *(To ZMEYUKINA.)* Have pity on me, please, enchanting Anna Martynovna!

ZMEYUKINA: You really are too much, aren't you…I already told you, I'm not in good voice tonight.

YAT: Sing something, I beg of you! Just one small note! Have pity on me! Just one small note, that's all!

ZMEYUKINA: You get on my nerves, really, you do…*(Sits and waves her fan.)*

YAT: But you simply have no heart! May I ask how one so cruel could have such a wonderful, wonnnnderful voice! You should pardon me for saying so, but with a voice like that, why is it you're a midwife? You ought to be a concert singer! How divinely you sang that grace note, for example...you know the one...*(Sings.)* "I loved you once, in vain I loved..." Sublime!

ZMEYUKINA: *(Sings.)* "I loved you once, and I might love again..." You mean that?

YAT: That's it, that's it! Sublime!

ZMEYUKINA: No, I can't, I'm not in good voice today. Here, fan me...It's hot! *(To APLOMBOV.)* Epaminond Maksimich, why so melancholy? That's no way for a groom to behave! Shame on you, to be so disagreeable. What's bothering you, anyway?

APLOMBOV: Marriage is a serious step! One must think it over carefully, thoroughly.

ZMEYUKINA: What repulsive cynics you all are! I'm suffocating to death in your company... Air! Do you hear me? I need air! *(Hums.)*

YAT: Sublime! Sublime!

ZMEYUKINA: Fan me! Fan me! Or else I think I'll burst! Tell me, please, why is it so stuffy in here?

YAT: Because you're sweating...

ZMEYUKINA: Ugh! How vulgar! Don't you dare speak like that in my presence!

YAT: Sorry! Of course, you're accustomed to high society, you should pardon the expression...

ZMEYUKINA: Oh, leave me alone! Give me poetry, give me ecstasy! Fan me, fan me...

ZHIGALOV: *(To DYMBA.)* Shall we have another? *(Pours.)* A drink is good for any occasion. The main thing, Kharlampy Spiridonich, is not to let it interfere with business. Go right ahead and do it, but keep your wits about you...And while we're on the subject of drinking, why not have a little drink? To your good health!

They drink.

Tell me something, do you have tigers in Greece?

DYMBA: Yes, tigers ve have.

ZHIGALOV: What about lions?

DYMBA: Lions ve have, too. In Russia is nossing, but in Greece is everysing. In Greece is my fazzer, and my uncle, and my brothers, and here is nossing.

ZHIGALOV: Hm...What about whales, are there any whales in Greece?

DYMBA: Is everysing in Greece.

NASTASYA TIMOFEEVNA: *(To ZHIGALOV.)* Why are we standing around nibbling and drinking? Everyone should be sitting down to supper. And don't go sticking your fork in the lobsters...They're reserved for the general. He still might be coming...

ZHIGALOV: Do you have any lobsters in Greece?

DYMBA: Yes, ve have...In Greece, ve have everysing.

ZHIGALOV: Hm...And what about civil servants?

ZMEYUKINA: How exotic Greece must be!

ZHIGALOV: And there is probably a lot of graft and corruption. The Greeks are just like the Armenians or the gypsies. They can't sell you a sponge or a goldfish without trying to bargain you down. How about another drink?

ZMEYUKINA: What's the point? Time to sit down to supper. It's already eleven o'clock...

ZHIGALOV: All right...if you want us to sit, we'll sit. Ladies and gentlemen, I most humbly beseech you! Please! *(Shouts.)* Supper time! Come on, you young people!

NASTASYA TIMOFEEVNA: Come one and all, dear guests. Please be seated!

ZMEYUKINA: *(Sitting at the table.)* Give me poetry!

"He sought the ocean's mighty roll,
To calm the storm within his soul."

Give me the storm!

YAT: *(Aside.)* A magnificent woman! I'm in love! I'm head-over-heels in love!

Enter DASHENKA, MOZGOVOY, the BEST MAN, young men and ladies, etc. They all sit down noisily around the table. There is a moment's pause; then the band plays a march.

MOZGOVOY: *(Standing.)* Ladies and gentlemen! I have an announcement to make...We have many addresses and speeches ahead. So, without further ado, ladies and gentlemen, I propose we drink a toast to our newlyweds!

The band plays a flourish. Cheers. Clinking of glasses.

MOZGOVOY: To the bride and bridegroom!

ALL: Make it sweet! Make it sweet!

APLOMBOV and DASHENKA kiss.

YAT: Sublime! Sublime! I must say, gentlemen, and let us give credit where credit is due: This hall, this entire establishment, in fact, is simply magnificent! Outstanding, superb! Only, guess what's lacking to set the whole thing off? Electric lighting, you should pardon the expression! Electric lighting has been introduced in all other foreign countries, only Russia lags behind...

ZHIGALOV: *(Thoughtfully.)* Electric lighting...Hmmm...Now in my opinion, electric lighting is only another form of fraud...You know, they slip in a piece of coal when they think you're not looking! No, my friend, if you're going to give us lighting, then don't give us coal, give us something substantial, you know, something impressive! Let there be *real* light — do you understand — real light, natural light, not intellectual light!

YAT: If you'd ever seen an electric battery, you'd be singing a different tune.

ZHIGALOV: I don't want to see one. It's just another fraud, to swindle the common man, to squeeze him dry...We know those swindlers, we know their type...And as for you, young man, instead of sticking up for swindlers, why not have another drink, and fill the glasses all around! Go on!

APLOMBOV: I agree with you completely, Papa dear. Why bother having intellectual conversations? I mean, I myself have no objection to discussing inventions of the scientific kind, but there's a time and a place for everything. *(To DASHENKA.)* What do you think, *ma chère*?

DASHENKA: He's just trying to show how smart he is, by speaking of things that others don't understand.

NASTASYA TIMOFEEVNA: We've managed to live our lives without education, thank God, and marry off three daughters to fine young men. So if you find us ignorant, then why do you come here! Go hang around your educated friends!

YAT: Dear Nastasya Timofeevna, I have the greatest respect for your family, so if I happened to bring up electric lighting, it wasn't to impress you with my superiority. Why, I can even join in the drinking, if you like. I have always wished with all my heart that Darya Yevdokimovna find a good husband. And in our day and age, Nastasya Timofeevna, a really good husband is hard to find. Nowadays everyone's trying to marry for money...

APLOMBOV: What are you insinuating!

YAT: *(Frightened.)* I'm not insinuating anything...Present company excluded, of course...I was only saying...that in general...Forgive me! Everyone knows you married for love...of course...The dowry is nonsense.

NASTASYA TIMOFEEVNA: Oh, no it's not! And watch what you're saying, sir. Besides a thousand rubles in cash, we also gave them three coats, a bed, and all their furniture. Let me see you find that size dowry anywhere else!

YAT: I didn't mean anything by it...Furniture, really, that's a very good thing...and coats too, of course. Now I'm afraid they're offended. I didn't mean to insinuate anything, really.

NASTASYA TIMOFEEVNA: Then don't. We invited you to the wedding out of respect for your parents, and here you go and say all sorts of things. If you really thought that Epaminond Maksimich was marrying for money, then why didn't you say so before? *(Tearfully.)* I have nursed her, coddled her, raised her…cared for her like a precious jewel, my little girl…

APLOMBOV: And you actually believed him? Well, I most humbly thank you. I'm much obliged! *(To YAT.)* As for you, Mr. Yat, you may be a friend of mine, but I will not permit you to behave like this in other people's houses! Will you kindly get out of here!

YAT: *What* did you say!

APLOMBOV: If only you were a gentleman, like me! I repeat, get out!

The band plays a flourish.

YOUNG GENTLEMEN: *(To APLOMBOV.)* Oh, let him stay! Calm down! What's the point! Sit down! Leave him alone.

YAT: I never meant anything by it…Really…I don't understand what the problem is…All right, all right, I'm leaving…Only give me back the five rubles you borrowed from me last year to buy that *piqué* waistcoat, you should pardon the expression. I'll have one more drink…and then I'll go, only first pay me back what you owe me.

GENTLEMEN: Stop it! Stop it! Please! Enough! What kind of nonsense is this?

BEST MAN: *(Shouting.)* A toast to the parents of the bride, Yevdokim Zakharich and Nastasya Timofeevna! To your good health!

The music plays a flourish. Cheers.

ZHIGALOV: *(Touched, bows to all.)* I thank you. Beloved guests! I'm eternally grateful to you that you're here, that you've come, that you haven't snubbed us!…And don't think I've invited you all here under false pretenses, not at all, I've invited you here out of feeling! Out of generosity! You're good people, and you can't do enough for good people! I humbly thank you! *(Exchanges embraces.)*

DASHENKA: *(To NASTASYA TIMOFEEVNA.)* Mama, why are you crying! I'm so happy!

APLOMBOV: *Maman* is upset that you're leaving her. But I've advised her to remember our little talk.

YAT: Don't cry, Nastasya Timofeevna! Just think about it: What are human tears, anyway? A psychological dysfunction, that's all!

ZHIGALOV: What about mushrooms? Do you have mushrooms in Greece?

DYMBA: Is mushrooms. Is everysing in Greece.

ZHIGALOV: I'll bet you don't have white mushrooms, though.

DYMBA: Is white mushrooms, too. Is everysing.

MOZGOVOY: Kharlampy Spiridonich, it's your turn to make a speech! Ladies and gentlemen, please, a speech!

ALL: *(To DYMBA.)* Speech! Speech! It's your turn!

DYMBA: But vy? I don't understand...Vat is zis?

ZMEYUKINA: Oh, no, you don't! It's your turn now! Come on, get up!

DYMBA: *(Stands, embarrassed.)* Zis is what I can say...Zere is Russia, and zere is Greece. In Russia, zere are Russian peoples, in Greece zere are Greek peoples...And on ze sea zere are sailboats, which ze Russians call sheeps, and on ze ground zere is somesing else which ze Russians call railvaze. I understand zis vell...Ve are Greeks, you are Russians, and I don't need notting...And zis is vat else...Zere is Russia. Zere is Greece.

Enter NYUNIN.

NYUNIN: Wait, ladies and gentlemen, don't start eating yet! Wait a minute! Nastasya Timofeevna, please! Come here for a moment! *(Takes NASTASYA TIMOFEEVNA aside, panting, out of breath.)* Listen...The general is coming...I finally got a hold of one...I'm exhausted...He's the real thing, a true-blue general, old, eighty, probably, or even ninety...

NASTASYA TIMOFEEVNA: When is he coming?

NYUNIN: Any minute. You'll be thanking me the rest of your life. He's better than a general, he's almost a Napoleon! And we're not talking infantry here, we're talking navy! Actually, he's a captain of the second class, but in the navy that's the equivalent of Major-General, or the civilian rank of State Councillor. Really, it's the same thing. Maybe even higher.

NASTASYA TIMOFEEVNA: You're not kidding me, are you, Andryushenka?

NYUNIN: Would I do a thing like that? Relax, don't worry about it!

NASTASYA TIMOFEEVNA: *(Sighing.)* We don't want to throw our money away for nothing, Andryushenka...

NYUNIN: Don't worry about it! He's not only a general, he's a masterpiece of a general! *(Raises his voice.)* So I say to him: "Your excellency," I say to him, "You've forgotten us. Shame on you, your excellency, shame on you, to have forgotten old friends! Nastasya Timofeevna," I say to him, "she's very annoyed with you." *(Goes to the table and sits down.)* And he says to me: "But really, my friend, how can I go, if I don't know the bridegroom?" "Oh come come, your excellency, why stand on ceremony?" I say to him. "The bridegroom is an excellent fellow, he's got a heart of gold, pure gold. Works as an appraiser in a pawnshop," I say to him, "but don't go thinking, your excellency, that's he's a no-good, or even a shady character, or anything like that. Nowadays," I say to him, "even respectable ladies work in pawnshops." So he slaps me on the shoulder, and we smoke a couple of Havana cigars together, and now he's coming…Wait, ladies and gentlemen, don't eat yet…

APLOMBOV: And when is he coming?

NYUNIN: Any minute. When I left him, he was putting his galoshes on. Wait, ladies and gentlemen, don't eat yet.

APLOMBOV: You'd better tell them to play a march…

NYUNIN: *(Shouts.)* Eh, musicians! A march!

The band plays a march for a minute.

A SERVANT: *(Announces.)* Mr. Revunov-Karaulov!

ZHIGALOV, NASTASYA TIMOFEEVNA, and NYUNIN rush to greet him.

Enter REVUNOV-KARAULOV.

NASTASYA TIMOFEEVNA: *(Curtseys.)* Welcome, your excellency! The pleasure is ours!

REVUNOV: Delighted!

ZHIGALOV: We are not celebrities, your excellency, we're not society, we're simple folk, but don't think that we're trying to pull the wool over anyone's eyes here, or anything of that sort. No, there's nothing we wouldn't do for nice people, nothing's too good for them. So please, welcome, and make yourself at home!

REVUNOV: Simply delighted!

NYUNIN: Allow me to make the introductions, your excellency! The bridegroom Epaminond Maksimich Aplombov with his newborn…that is to say his newly *wedded* wife! Ivan Mikhailich Yat, telegraph clerk! A foreign gentleman of Greek extraction, in the confectionary trade, Kharlampy Spiridonich Dymba! Osip Lukich Babelmandebsky! And so on, and so on…Forget about the rest of them. Sit down, your excellency!

REVUNOV: Delighted! Forgive me, ladies and gentlemen, I'd like to have a word with Andryusha here. *(Takes NYUNIN aside.)* My friend, I'm somewhat confused…Why are you calling me "your excellency?" I'm not a general, no indeed! I'm a captain, second class — that's even lower than a colonel.

NYUNIN: *(Speaks into his ear, as if he were deaf.)* I know, but Fyodor Yakovlevich, please, kindly permit us to call you "your excellency!" This family here, you know, they're very patriarchal, they have great respect for age and rank…

REVUNOV: Well, in that case, then of course…*(Goes to the table.)* Delighted!

NASTASYA TIMOFEEVNA: Sit down, your excellency! Be so kind! And please partake, your excellency! Forgive us, please, you must be accustomed to nice manners, but here we are simple people!

REVUNOV: *(Not hearing.)* How's that? Hm...yes, yes.

Pause.

Yes...In the olden days people always lived simply, and everyone was content. I live simply too, in spite of my officer's rank...So today, Andryusha comes to see me and invites me here to this wedding. How can I come, says I, if I don't know anyone? Won't it be rather awkward! And he says to me: "They're simple, old-fashioned people, everybody's welcome there..." Well, of course, if that's the case...then why not? Delighted. It's boring staying home alone, says I, and if my presence at a wedding can give anybody pleasure, then I'm only too happy to oblige them...

ZHIGALOV: Do you mean it, your excellency? Really? I commend you! I'm a simple man, an honest man, I respect like-minded people. Eat and drink to your heart's content, your excellency!

APLOMBOV: Have you been retired long, your excellency?

REVUNOV: Wha-? Yes, yes...You're right...It's true. Yes...Excuse me please, but what is this? The herring is bitter...and the bread tastes bitter, too. How can this be!

ALL: Make it sweet! Make it sweet!

APLOMBOV and DASHENKA (the bride and bridegroom) kiss.

REVUNOV: Ho-ho-ho! To your good health!

Pause.

Yes...In the olden days life was simple, and everyone was content...I love simplicity...I'm very old indeed, I retired in 1865...I'm seventy-two years old... Yes. Of course, there were times then, too, when they liked to put on a bit of a show, but...*(Sees MOZGOVOY.)* You...er...you're a sailor, aren't you?

MOZGOVOY: Yes, indeed I am.

REVUNOV: Aha...Right...Yes...A sailor's life has always been hard. It tests a man's mind. Every single word has its own special meaning, so to speak! For example: "Hands aloft, to the foresail and mainsail." Now, what does that mean, exactly? Well, any good sailor knows that! Ho-ho...It's as slippery as mathematics!

NYUNIN: To the good health of his excellency, Fyodor Yakovlevich Revunov-Karaulov!

The band plays a flourish. Cheers.

YAT: Your excellency, you were kind enough, just now, to wax eloquent on the difficulties of the naval service. But do you really think that the telegraph service is any easier? Nowadays, your excellency, no one can get into the telegraph service, unless they can read and write in French and German. Because the most difficult work in our service is the transmission of telegrams. It's murderously difficult! Do me the honor and listen to this, sir. *(Knocks on the table with a fork, imitating a telegraph transmission.)*

REVUNOV: What does that mean?

YAT: It means: "I hold you in the highest esteem," your excellency. Think it's so easy, eh? Listen to this...*(Knocks.)*

REVUNOV: Louder, please...I can't hear it...

YAT: Now this means: "*Madame*, how happy I am, to hold you in my arms!"

REVUNOV: What *madame* are you talking about? Oh, yes...I see...*(To MOZGOVOY.)* As I was saying, suppose you're running free and you have to set your topgallants and royals! Then you have to order: "Upper yardmen to the topgallants and royals...and at the same time that they are setting the sails on the yards, you have to stand by your royal and topgallant sheets, halyards, and braces on deck...

BEST MAN: *(Stands.)* Distinguished ladies and gentlemen...

REVUNOV: *(Interrupting.)* Yes, sir...We have plenty of commands...Yes... "Pull in the topgallant and royal sheets!" Isn't that a good one? But what does it mean, what sense does it make? Well, now, that's easy! You see, they pull in the topgallant and royal top sheets...all at once! Meanwhile, they square off the royal sheets and halyards as they're hoisting, and at the same time they pay out a little on the braces from the sails as the occasion demands, and so in the end when the sheets are brought home and the halyards all run right up, then they pull in the topgallant and royal braces, and the yards are lined up according to the direction of the wind...

NYUNIN: *(To REVUNOV.)* Fyodor Yakovlevich, our host kindly asks that you talk about something else. The other guests don't know what you're talking about, and it's very boring for them...

REVUNOV: What? Who's bored? *(To MOZGOVOY.)* Young man! Now suppose the boat is closehauled under full sail on the starboard tack and you have to jibe, what order do you give? Well, I'll tell you what order you give: You call all hands on deck, and you call out: "Prepare to jibe!"...Ho-ho...

NYUNIN: Fyodor Yakovlevich, enough! Please eat.

REVUNOV: And as soon as they've all run up on deck, then you call out: "Take your places! Jibe ho!" Ah, what a life! You give the command, and you watch the sailors run to their places like lightning, laying out the topgallants and braces. And you simply can't bear it any more, and you cry at the top of your lungs: "Well done, lads! *(Chokes and coughs.)*

BEST MAN: *(Hastens to take advantage of the ensuing pause.)* As we gather together today, so to speak, to celebrate our beloved…

REVUNOV: *(Interrupting.)* Yes! You see, there are so many commands to remember! For example: "Let fly the fore-sheet! Let fly the main!…"

BEST MAN: *(Offended.)* Why does he keep on interrupting! We'll never get through one single speech!

NASTASYA TIMOFEEVNA: We're ignorant people, your Excellency, we don't understand any of this, so what's the use, why don't you tell us something about…

REVUNOV: *(Not hearing.)* I've already eaten, thank you very much. Goose, did you say? No, thank you…Yes…Those were the good old days, young man…I remember them well! You sail along the sea, not a care in the world…and *(his voice trembles)* remember the joys of tacking? What sailor doesn't thrill to the memory of that manoeuvre?! You only have to hear the command: "All hands on deck! Ready about!"— it's like a bolt of electricity running through them all! From the commander to the lowliest sailor — every heart beats faster…

ZMEYUKINA: My God, this is boring! Boring! Please!

General grumbling.

REVUNOV: *(Not hearing.)* Thank you, really, I've already eaten. *(Passionately.)* Everything is ready, all eyes are on the first lieutenant…"Man the starboard fore and main braces and the port mizzen top braces and counter brace on the port side," orders the first lieutenant. It's all done in a flash…"Let fly the head and fore-sheets…Hard-a-lee!" *(Stands.)* The ship has come up into the wind, and at last the sails begin to shake. The first lieutenant shouts: "Look lively on those braces" — while his eyes are fixed frozen on the main topsail, and when finally, the great moment comes, and at last that sail starts shaking, too, that is to say the ship has begun to luff, you hear the thunderous command: "Let go the main top bowline, haul aft the braces!" And then it's like the fall of the Tower of Babel — everything's flying and cracking and crashing — and it all comes off without a hitch. The ship has turned triumphantly!

NASTASYA TIMOFEEVNA: *(Flaring up.)* General, this is disgraceful…And at your age, you ought to be ashamed of yourself! Enough of this!

REVUNOV: Cutlets? No, I haven't had any yet…thank you very much.

NASTASYA TIMOFEEVNA: *(Loudly.)* I said, you should be ashamed of yourself at your age! Really, General, it's disgraceful!

NYUNIN: *(Embarrassed.)* Ladies and gentlemen, really…must we? Come now…

REVUNOV: First of all, I'm not a general, I'm a captain of the second rank, which in the military corresponds to a lieutenant colonel.

NASTASYA TIMOFEEVNA: If you're not a General, then why did you take our money? We didn't pay you money for you to make a fool of yourself!

REVUNOV: *(In disbelief.)* What money?

NASTASYA TIMOFEEVNA: You know very well, what money. Haven't you already received your twenty-five rubles from Andrey Andreevich?…*(To NYUNIN.)* Shame on you, Andryushenka! I never asked you to hire someone like this!

NYUNIN: Really…Stop it! Must you?

REVUNOV: Hired…Paid…What's going on?

APLOMBOV: One moment, please…Did you really receive twenty-five rubles from Andrey Andreevich?

REVUNOV: What twenty-five rubles? *(Thinks for a moment.)* So that's what this is! Now I understand everything…What a vile trick! A vile and dirty trick!

APLOMBOV: You really took money for this?

REVUNOV: I took no money of any kind! Get away from me! *(Stands up from the table.)* What vileness! What baseness! To insult an old man, a sailor, an officer emeritus!…If this were a respectable household, I could challenge someone to a duel, but what can I do here? *(Dismayed.)* Where is the door? Which way out? Waiter, show me out? Waiter! *(Exiting.)* What baseness! What vileness! *(Exits.)*

NASTASYA TIMOFEEVNA: Andryushenka, where are the twenty-five rubles?

NYUNIN: Who cares? Big deal! Everyone is celebrating, and you're talking nonsense…*(Shouts.)* To the good health of the happy couple! Musicians! Play a march! Let's have music!

The band plays a march.

To the good health of the happy couple!

ZMEYUKINA: I can't breathe! Air, give me air! When you're near me, I can't breathe!

YAT: *(In ecstasy.)* Sublime! Sublime!

General pandemonium.

BEST MAN: *(Trying to be heard.)* Esteemed ladies and gentlemen! On this day, so to speak…

Curtain.

1889

THE JUBILEE

A Farce in One Act

CAST OF CHARACTERS

ANDREY ANDREEVICH SHIPUCHIN, Chairman of the Board of
Directors of the Mutual Bank of N—., a man in his prime; wears a
monocle

TATYANA, his wife, aged twenty-five

KUZMA NIKOLAEVICH KHIRIN, an elderly bank clerk

NASTASYA FYODOROVNA MERCHUTKINA, an old woman in a
cloak

A BANK DELEGATE

Shareholders of the bank

Bank clerks

The action takes place in the offices of the Mutual Bank of N —.

The Jubilee

The office of the Chairman of the Board of Directors. There is a door to the left, leading into the main bank office. There are two writing desks. The furnishings are extremely luxurious: velvet-upholstered furniture, flowers, statues, carpets, and a telephone. It is noon.

KHIRIN is alone. He is wearing felt boots.

KHIRIN: *(Shouts at the door.)* Send somebody out to get fifteen kopeks worth of valerian drops, and have some fresh water brought into the Chairman's office! How many times do I have to tell you? *(Goes to the desk.)* I'm all worn out. I've been writing for three whole days and nights, I haven't even closed my eyes; all day long I write here, all night long I write at home. *(Coughs.)* My whole body aches. I've got chills, and a fever, and a cough, and my legs ache...what's more, I keep seeing stars, or exclamation marks, or something like that. *(Sits.)* And that pompous phony, that fraud, our chairman, today he'll give a speech at our general meeting: "Our bank: present and future." Thinks he's a real orator, that one...*(Writes.)* "Two... one...one...six...zero...seven...And: six...zero...one...six..." Thinks he can put on a big show, while I sit here slaving away like a convict...Thinks he can fabricate a fantasy report, while I sit here counting away, day after day, till I'm blue in the face, curse him!...*(Clicks on the abacus.)* I can't bear it any longer! *(Writes.)* And: "one...three...seven...two...one...zero..." He promised to reward me for my diligence. If all goes well today, if he pulls the wool over their eyes, he's promised me a gold medal and three hundred rubles...a bonus!...We'll see. *(Writes.)* And if I get nothing for my pains, then watch out, my friend...I've got a short fuse...I can be dangerous...Oh, yes, I can!

Offstage, there is noise and applause. SHIPUPCHIN's voice: "Thank you! Thank you! I'm deeply moved." Enter SHIPUCHIN. He is wearing tails and a white tie; he carries an album that has just been presented to him.

SHIPUCHIN: *(Standing in the doorway and turning to the main office.)* Your gift, dearest colleagues, I shall treasure till my dying day as a memento of the happiest years of my life! Yes, gentlemen! Once again, I thank you!

(Blows a kiss in the air and goes to KHIRIN.) My dearest, most esteemed Kuzma Nikolaich!

While he is speaking on stage, clerks come and go with papers for him to sign.

KHIRIN: *(Standing.)* May I have the honor of congratulating you, Andrey Andreich, on this, the fifteenth anniversary of our bank, and to wish you…

SHIPUCHIN: *(Firmly shakes his hand.)* I thank you, my dear fellow! I thank you! And on this most auspicious of days, our jubilee, it is fitting that we embrace!…

They embrace.

I'm very very happy indeed! Thank you for your services, for your loyalty, for everything! Any contribution I have had the honor of making as president of this bank, I have made thanks to my colleagues. *(Sighs.)* Yes, my friend, fifteen years! Fifteen years, or my name's not Shipuchin! *(Quickly.)* So, how's my report? Is it coming along?

KHIRIN: Yes, sir. Only five pages left to go.

SHIPUCHIN: Excellent. Will it be ready by three?

KHIRIN: If I'm not interrupted, it will. There's only a little bit left.

SHIPUCHIN: Magnificent. Magnificent, or my name's not Shipuchin! The general meeting begins at four. Please, my dear fellow. Give me the first part, I'll study it carefully…Go on, hurry up…*(Takes the report.)* There's a lot riding on this report…It's my *profession de foi*, or, how shall I put it, my fireworks!…Yes, fireworks! or my name's not Shipuchin! *(Sits and reads the report to himself.)* God, I'm tired, I'm dead on my feet…Last night I had an attack of gout, all morning I've spent rushing around doing errands, and now there's all this excitement, and applause, and tumult…I'm exhausted!

KHIRIN: *(Writes.)* "Two…zero…zero…three…nine…two…zero…" These numbers make my head spin…"Three…one…six…four…one…five…" *(Clicks on the abacus.)*

SHIPUCHIN: Oh, by the way, there was more unpleasantness…This morning your wife came to complain about you again. She said that you went after her with a knife last night, and your sister-in-law, too. What kind of behavior is that, Kuzma Nikolaich? Ay-ay-ay!

KHIRIN: *(Severely.)* May I dare to make one small request, Andrey Andreich, on the occasion of this jubilee? I ask, out of respect for my painstaking drudgery, that you not interfere in my private affairs. I do beseech you!

SHIPUCHIN: *(Sighs.)* You really are impossible, Kuzma Nikolaich! You're an excellent man, well-respected, too, but you carry on about women like Jack the Ripper. Really, you do. I don't understand: Why do you hate them so?

KHIRIN: And I don't understand why you love them so much!

Pause.

SHIPUCHIN: The clerks have just presented me with an album, and the shareholders, I've been told, want to give me a speech and a silver mug…*(Plays with his monocle.)* Well, that's just fine, or my name's not Shipuchin! It's just as it should be…Nice to have a little ceremony, it's good for the bank's reputation, damn it! You're one of the family, you know what's going on, so I can tell you…I wrote the speech myself, and I bought the silver mug, too…And the folder for the speech cost me forty-five rubles, but, really, it was absolutely necessary. And anyway, *they* would never have thought of it. *(Looks around.)* Just look! Look at all this furniture! They say I'm a slave to detail! They say I only care that the doornobs are polished, and the clerks wear the latest ties, and a big fat doorman stands at the entrance. But no, gentlemen, no. Doornobs and doormen are not just details. Now at home I can be just another bourgeois, eat myself sick, sleep all the time, drink like a fish…

KHIRIN: Please refrain from insinuations, sir, thank you very much!

SHIPUCHIN: Oh, for God's sake! No one's insinuating anything! Really, you're insufferable…Where was I? Oh, yes. As I was saying, at home I can be a bourgeois, *nouveau riche*, I can be whatever the hell I want to be. But here we must be grandiose! This, sir, is a bank! Here every detail must impress, there must be an air of solemnity! *(Picks up a piece of paper from the floor and throws it into the fireplace.)* That's how I've enhanced this bank's reputation! Tone is everything, and everything is tone, or my name's not Shipuchin! *(Glances at KHIRIN.)* My dear man, any moment now a delegation of shareholders is arriving at the bank, and you're standing there in felt boots and a scarf…and some wildly colored jacket…You might have worn tails, you know, or at least a black frock coat…

KHIRIN: My health is more important to me than your shareholders. I ache all over.

SHIPUCHIN: *(Agitated.)* But you look like a wreck. You'll spoil the ambience!

KHIRIN: When the delegation arrives, I'll hide. No harm done…*(Writes.)* "Seven…one…seven…two…one…five…zero." I don't like disorder, either… "Seven…two…nine…" *(Clicks on the abacus.)* In fact, I can't bear it! You shouldn't have invited any ladies to the jubilee dinner…

SHIPUCHIN: What nonsense…

KHIRIN: You'll fill the hall with ladies just for show, I know, but they'll spoil everything, just you wait and see. Evil and chaos — that's what they'll bring.

SHIPUCHIN: On the contrary, the company of ladies is elevating.

KHIRIN: Oh, really…Your wife is an educated woman, or so it seems, so why is it, then, that last Monday she blurted out something that took me two days to recover from? All of a sudden, right out in public, right in front of strangers, she says: "Is it true that my husband bought shares from the Dryazhsko-Pryazhsky concern for our bank, and the price took a nosedive on the stock exchange? Oh, my husband was so upset!" Right out in public, she says it! Why you confide in them, I don't understand! Do you want them to get you convicted?

SHIPUCHIN: All right, all right, enough! This is all too gloomy for a jubilee. By the way, you just reminded me. *(Looks at his watch.)* My wife's due here at any moment. As a matter of fact, I should have gone to the station to meet her, poor thing, but I didn't have the time…and anyway, I'm tired. The truth of it is, I'm not particularly glad that she's coming! That is to say, I'm glad, but I'd have been much happier if she'd gone to her Mother's for a day or two. She'll insist I spend the whole evening with her, and meanwhile, we'd planned a little outing after dinner…*(Shudders.)* I've even started getting nervous twitches. I'm so tense, the slightest nonsense could provoke me into tears! No, I must be strong, or my name's not Shipuchin!

Enter TATYANA ALEKSEEVNA in a raincoat, with a travel bag across her shoulder.

Bah! Speaking of the devil!

TATYANA ALEKSEEVNA Darling! *(Runs to her husband, gives him a prolonged kiss.)*

SHIPUCHIN: We were just talking about you!…*(Glances at his watch.)*

TATYANA ALEKSEEVNA: *(Out of breath.)* Did you miss me? Are you well? I haven't even been home, I came here straight from the station. I have so much to tell you, I can't bear it…I won't even take off my coat, I've only stopped by for a minute. *(To KHIRIN.)* Hello, Kuzma Nikolaich! *(To SHIPUCHIN.)* Everything all right at home?

SHIPUCHIN: Fine. And you've gotten plumpier and prettier in only a week…So, how was your trip?

TATYANA ALEKSEEVNA: Wonderful. Mama and Katya send their love. Vasily Andreich made me promise to give you a kiss. *(Kisses him.)* Aunty has sent you a pot of preserves, and everyone's angry that you haven't written.

Zina made me promise to give you a kiss, too. *(Kisses him.)* Oh, if only you knew what's been going on! If only you knew! I'm afraid to tell you! If only you knew! But I can see it in your eyes that you're not glad to see me!

SHIPUCHIN: On the contrary...Darling...*(Kisses her.)*

KHIRIN gives an angry cough.

TATYANA ALEKSEEVNA: *(Sighs.)* Ach, poor Katya, poor poor Katya! I feel so sorry for her, really, I do!

SHIPUCHIN: We're having a jubilee today, darling, a delegation of shareholders is arriving any minute, and you're not even dressed!

TATYANA ALEKSEEVNA: Oh, that's right! A jubilee! Congratulations, gentlemen...I wish you...Oh! That means there will be a meeting and then a dinner...I love it. Do you remember that marvelous shareholder's speech that took you so long to write? Are you going to give it today?

KHIRIN gives another angry cough.

SHIPUCHIN: *(Embarrassed.)* Darling, let's not talk about it...Really, you ought to go home.

TATYANA ALEKSEEVNA: Yes, yes, right away. Just let me tell you a story — it'll only take a minute, and then I'll go. I'll start from the beginning. All right...After you'd seen me off on the train, do you remember, I sat down next to a very large lady and started to read. I don't like talking on trains. I kept on reading and reading for three station stops, I never uttered a word to a single soul...And then night fell, and, you know, I started getting such depressing thoughts! A young man was sitting opposite me, not bad-looking, rather handsome, actually, a brunette...Well, we started talking... Then a handsome young sailor joined us, and then a young student... *(Laughs.)* I told them I wasn't married...How they flirted with me! We talked and talked till midnight, the brunette told some frightfully funny stories, and the sailor sang all night long. I laughed until my sides ached. And then, when the sailor — I mean, really, those sailors — when he found out by chance that my name was Tatyana, do you know what he sang? *(She sings in a bass voice.)* "Onegin, I'll confess it gladly,/It's true I love Tatyana madly!"...*(Laughs uproariously.)*

KHIRIN gives yet another angry cough.

SHIPUCHIN: Listen, Tanyusha, please, we're keeping Kuzma Nikolaich from his work. Go home, darling, please...Later...

TATYANA ALEKSEEVNA: No, wait, let him hear this, really, it's very interesting. I'm almost finished. Seryozha met me at the station. And then another young man appeared, I think he was a tax inspector, or something...not bad looking, very handsome actually, especially his eyes... Seryozha introduced him, and off we went, the three of us...The weather was wonderful...

Offstage, a voice: "You can't go in there! No! What is it you want?"

Enter MERCHUTKINA.

MERCHUTKINA: *(In the doorway, brushing people aside.)* What do you think you're doing! Get your hands off me! It's him I'm looking for!... *(Enters, to SHIPUCHIN.)* May I introduce myself, your honor...Natasya Fyodorovna Merchutkina, my husband is a civil servant.

SHIPUCHIN: And what may I do for you?

MERCHUTKINA: Permit me to explain, your honor, my husband, Merchutkin, the civil servant, has been sick for five months, and while he was home recuperating, he was fired for no reason whatsoever, your honor, and when I went to collect his pay, do you know what they'd done? They'd gone and deducted twenty-four rubles and thirty-six kopeks from his wages. "What for?" I asked. "He had borrowed it from the cash box, and other people had to cover for him," they said. Well, imagine him doing a thing like that, without my knowing it! It's impossible, your honor! I am a poor woman, I take in boarders...A weak, defenseless woman...I have to put up with such insults, I never get a kind word from anyone.

SHIPUCHIN: Let me see this...*(Takes the petition from her and reads it while standing in place.)*

TATYANA ALEKSEEVNA: *(To KHIRIN.)* Anyway, let me begin all over again...Last week, all of a sudden, I got a letter from Mama. She wrote that my sister Katya had received a proposal from a certain Grendilevksy. A fine man, a decent young man, but with no means and no position whatsoever. And to make matters worse, as you can imagine, Katya was very keen on him. So, what was to be done? Mama wrote that I should come as soon as possible, and try to dissuade Katya...

KHIRIN: *(Sternly.)* Excuse me, madam, you've made me lose my place. Mama, Katya, I'm all mixed up, I don't understand what's going on.

TATYANA ALEKSEEVNA: Too bad! Why don't you listen when a lady is speaking to you? What's your problem? Are you in love? *(Laughs.)*

SHIPUCHIN: *(To MERCHTKINA.)* Excuse me please, but what's this all about? I don't understand any of it...

TATYANA ALEKSEEVNA: Are you in love? A-a-ah! You're blushing!

SHIPUCHIN: *(To TATYANA ALEKSEEVNA.)* Tanyusha, step into my office for a moment, darling. I'll be right there.

TATYANA ALEKSEEVNA. Very well. *(Exits.)*

SHIPUCHIN: I simply don't understand it. You've obviously come to the wrong place, madam. Your petition has nothing to do with us whatsoever. You really should address this to the office where your husband was employed.

MERCHUTKINA: I've already been to five different offices, sir, and they won't even read my petition. I was almost at my wits' end, until Boris Matveich — he's my son-in-law — advised me to come and see you. "Go see Mr. Shipuchin, Mama," he said, "He's a very influential man, he can do anything…" Please help me, your honor!

SHIPUCHIN: There's nothing we can do for you, madam. Please understand — your husband, as far as I can tell, was working in the medical office of the War Department, while our establishment here is completely private, commercial, we're a bank. Don't you understand?

MERCHUTKINA: Your honor, about my husband's illness, I have a doctor's certificate. Please, if you would kindly have a look at it…

SHIPUCHIN: *(Irritated.)* That's wonderful, I believe you, I do, but, I repeat, we have nothing to do with it.

Offstage, TATYANA ALEKSEEVNA's laughter can be heard, followed by a man's laughter.

SHIPUCHIN: *(Watching the door.)* She's keeping them from working out there. *(To MERCHUTKINA.)* Really, it's odd — and a bit funny, too. Doesn't your husband even know where to send you?

MERCHUTKINA: He knows nothing, your honor. "Go away! It's none of your business!" That's all he says…

SHIPUCHIN: I repeat, madam: Your husband worked in the medical office of the War Department, this is a bank, a private, commercial establishment…

MERCHUTKINA: Right, right, right…I understand, sir. In that case, your honor, tell them to give me just fifteen rubles! I can wait for the rest.

SHIPUCHIN: *(Sighs.)* Ach!

KHIRIN: Andrey Andreich, if this keeps up, I'll *never* finish this report!

SHIPUCHIN: Just a minute. *(To MERCHUTKINA.)* You just can't get it into your head, can you. Please understand, coming to us with a request like this is as strange as, let us say, filing a divorce petition at a chemist's or a surveyor's office.

A knock at the door. TATYANA ALEKSEEVNA's voice: "Andrey, may I come in?"

(*Shouts.*) Wait just a minute, please, darling! So they underpaid you, but what's that got to do with us? And furthermore, madam, it's our jubilee today, we're very busy...people are arriving any minute...Excuse me, please...

MERCHUTKINA: Your honor, have pity on a poor poor orphan! I'm a weak, defenseless woman...I'm dead tired, too...There's trouble with my lodgers, and this business with my husband, and the household to look after, and my son-in-law's out of work, too.

SHIPUCHIN: Madame Merchutkina, I...No, never mind, really, I don't have time to speak with you. My head is spinning from all this...You're interfering here, and you're wasting your time...(*Sighs, aside.*) The woman's an idiot, or my name's not Shipuchin! (*To KHIRIN.*) Kuzma Nikolaich, explain it to Madame Merchutkina, if you please...(*Waves his hands and exits into the board room.*)

KHIRIN: (*Goes up to MERCHUTKINA. Sternly.*) And what may I do for you?

MERCHUTKINA: I'm a weak, defenseless woman...I may look strong, but if you took me apart you wouldn't find one healthy nerve in my body! I can hardly stand on my own two feet, I've lost all my appetite. I drank some coffee this morning, and I couldn't even enjoy it.

KHIRIN: I'm asking you, what may I do for you?

MERCHUTKINA: Ask them to pay me back my fifteen rubles, and the rest they can give me in a month.

KHIRIN: But you were told just now, and in the Russian language, I believe, that this is a bank!

MERCHUTKINA: Yes, yes, of course...But I can present you with a medical certificate, if necessary.

KHIRIN: Have you lost your mind, or what?

MERCHUTKINA: I'm only asking for what's owed to me by law, dear sir. I don't want what isn't mine.

KHIRIN: And I'm asking you if you've lost your mind. Oh, the hell with it, I don't have the time to talk to you! I'm busy. (*He shows her the door.*) Allow me!

MERCHUTKINA: (*Surprised.*) But what about the money?...

KHIRIN: The fact of the matter is, you don't have a mind to lose...(*Taps his finger on the table, and then on his forehead.*)

MERCHUTKINA: (*Taking offense.*) What? Who do you think you are, anyway? Go talk like that to your *own* wife...*I* am the wife of a civil servant...So don't start that with me!

KHIRIN: (*Incensed, and in a low voice.*) Get out of here!

MERCHUTKINA: But, but, but… Watch it, you!

KHIRIN: *(In a low voice.)* If you don't leave this very instant, I shall send for the porter! Out! *(Stamps his foot.)*

MERCHUTKINA: Who do you think you are! I'm not afraid of you! I know your type…Cheapskate!

KHIRIN: I've never seen anything more disgusting in my entire life…Ugh! What a pain in the neck…*(Breathes heavily.)* For the last time…Do you hear me! If you don't get out of here, you old witch, I'll grind you up into little bits! I'll cripple you for life! I'm homicidal!

MERCHUTKINA: All bark and no bite, that's what you are. I'm not afraid of you. I know your type.

KHIRIN: *(In despair.)* I can't bear the sight of her any more! I feel faint! I can't bear it! *(Goes to the table and sits down.)* The bank is swarming with women, and I can't get the report done! I simply can't!

MERCHUTKINA: I only want what is rightfully mine, by law. Look at him, what a disgrace! Sitting around in an office with his boots on…The peasant…

Enter SHIPUCHIN and TATYANA ALEKSEEVNA.

TATYANA ALEKSEEVNA: *(Enters after her husband.)* We'd just come back from a party at the Berezhnitsky's. Katya was wearing a pale blue silk dress trimmed in delicate lace, with an open neck…She looked lovely with her new coiffure…I fixed it for her myself…She was stunning!

SHIPUCHIN: *(Who by now has a migraine.)* Yes, yes…stunning… Any moment someone might come.

MERCHUTKINA: Your honor!…

SHIPUCHIN: *(Despondently.)* Now what? What do you want?

MERCHUTKINA: Your honor!…*(Points to KHIRIN.)* This person here, this individual…first he taps on his forehead and then on the table…You ask him to deal with my situation, and what does he do? He mocks me and says all kinds of things. I am a weak, defenseless woman…

SHIPUCHIN: Very well, madame, I'll deal with it…I'll take the necessary steps…Only please leave…I'll deal with it later!…*(Aside.)* My gout is acting up!…

KHIRIN: *(Goes up to SHIPUCHIN, softly.)* Andrey Andreich, please, send for the doorman, and have her thrown out by her neck. Have you ever seen anything like it?

SHIPUCHIN: *(Frightened.)* No, no! She'll start screaming, and there are a lot of apartments in this building.

MERCHUTKINA: Your honor!…

KHIRIN: *(In a tearful voice.)* But I must write this report, I must! I won't get it done!…*(Returns to the table.)* I won't!

MERCHUTKINA: Your honor, when will I get my money? I need it now.

KHIRIN: *(Aside, with indignation.)* What an ab-so-lu-tely *horrible* woman! *(Gently, to MERCHUTKINA.)* Madam, I've already told you. This is a bank, a private commercial establishment…

MERCHUTKINA: Take pity on me, your honor, think of yourself as my own dear father…If the medical certificate will not suffice, I can bring one from the police department as well. Please, tell them to give me the money!

SHIPUCHIN: *(Sighs heavily.)* Ugh!

TATYANA ALEKSEEVNA: *(To MERCHUTKINA.)* Look, old woman, don't you get it? They're telling you you're in the way. Really.

MERCHUTKINA: Madam, lovely lady, please understand, no one will help me. Even food and drink are no comfort. I drank some coffee today, and I didn't even enjoy it.

SHIPUCHIN: *(Exhausted, to MERCHUTKINA.)* How much do you want?

MERCHUTKINA: Twenty-four rubles and thirty-six kopeks.

SHIPUCHIN: Fine! *(Takes twenty-five rubles from his wallet and gives them to her.)* Here's twenty-five rubles. Take it…and get out of here.

KHIRIN gives an angry cough.

MERCHUTKINA: I humbly thank you, your honor…*(Hides the money.)*

TATYANA ALEKSEEVNA: *(Sits next to SHIPUCHIN.)* Oh well, I'd better be going home now…*(Looks at her watch.)* But wait, I still haven't finished my story…It'll only take a minute, and then I'll go home…Such goings on! Such goings-on! As I was saying, we went to the Berezhnitsky's party…It was fine, it was pleasant, nothing special…And of course, Katya's admirer Grendilevsky was there…So I had a little talk with Katya, and I shed a few tears, and dissuaded her, so she had it out with Grendilevsky right there at the party and turned him down. Fine, I thought, everything turned out beautifully, I couldn't have hoped for better: I've placated Mama, I've saved Katya, now I can relax…Then what do you suppose happened? Katya and I are walking in the garden just before supper, when suddenly…*(agitated)* when suddenly, we hear a shot…No, I can't even talk about it, I'll get too upset! *(Fans herself with a handkerchief.)* I can't!

SHIPUCHIN: *(Sighs.)* Ach!

TATYANA ALEKSEEVNA: *(Weeps.)* We rush out to the summerhouse, and…there lies poor Grendilevsky…with a pistol in his hand…

SHIPUCHIN: No, I can't bear it! I can't bear it! *(To MERCHUTKINA.)* What more do you want?

MERCHUTKINA: Your honor, please, can my husband possibly have his job back?

TATYANA ALEKSEEVNA: *(Weeping.)* He shot himself right in the heart... Right here...Katya fainted, poor thing...And he's lying there, paralyzed with fear...and begs us to send for the doctor. The doctor comes right away...and saves the poor fellow...

MERCHUTKINA: Please, your honor, can my husband have his job back?

SHIPUCHIN: No, I can't bear it! *(Weeps.)* I can't! *(Reaches out to KHIRIN in despair.)* Get her out of here! Get her out, I beg of you!

KHIRIN: *(Goes up to TATYANA ALEKSEEVNA.)* Out!

SHIPUCHIN: No, not her, this one...the nightmare...*(indicates MER-CHUTKINA)* this one!

KHIRIN: *(Not understanding him, again to TATYANA ALEKSEEVNA.)* Get out of here! *(Stamps his foot.)* Out!

TATYANA ALEKSEEVNA: What? What did you say? Have you gone mad?

SHIPUCHIN: This is terrible! I am so unhappy! Get her out of here! Out, I tell you!

KHIRIN: *(To TATYANA ALEKSEEVNA.)* Out! Or else I'll cripple you! I'll mutilate you! I'll tear you apart! I'll stop at nothing!

TATYANA ALEKSEEVNA: *(Runs away, chased by KHIRIN.)* How dare you! *(Shouts.)* Andrey! Help! Andrey! *(Shrieks.)*

SHIPUCHIN: *(Chases after them.)* Stop! I beseech you! Quiet, please! Have mercy on me!

KHIRIN: *(Chases after MERCHUTKINA.)* Get out of here ! Grab her! Beat her! Slit her throat!

SHIPUCHIN: *(Shouts.)* Stop it! I beg you! I beseech you!

MERCHUTKINA: Good heavens!...Good Heavens...*(Screams.)* My God!...

TATYANA ALEKSEEVNA: *(Shouts.)* Save me! Save me!... Ach, ach...I'm fainting! Fainting! *(Leaps up on a chair, then falls on the divan, moaning, as if in a faint.)*

KHIRIN: *(Chases after MERCHUTKINA.)* Beat her! Flog her! Slash her to pieces!

MERCHUTKINA: Oh, oh...Good heavens, everything's going dark! Oh! *(Faints into SHIPUCHIN's arms.)*

There is a knock at the door, and a voice offstage: "The delegation has arrived!"

SHIPUCHIN: Delegation...Reputation...Occupation...

KHIRIN: *(Stamps his feet.)* Out, goddammit! *(Rolls up his sleeves.)* Give her to me! I'm going to kill her!

Enter a delegation of five men; all are dressed in tails. One carries a speech bound in velvet, another carries a tankard. Bank clerks peer through the door to the board room. TATYANA ALEKSEEVNA lies on the divan, MER-CHUTKINA lies in the arms of SHIPUCHIN; both are moaning softly.

A BANK DELEGATE: *(Reads in a loud voice.)* "Most esteemed and beloved Andrey Andreich! Casting a retrospective eye on the estimable past of our financial establishment, calling to mind the history of its gradual evolution, the impression we receive is favorable to the highest degree. True: in the earlier years, the limited financial resources, the absence of a serious and solid administrative base, and to be sure, the vagueness of our own institutional goals: all these factors brought to mind the fundamental question of Hamlet: "to be or not to be"; at one time, even, there were voices heard in favor of closing the bank. And then who ascended to the throne of institutional leadership, but — you. Your broad knowledge, your vitality, your innate sense tact — these were the cause of the extraordinary success, the remarkable prosperity of our institution. The bank's reputation… *(coughs)* the bank's reputation…"

MERCHUTKINA: *(Moans.)* Ach! Ach!

TATYANA ALEKSEEVNA: *(Moans.)* Water! Water!

DELEGATE: *(Continues.)* The bank's reputation…*(coughs)* the bank's reputation has been elevated by you to such lofty heights that our establishment may now compete with the finest foreign concerns…

SHIPUCHIN: Delegation…reputation…occupation…
    "One night two friends went for a walk
    And on that walk they had a talk…"
    "Don't say that our youth has been wasted,
    Tormented by my jealousy."

DELEGATE: *(Continues, in embarrassment.)* "And thus, casting an objective eye on the present, we, most esteemed and beloved Andrey Andreevich…" *(lowering his voice)*…have decided, actually, to come back later, that is, under the circumstances…Later is better…

They exit in embarrassment.

Curtain.

1891

THE NIGHT
BEFORE THE TRIAL

CAST OF CHARACTERS

FYODOR NIKITICH GUSEV, a gentleman of considerable years

ZINOCHKA, his young wife

ALEKSEY ALEKSEICH ZAYTSEV, a traveler

STATIONMASTER

The action takes place at a postal way station, one winter's night.

The Night before the Trial

A postal way station. A gloomy room whose walls are blackened with soot. Large sofas covered in oilcloth. A cast-iron stove with a chimney stretching across the entire room.

Enter ZAYTSEV with a suitcase, and the STATIONMASTER with a candle.

ZAYTSEV: God! It stinks in here, man! You can't even breathe! There's a sourish sort of smell…like sealing wax, or squashed bedbugs, or something… Ugh!

STATIONMASTER: Smells the way it always does.

ZAYTSEV: Wake me at six in the morning, would you…and make sure there's a troika ready…I've got to be in town by nine.

STATIONMASTER: Right-o…

ZAYTSEV: What time is it, anyway?

STATIONMASTER: Half past one…*(Exits.)*

ZAYTSEV: *(Removing his fur coat and felt boots.)* God, it's freezing! My brain's gone numb, it's so cold…Feel as if I've been smothered with snow, doused with water, and then flogged senseless…I mean, what with the snow drifts and this hellish blizzard, five minutes more out there and I'd be at death's door. I'm half-dead already. And for what? It'd be one thing if I were on my way to a *rendezvous,* or to collect an inheritance or something, but no, here I am, on the road to ruin…Can't even think about it, it's so terrible…Tomorrow there's a session of the circuit court in town, and guess who's the defendant?!…They'll charge me with bigamy, forgery of my grandmother's will to the tune of three hundred rubles, roughly, and attempted murder of a billiards' marker. The jury'll throw me in prison — no doubt about it. Here today, imprisoned tomorrow, and in six month's time — it's the frozen wilds of Siberia…Brrrrr! *(Pause.)* However, there is a way out of this terrible fix. Indeed, there is! If the jury finds me guilty, I shall turn to the aid of an old, old friend…A true and trusty friend! *(Pulls a large pistol from his suitcase.)* Ta-da! What a pal! Swapped him with Cheprakov for a couple of hounds. What a beauty! I mean, even to shoot yourself with him would bring you pleasure…of sorts…*(Gently.)* You loaded, fella? Eh? *(In a light voice, as if answering for the pistol.)* Yes, I am…*(In his own voice again.)* You'll make a lot of noise, won't you? A great big bang, right? *(In a light voice.)* A great big bang…*(In his own voice again.)* You clown, you…you old sweetheart…Go on, take a rest, go to sleep, "'night 'night"…*(Kisses the pistol and hides it in his suitcase.)* Soon as I hear "yes, guilty," then it's "bang!"—I'll put a bullet through my brain, and that's that…If only I weren't so frozen stiff…Brrrrr! Got to warm up…*(Waves his arms about, jumps up and down next to the stove.)* Brrrr!

ZINOCHKA peers through the doorway, and immediately disappears again.

What's going on here? Someone just looked through the door…Hm…Yes, I'm sure they did…Guess I've got neighbors then, eh? *(Eavesdrops through the door.)* Can't hear a thing…Not a sound…Probably fellow travelers, just passing through…Maybe they're a decent sort, why not wake 'em up, let's have a hand of bridge, why don't we…A grand slam in no trump! It'll keep me occupied, heaven help me…Especially if it's a woman. There's nothing better than a one-night stand, I always say…Sometimes, when you're on the road, you'll run across a romance better than any Turgenev novel, even…I remember, once, when I was traveling in the Samara province. I stopped at a way station…It was nighttime, I remember, and the crickets were chirping in the hearth…it was quiet…I was sitting at the table, drinking tea…When all of a sudden I hear this mysterious rustle…The door flings open, and…

ZINOCHKA: *(From behind the door.)* It's absolutely disgusting! I've never seen anything like it! This isn't a way station, it's a outrage! *(Peeps out from behind the door, shouting.)* Proprietor! Proprietor! Where are you?

ZAYTSEV: *(Aside.)* Well, isn't *she* lovely! *(To ZINOCHKA.)* The proprietor's not here, dear lady. The boor's asleep, he's out cold. What may I do for you? Can I be of any help?

ZINOCHKA: It's awful, absolutely awful! Bedbugs, and they're eating me alive!

ZAYTSEV: Bedbugs? You don't say! Really…how dare they?

ZINOCHKA: *(In tears.)* It's awful, I tell you! I'm leaving this instant! Tell that scoundrel proprietor to harness the horses! Those bedbugs have drunk up all my blood!

ZAYTSEV: Poor thing! You're so lovely, and now all of a sudden…No, this is monstrous!

ZINOCHKA: *(Shouts.)* Proprietor!

ZAYTSEV: Dearest lady…*mademoiselle*…

ZINOCHKA: I'm not a *mademoiselle*…I'm married…

ZAYTSEV: So much the better…*(Aside.)* How adorable! *(To ZINOCHKA.)*

What I mean to say is, not having the honor of knowing your name and patronymic, *madame*, and, by the same token, being an honorable, respectable individual, I am, therefore taking the liberty of offering you my services...so that I might assist you in your time of misfortune...

ZINOCHKA: How?

ZAYTSEV: I always follow the golden rule of carrying insect powder with me wherever I go...a superb practice...Allow me to offer it to you with all my heart, from the depths of my soul!

ZINOCHKA: Oh, please!

ZAYTSEV: In that case, I'll give it to you this very minute...I've got it right here in my valise. *(Runs to the valise and rummages through it.)* Those eyes, that precious little nose...A romance! I can feel it coming! *(Rubs his hands.)* Fortune smiles on me: I stop at a way station, and there I find romance... She's so beautiful, I'm all starry-eyed...Here we are! *(Goes back to the door.)* Here we are, your salvation...

ZINOCHKA extends her hand from behind the door.

No, no, please, allow me to come into the room and sprinkle it on myself...

ZINOCHKA: No, no...Come into my room? How could you?

ZAYTSEV: Why not? There's nothing wrong with it, especially...especially since I am a doctor, and doctors and hairdressers always intrude on people's privacy...

ZINOCHKA: You aren't making it up, are you? You're really a doctor?

ZAYTSEV: Word of honor!

ZINOCHKA: Well then, of course, if you're a doctor...then please, by all means...Only why should you put yourself out like this? I'll send my husband out...Fedya! Fedya! Wake up, you clod!

FEDYA's voice, offstage: "Wha-?"

Come here, the doctor has kindly offered us some insect powder. *(She disappears.)*

ZAYTSEV: "Fedya!" Now that's a surprise! Much obliged, I'm sure! What do I need this Fedya for! He can go take a flying leap, that's what he can do! No sooner do we get acquainted, no sooner do I start playing "doctor," then suddenly up pops Fedya...It's like getting doused with cold water...To hell with the insect powder! And anyway, she's nothing special...That face of hers...not much to look at...She's not my type!

Enter GUSEV, wearing a dressing gown and a nightcap.

GUSEV: Pleased to meet you, doctor…My wife just told me you've got some insect powder.

ZAYTSEV: *(Gruffly.)* That's right!

GUSEV: Please, lend us a little, would you, these bedbugs are eating us alive…

ZAYTSEV: Go ahead…take it!

GUSEV: I humbly thank you…I'm much obliged. You got caught in the blizzard, too?

ZAYTSEV: Yes!

GUSEV: I see…Terrible weather…And whereabouts are you headed?

ZAYTSEV: To town.

GUSEV: So are we. Hard work ahead tomorrow, got to get some sleep, but what an ordeal this is, I simply can't bear it…Our way stations are a disgrace, they truly are, they're shocking. Bedbugs, cockroaches, all kinds of creatures…If I had my way, I'd slap a penalty on all proprietors having bedbugs in their establishments, under the terms of Article 112, for "not keeping their domestic animals under control." I'm much obliged, doctor… And what is your specialty, may I ask?

ZAYTSEV: Chest and…head ailments.

GUSEV: I see…Nice meeting you…*(Exits.)*

ZAYTSEV: *(Alone.)* Scarecrow! If it were up to me, I'd bury him in insect powder up to his neck! I'd cream him in cards ten times over! Better yet, I'd play him in billiards and accidentally give him a bop with a billiard cue that he'd remember for a week…Look at him: a lump instead of a nose, those creepy blue veins all over his face, a wart on his forehead…and he has the nerve to marry a woman like that! How dare he? It's scandalous! It's downright obscene…And they ask me why I'm such a pessimist? How could I *not* be, under such circumstances?

GUSEV: *(In the doorway.)* Now don't be shy, Zinochka…After all, he's a doctor! Don't stand on ceremony, go ahead and ask him…There's nothing to be afraid of…Shervetsov didn't help you, so perhaps *he* will… *(To ZAYTSEV.)* Forgive me for disturbing you, doctor…Can you tell me, please, why my wife has this tightness in her chest? She has this cough, you see…and she's all congested…What could it be from?

ZAYTSEV: Well, that's a long story…I couldn't make an immediate diagnosis…

GUSEV: Oh, that's all right. We've got plenty of time…who can sleep, anyway?! Be a good fellow, would you, have a look!

ZAYTSEV: *(Aside.)* This is getting tricky!

GUSEV: *(At the top of his voice.)* Zina! You're being foolish…*(To ZAYTSEV.)* She's shy…She's bashful, just like I am…Virtue is all well and good, but how far can you go? To be bashful with your doctor, when you're sick, now, really, that's going too far…

Enter ZINOCHKA.

ZINOCHKA: You're right, I'm ashamed…

GUSEV: There, there…*(To ZAYTSEV.)* I should tell you, she's been seeing Dr. Shervetsov. He's a good man, the life of the party and all that, he knows his medicine, but…I don't know, I just don't trust him! As a matter of fact, I don't like him, either! I can see, dear doctor, that you're not in the mood, but please, oblige us!

ZAYTSEV: I…I have no objection…Really…*(Aside.)* This is quite a situation we've got here!

GUSEV: Please, examine her, I'll go ask the proprietor to light the samovar. *(Exits.)*

ZAYTSEV: Sit, please, I beg of you…

They sit.

How old are you?

ZINOCHKA: Twenty-two…

ZAYTSEV: Mm…A dangerous age. Let me take your pulse! *(Feels her pulse.)* Mm…yes…

Pause.

What are you laughing at?

ZINOCHKA: You're not deceiving me…that you're a doctor?

ZAYTSEV: How could you say such a thing! What do you take me for! Hm…pulse is fine…Hm…yes…What plump little hands …God, how I love roadside romances! You travel, and you travel, and then suddenly you encounter such a…pulse…Do you like the art of medicine?

ZINOCHKA: Yes.

ZAYTSEV: Lovely! Absolutely lovely! Allow me to examine you!

ZINOCHKA: Wait, wait, wait…please, mind that you don't go…too far!

ZAYTSEV: That lovely little voice, those positively sparkling eyes…One smile and I'm out of my mind…Is your husband jealous? *Very* jealous? Your pulse…just let me feel your pulse, and I'll die of happiness!

ZINOCHKA: No, wait, please, kind sir…Sir! I see that you take me for another sort of woman.…You are mistaken, sir! I'm married, my husband has a reputation to uphold.

ZAYTSEV: I know, I know, but is it my fault that you're so beautiful?

ZINOCHKA: I simply won't allow it, sir…Leave me alone, or I'll be forced to press charges… Sir! I love my husband, I respect him too much to permit some sweet-talking wayfarer to seduce me with a few silly words…You are sorely mistaken, sir, if you imagine that I…I think I hear my husband coming now…Yes, he's coming…Why don't you say something? What are you waiting for…Go on, kiss me, for Christ's sake!

ZAYTSEV: Darling. *(They kiss.)* Precious! Puppy dog! *(They kiss again.)*

ZINOCHKA: Wait, wait, wait…

ZAYTSEV: My little kitten…*(They kiss.)* My fluffy little… *(Sees GUSEV entering.)* One more question: When do you cough more, on Tuesdays or on Thursdays?

ZINOCHKA: Saturdays…

ZAYTSEV: Hm…Let me feel your pulse!

GUSEV: *(Aside.)* Looks as if there's been some kissing going on here…Just like the time with Shervetsov…I just don't understand the practice of medicine…*(To ZINOCHKA.)* Zinochka, be serious…You can't behave like this…You can't neglect your health! You must listen to what the doctor tells you to do. Medicine is making enormous strides these days! Enormous strides!

ZAYTSEV: Oh, yes! Now, listen to my diagnosis…At this time your wife is not in danger, but unless she submits to serious treatment, her illness may take a severe turn for the worse: heart attack, inflammation of the brain…

GUSEV: You see, Zinochka! You see! What trouble you cause me…I wouldn't have known any of this…

ZAYTSEV: I'll write a prescription immediately…*(Tears a piece of paper from the ledger book, sits and writes.)* Sic transit…two drams…Gloria mundi… one ounce…Aqua destillatae…two grains…Now take a dose of this powder three times a day…

GUSEV: In water or in wine?

ZAYTSEV: In water…

GUSEV: Boiled water?

ZAYTSEV: Absolutely…boiled water.

GUSEV: Please accept my heartfelt expression of gratitude, doctor…and so, goodnight. Thanks to you, we can sleep, we can breathe again, can't we, Zinochka?

ZINOCHKA: Mmm…but —

ZAYTSEV: No, don't speak — your condition might worsen considerably — drastically, even, there might be serious complications…

ZINOCHKA: But —

GUSEV: Listen to the doctor, dearest!

ZAYTSEV: Yes, always, listen to the doctor. In fact, your pulse, one more time —

ZINOCHKA: But —

GUSEV: That's enough, thank you, doctor. We've troubled you too long. Good night now.

ZINOCHKA: Yes, goodnight, "doctor."

ZAYTSEV: Good night, I —

GUSEV: No, please, we'll inconvenience you no longer. You have to be in town tomorrow, and so do I…

They exit.

ZAYTSEV: Good night. Roadside romances be damned.

GUSEV: *(Reappears once more.)* Oh, and one more thing, doctor. Your payment, allow me…*(Offers him ten rubles.)*

ZAYTSEV: Oh, no, please, it's my pleasure…professional courtesy…You know, fellow travelers, and all that…

GUSEV: I insist. I always pay for honest labor! You've studied long and diligently! You've toiled and sweated blood to acquire your knowledge! How well I understand!

ZAYTSEV: But —

GUVEV: Good night, doctor.

ZAYTSEV: Good night, sir. *(GUSEV exits)*…Sweet dreams…

Pause.

(Alone.) Roadside romances, curse them. I'm left to scratch…and dream… of the softness of her skin, so warm, so fragrant…those plump little hands… that pulse…

Pause.

And that is how I spent the night before my trial. Alone, miserable, barely thawed, with no romance to warm me. But there's more…I fall asleep, in the stillness and the darkness, with only the sound of the bedbugs biting… I scratch…and I dream…dream of the proceedings yet to come, tomorrow, at the session of the circuit court in town, alone on the day of my destiny. Imagine the feeling…the door to the courtroom opens and the bailiff escorts me to the dock. Trembling and confused, I see thousands of eyes fixed upon me…I feel my hour of judgment come at last when I glance at the serious, solemn faces of the jury…And now my dream turns into nightmare! Omigod! I raise my eyes to the table, covered with red cloth, and whom do I see in the public prosecutor's place? — but *him!* "Fedya!" *Her* husband! The husband of my roadside romance! With his lumpy, warty, blue-veined face...What horror! He sits and writes something. Looking at him, I remember the bugs, and Zinochka, and my diagnosis, and I feel not only shivers running down my spine, but the entire Arctic Ocean! He lifts his eyes toward me...wait...at first, he doesn't recognize me...but then his pupils dilate, his jaw drops...his hands shake... And slowly, slo-o-wly, he rises, and fastens his glassy stare upon me. I, too, get up, I don't know why, and stare back...

"Will the defendent please tell the court his name and so on and so on?" — says the judge.

The prosecutor sits and drinks a glass of water. Beads of cold sweat break out on his forehead.

"Well, now I've had it!" I think to myself...

The prosecutor is purple with rage. He opens his mouth to speak —

And suddenly, I wake with a start. A cold dawn is breaking, dimly... the stench hangs thick in the air, the bedbugs pause...not a sound comes from the next room...Stillness.

How will it all end?

1890s

IN MOSCOW

(A Moscow Hamlet)

Translator's note: This *feuilleton* was published in *Novoe Vremya (New Times)*, #5667, December 1891, under a pseudonym. Its contents provide a fitting epilogue to the period during which Chekhov wrote his one-act plays. It also lends itself readily to be performed as a monologue. The identity of the narrator (a.k.a. "a Moscow Hamlet") and the *mise en scène* can be left to the imagination of the actor and director.

In Moscow

I am a Moscow Hamlet. Yes. In Moscow, I wander, from other people's houses to the theatres, from the theatres to the restaurants, from the restaurants to the publishers, and everywhere I go, I say the same thing:

"God, how boring it is! How oppressively boring!"

And I always get the same, sympathetic reply:

"Yes it is, it really is, it's terribly boring."

And that's how it goes, from morning till evening. And at night, when I'm home, and I lie down to sleep, and in the darkness I ask myself *why* is it all so painfully boring, then I get this heavy, restless feeling in my chest, and I remember how, a week ago, at someone else's house, when I asked what to do for this boredom, some fellow, I don't know who, obviously not a Muscovite, turns to me suddenly and says in an irritated voice:

"Oh, well, you simply take a piece of telephone cord and you hang yourself on the nearest telegraph pole. That's all that's left for you to do!"

Yes. And meanwhile, alone at night, in the darkness, I begin to understand *why* it is all so terribly boring. Why, indeed? Why? Here, I believe, is the reason…

First of all, I know absolutely nothing. Once upon a time I learned something, but God only knows what it was, I've forgotten everything I've ever known, and what I *do* know isn't worth a damn anyway, and so it seems that every other minute I'm discovering America. For example, when they tell me that Moscow needs a sewer system, or that cranberries don't grow on trees, I ask in amazement:

"Really?"

Ever since I was born, I've lived in Moscow, but for the life of me I don't know where Moscow came from, why it exists, for whom, for what reason, for what purpose or benefit. At council meetings and gatherings, I talk with others about the municipal economy, but I have no idea what the size of Moscow is, or the population, or the number of births or deaths, how much we earn and how much we spend, how much we trade and with whom…Which town is more prosperous: Moscow or London? If London, then why? God only knows! And when in the council the question arises, I shudder and am the first to call out: "Give it to a committee! A committee!"

I mutter to the merchants that it's high time Moscow conducted trade with China or Persia, but we haven't the faintest idea where China and Persia are, or what they might need from us besides moldy, damp silk. From morning till night I sit stuffing myself at Testov's and I don't know why I am doing it. I play a part in someone or other's play, and I don't even know what the play's about. I go to hear *The Queen of Spades* and only after they raise the curtain do I remember that I haven't even read Pushkin's story or else I've simply forgotten it. I write a play and produce it myself, and only when it flops do I realize that the same play was already written by Vladimir Aleksandrov, and before him by Fedotov, and before Fedotov, by Shpazhinsky. I can't speak, or argue, or hold a conversation, even. When I'm out in society, and they talk to me of something I know nothing about, I simply bluff my way out of it. I put on a sad, ironic expression, I take the person I'm speaking to by the collar, and say: "That's old, my friend," or "You're contradicting yourself, dear fellow…Maybe some other time we'll settle this fascinating question, but in the meantime, tell me, for God's sake: Have you seen *Imogen*?" In this respect I've learned a little something from the Moscow critics. When they talk to me about the theatre and modern drama, for example, I don't know the first thing about it, but when they put the question to me directly, I have no difficulty whatsoever in answering: "Right you are, gentlemen…Let us assume this is so…But where are the ideas? The ideals?" or else sighing, I exclaim: "O immortal Molière, where are thou?!" and, sadly waving my hand, I leave by another door. There's some Danish playwright or other named Lope de Vega. So sometimes I bewilder the public with him. "I'll tell you a secret," I whisper to my neighbor, "Calderon stole that phrase from Lope de Vega…" And they believe me…Who cares — let them find out for themselves!

Because I know nothing, I am completely uncultured. True, I dress fashionably, have my hair cut at Teodor's, my decor is *chic;* but nevertheless, I'm

Asiatic, and therefore *mauvais ton*. My writing table cost me four hundred rubles, it's all inlaid, my upholstery is velvet, there are paintings, rugs, statuettes and tigerskins, but if you look closely, the flue in the stove is stopped up with a woman's blouse, and there's no spittoon, so my guests and I have to spit on the floor. There's the smell of fried goose on the staircase, there's a sullen look on my servant's face, there's dirt and filth in the kitchen, and under the bed and behind the wardrobes there are cobwebs, dust, old boots covered with green mold, and papers smelling of cat. There's always some calamity: either the stove's smoking, or the lavatory's cold, or the casement window won't close, and so that it doesn't snow into the study, I stop up the window with a cushion. And then, from time to time, I live in furnished quarters. I lie there on the sofa and I think about boredom, and in the adjacent room on the right, some German lady is frying cutlets on the stove, while in the room on the left some girls are banging beer bottles on the table. From my own room I study "life," I look at everything from the point of view of what goes on in furnished quarters, so now I write only of the *fräulein,* the girls, and dirty linen. Or else I play the role of drunkard and disillusioned idealist, and maintain that the most important question of the day is that of flophouses and the intellectual proleteriat. And yet, all the while, I feel nothing, I notice nothing. I'm completely at home with the low ceilings, and the cockroaches, and the dampness, and the drunken companions who stretch out on my bed with their filthy boots on. Neither pavements covered with yellowish-brown slime, nor rubbish heaps, nor filth-encrusted gates, nor illiterate signboards, nor raggedy beggars — none of it offends my aesthetic. Like a specter, I shrink into the narrow sleigh, and the wind pierces right through me; the driver's whip lashes 'round my head, the mangy little horse trudges through the streets, and still I notice nothing. What do I care! They tell me that Muscovite architects are building little soapboxes for houses, and are ruining Moscow. But I don't think those soapboxes are bad at all, really. They tell me our museums are ill-conceived, inconvenient, and dysfunctional. But I never go to museums. It's a pity that Moscow had only one decent picture gallery, and that one was closed by Tretyakov. Oh, well, let him close it, if he wants to…

But let us turn then, shall we, to the second cause of my boredom: I think I am exceptionally intelligent and important. Whether I'm out visiting, or conversing, or keeping silent, or giving readings at a literary soirée, or stuffing myself at Testov's — all this I do with the greatest aplomb. There isn't a discussion I wouldn't interfere with. It's true, I don't know how to speak, but I know how to smile ironically, to shrug my shoulders, and say "ah!" As an ignorant, uncultured Asiatic, in essence I'm very content, but I know how to give the impression that I'm not at all content, and I'm so subtle and successful that at times I believe it myself. When something funny is playing at the theatre, I often feel like laughing, but I hasten to adopt a serious stare; God forbid I should smile, what will the neighbors say? Someone laughs behind me, and I look around sternly: An unfortunate lieutenant, another Hamlet like me, is embarrassed, and in order to apologize for his inadvertent laughter, says:

"How vulgar! What a farce!"

At intermission, I loudly announce at the buffet:

"God only knows what kind of play this is! It's disgraceful!"

"Yes, it's a circus," someone else replies, "but you know, it's got an *idea*…"

"Oh come, come! That theme's been worked to death long ago by Lope de Vega, and of course, there's no comparison! And how boring it is! How god-awful boring!"

At *Imogen*, while stifling a yawn, my jaw almost dislocates; my eyes roll out of my head from boredom, my mouth goes dry…but on my face is a blissful smile.

"What a pleasure," I say *sotto voce*. "How long it has been since I've enjoyed myself so much!"

Sometimes — I don't know why — I feel like acting in a vaudeville, and in our depressing day and age, now wouldn't a vaudeville be just "the thing!" — but…what would the editors of *The Artist* say?

No, God forbid!

At picture exhibitions, my eyes often narrow, I shake my head meaning-fully, and exclaim in a loud voice:

"Everything seems to be here: atmosphere, expression, color…But what's going on here? Where are the ideas? Are there *any*?"

With respect to reviews, I demand honesty, and above all, I demand they be written by professors or people who have been to Siberia. For he who is not a professor, or has not been to Siberia — then *he* is not a man of true talent. I demand that M H. Yermolova play only virgins of no more than twenty-one. I demand that classical plays at the Maly Theatre be staged exclusively by professors...and I mean *exclusively!* I demand that even the most minor actors, before they learn their roles, familiarize themselves with Shakespeare, so that when an actor says, for example: "Good night, Bernardo!" the entire audience feels as if he's read all eight volumes.

I am very very frequently in print. As recently as yesterday I was on my way to the publisher of a very thick journal, to ask when my novel of many pages would be published.

"Really, I don't know what to do," replied the editor, embarrassed. "It's soooo long, you see, and...so boring."

"Yes," I said, "but on the other hand, it's honest!"

"Yes, you're right," agreed the editor, even more embarrassed. "Of course, I'll publish it..."

The young girls and ladies, with whom I am acquainted, are also unusually intelligent and important. They're all alike; they dress alike, they talk alike, they walk alike, and the only difference is that one has heart-shaped lips, while the other, when she smiles, has a mouth as wide as an eel-trap.

"Have you read Protopopov's latest article?" asks heart-lips. "It's a revelation!"

"And don't you agree," says eel-trap, "that Ivan Ivanich Ivanov, with his passion and conviction, reminds one of Belinsky? He is my only hope."

I confess, there was someone once, a *"she"*...How well I remember our declaration of love. She sat on the sofa. Her lips were heart-shaped. She was dressed very badly, "unpretentiously," as they say, her coiffure was ridiculous; I take her by the waist — her corset scrunches; I kiss her cheek — her cheek is salty. She is embarrassed, stunned, bewildered: "Forgive me," says she, "but how can one reconcile honest principles with such a vulgarity as love?" or "What would Protopopov say, if he could see this? Oh no, never! Leave me alone! I offer you my friendship!" And I say: "Friendship alone is not enough"…Then she shakes her finger coquettishly at me and says:

"Good, I shall love you, but on the condition that you hold your banner high."

And when I hold her in my arms, she whispers:

"We shall struggle together…"

Then, living with her, I find that she, too, has a jacket stuffed into the flue in her stove, and that the papers under her bed smell of cat, and she also plays devil's advocate in arguments, and at art exhibits, she babbles like a parrot about "atmosphere" and "expression." And she, too, has a "an idea!" She drinks vodka on the sly, and in bed at night she smears her face with sour cream to look younger. In her kitchen there are cockroaches, dirty mops, and filth; and when the cook bakes pies, before she puts them in the stove, she takes the comb out of her hair and buries it into the upper crust; and what's more, when she makes pastries, she moistens the raisins with saliva so that they stick better into the dough. And I flee! Flee! My romance flies out the window, and meanwhile *she*, Miss Clever, Miss Confident, Miss Contemptuous, goes around squealing on me, saying:

"He has betrayed his convictions!"

The third reason for my boredom is my furious and excessive envy. When they tell me that so-and-so has written a very interesting article, and that such-and-such a play is a success, and this one has won two thousand in the lottery, and that one's speech has made a tremendous impression, then my eyes start to narrow, and I say:

"I'm so happy for him, but, really, you know, he was convicted for theft in '74!"

My soul turns into a lump of lead, and I despise him to the depths of my soul, he who has been so successful, and on and on I go, saying:

"He tortures his wife, he has three lovers, and he's always buying the reviewers free dinners. In short, he's a regular beast…His novel's not so bad, but no doubt he's stolen it from somebody else. His lack of talent is scandalous…Yes, and to tell you the truth, I didn't find anything particularly distinctive in that novel, anyway…"

On the other hand, if somebody's play should flop, then I'm absolutely ecstatic and rush to take the author's side.

"No, gentlemen, no!" I cry. "There is *something* in that play. In any event, it is *literary*."

Did you know that everything mean and base and vile and spiteful that is said about anybody of note has been spread around Moscow by me? Let the mayor know that if he's managed to build us good roads, for example, then I'll start to hate him and I'll put out a rumor that he's a highway robber!…If they say to me that such-and-such a newpaper already has fifty thousand subscribers, then everywhere I go, I'll say the editor's been taking bribes. Other people's successes are my shame, my humiliation, a stab in my heart…And what question can there be of a social, civic, or politial conscience? If ever I had one, envy has gobbled it up long ago.

And so, ignorant, uncultured, unusually superficial and extremely self-important, cross-eyed with envy, liver distended, yellow, grey, and balding, I wander through Moscow from house to house, casting a spell, until everything else seems yellow, grey, and balding, too…

"God, how boring it is!" say I, with despair in my voice. "How oppressively boring!"

I'm infectious, like influenza. I complain of boredom, I posture, put on airs, I slander my nearest and dearest from sheer envy; and meanwhile, some young, impressionable student has heard me, and already he's running his hands through his hair self-consciously, and throwing aside the book he's been reading, says:

"Words, words, words…God, how boring it is!"

And his eyes start to narrow like mine, and he says:

"Our professors are delivering lectures now for the benefit of the famine-stricken. But I fear that they'll pocket half the money they're receiving."

I wander like a shadow, doing nothing, my liver grows and grows...And meanwhile, time passes and passes, I grow older, and weaker; and you'll see, one day soon, tomorrow maybe, even, I'll catch influenza and die, and they'll drag me off to the Vaganka Cemetery; and my friends will remember me for a few days, and then they'll forget me, and my name will cease to be a sound...Life does not repeat itself, and if you don't live the days that were given you, then you count them as lost...Yes, lost, lost!

And meanwhile, I could have learned anything, I could have mastered everything; if only I had exorcised the Asiatic in me, I might have studied and adored European culture, commerce, trade, agriculture, literature, music, painting, architecture, public health; I might have paved the streets of Moscow, traded with China and Persia, decreased the death rate, fought ignorance, debauchery and all kinds of depravity that prevent us from leading our lives; I might have been modest, affable, cordial, merry, even; I might have truly rejoiced at others' successes, since every success, no matter how small, is already one step toward happiness and truth.

Yes, I might have done it all! I might have! But I am a rotten old rag, a spineless creature, a miserable good-for-nothing, I am a Moscow Hamlet. Drag me off to the Vaganka Cemetery!

I toss and turn under the bedcovers, sleepless, thinking, wondering why am I tortured by boredom, and until the dawn, the words ring in my ears:

"You take a piece of telephone cord and you hang yourself on the nearest telegraph pole! That's all that's left for you to do."

1891

A Chronology
of the Moscow Period

The following is a chronology of the dates of Chekhov's one-act and full-length plays during the Moscow period, indicating when the plays were written, and giving premiere dates for those which were produced during that time. This chronology will give a picture of the intensity of Chekhov's involvement in the theatre during that hectic and exciting period.

ON THE HIGH ROAD	May, 1885
ON THE HARMFUL EFFECTS OF TOBACCO *(five subsequent revisions; final revision, 1902)*	February, 1886
SWAN SONG	January, 1887
IVANOV *premiere*	October, 1887 November 19, 1887
SWAN SONG premiere	February 19, 1888
THE BEAR *premiere*	February, 1888 October 28, 1888
THE PROPOSAL	October, 1888
IVANOV second premiere (St. Petersburg)	January 31, 1889
TATYANA REPINA	March, 1889
THE PROPOSAL premiere	April 13, 1889
THE TRAGEDIAN IN SPITE OF HIMSELF *premiere*	May, 1889 October 1, 1889
THE WEDDING	October, 1889
THE WOOD DEMON *premiere*	October, 1889 December 27, 1889
THE JUBILEE	December, 1891
THE NIGHT BEFORE THE TRIAL	1890s (actual date of writing unknown)

Chronology of the Plays

PLATONOV   1880–81

* ON THE HIGH ROAD   1885
  a dramatic study in one act

* ON THE HARMFUL EFFECTS OF TOBACCO   1886–1902
  a monologue in one act

* SWAN SONG   1887–1888
  a dramatic study in one act

  IVANOV   1887–1889
  a drama in four acts

* THE BEAR   1888
  a farce in one act

* THE PROPOSAL   1888
  a farce in one act

* TATYANA REPINA   1889
  a drama in one act

* A TRAGEDIAN IN SPITE OF HIMSELF   1889
  a farce in one act

* THE WEDDING   1889
  a play in one act

  THE WOOD DEMON   1889
  a comedy in four acts

* THE JUBILEE   1891
  a farce in one act

* THE NIGHT BEFORE THE TRIAL	1890s
THE SEAGULL *a comedy in four acts*	1896
UNCLE VANYA *scenes from country life in four acts*	1899
THE THREE SISTERS *a drama in four acts*	1901
THE CHERRY ORCHARD *a comedy in four acts*	1904

* The one-act plays

Translator's Note: The subtitles listed above are those given to the plays by their author.

Biographical Chronology:
Anton Pavlovich Chekhov

1860 January 17. Anton Pavlovich Chekhov, born in Taganrog, a town on the Azov Sea, son of a shopkeeper. (One of six children: Aleksandr, Nikolai, Anton, Masha, Ivan, Mikhail.) Of peasant lineage: His grandfather was a serf in the Voronezh province.

1869 enters grammar school, is required to work in his father's grocery store and to sing in the church choir along with his other siblings.

1876 Anton's father's bankruptcy forces the family to flee to Moscow; Anton is left behind to complete his education; supports himself by tutoring.

1877 sends his first serious full-length play, a lost manuscript whose title is purported to have been *Bezotsovshchina (Fatherless)* to his brother Aleksandr, along with several short comedic ones, which Aleksandr sends to journals for publication.

1879 passes his exams, joins his family in Moscow, enrolls in the medical school at Moscow University; to support his family and his education, begins writing sketches for humorous publications.

1880 first story published in *Strekoza (The Dragon Fly)*, a humorous journal; from 1880–87, writes over 400 stories and sketches for numerous journals under a variety of *"noms de plume"*.

1882 begins to contribute stories regularly to the weekly *Oskolki (Fragments)* for a five year period; its editor, Leykin, limits him to comedic sketches of less than 1000 words, signed primarily by Antosha Chekhonte; this becomes the main source of income for himself and his family.

1884 receives medical degree; begins to practice medicine; experiences his first lung hemorrhage; *Tales of Melpomena,* a collection of humorous short stories, is published.

1885 begins to contribute weekly to the *Petersburg Gazette* — no longer limiting him to strictly humorous pieces, and permitting him to write more lengthy stories; his collection *Motley Stories* is published; writes a dramatic study, *On the High Road.*

1886 invited to contribute to *Novoe Vremya (New Times)* by its prestigious publisher, Suvorin, enabling him to begin his more serious work and to publish under his true name with no space restrictions; experiences his second lung hemorrhage; writes *On the Harmful Effects of Tobacco;* continues writing dozens of short stories.

1887 premiere of *Ivanov* at the Korsh Theatre, Moscow, and then in St. Petersburg, with mixed and good reviews respectively; *At Twilight,* a volume of short stories, is published by Suvorin, establishing Chekhov as a writer of increased stature; writes *Calchas* (later retitled *Swan Song*).

1888 awarded Pushkin Prize in literature by the Imperial Academy of Sciences in St. Petersburg; premieres of *The Bear* and *Swan Song;* writes *The Proposal;* publication of a story, *The Steppe* in *The Northern Herald,* his first appearance in a so-called 'thick journal', the serious monthlies of the Moscow literary establishment, further enhancing his stature as a writer; *Stories,* a volume of short stories, is published by Suvorin.

1889 writes *The Wedding;* premieres of *The Proposal* and *The Tragedian in Spite of Himself;* premiere of *The Wood Demon* in Moscow, which closes after three performance to uniformly negative reviews; death of his brother, Nikolai, of consumption; writes stories: *A Dreary Story, The Bet.*

1890 journeys across Siberia to the island of Sakhalin off the Pacific Coast of Siberia to study the penal colony; experiences symptoms of coughing, heart palpitations; writes stories: *The Horse-Thieves, Gusev.*

1891 travels in Western Europe; writes *The Jubilee;* writes story *The Duel,* beginning the period of the longer and more serious stories.

1892 journeys to Novgorod province to join the fight against famine; purchases his "estate" in Melikhovo, fifty miles south of Moscow, and moves from Moscow with his family; appointed honorary medical superintendant of Serpukhov, his district, in the fight against cholera; his notes on the Sakhalin journey are published in *Russian Thought;* writes stories: *Ward No. 6, The Grasshopper, In Exile, Neighbors, The Wife.*

1893 increased symptons of his illness: coughing, heart palpitations, indigestion, headache; writes stories: *An Anonymous Story, The Two Volodyas.*

1894 his cough worsens; writies stories: *The Black Monk, The Student, The Teacher of Literature.*

1895 completes *The Seagull;* first meeting with Tolstoy; writes stories: *The Murder, Ariadne, Anna on the Neck.*

1896 October 17: *The Seagull* premieres at the Aleksandrinsky Theatre in St. Petersburg; it is a critical failure; writes stories: *The House with a Mezzanine, My Life.*

1897 continues his humanitarian work in the Serpukhov district (Melikhovo), building schools (at his own expense), census-taking; experiences a major lung hemorrhage; is formally diagnosed with consumption and advised by his doctors to move to the south; Stanislavsky and Nemirovich-Danchenko make plans for the founding of the Moscow Art Theatre; Chekhov spends winter in France; writes stories: *Peasants, The Schoolmistress.*

1898 inaugural season of the Moscow Art Theatre; December 17: *The Seagull* is produced there with great success; performances of *Uncle Vanya* are well-received in the provinces; Chekhov shows interest in the Dreyfus affair; Chekhov's father dies; owing to his declining health, Chekhov buys a plot of land in Yalta and builds a house; writes stories: *Man in a Case, The Husband, Gooseberries, About Love.*

1899 sells Melikhovo and moves to the Yalta with his mother and sister; sells all the rights for his works, past and future to St. Petersburg publisher Marks; October 26: *Uncle Vanya* is produced at the Moscow Art Theatre; writes stories: *The Darling, The Lady with the Dog, On Official Duty.*

1900 spring: the Moscow Art Theatre comes to Yalta to visit the ailing Chekhov, and performs *Uncle Vanya* for Chekhov, with Gorky, Bunin, Kuprin, and Rachmaninov in attendance. Chekhov is elected member of the Academy of Sciences; writies stories: *In the Ravine, At Christmas-Time.*

1901 January 31: *The Three Sisters* premieres at the Moscow Art Theatre; May 25, Chekhov marries Olga Knipper.

1902 resigns from the Academy of Sciences in protest against exclusion of Gorky; writes story: *The Bishop;* completes the final revision of *On the Harmful Effects of Tobacco.*

1903 his health declines; elected president of the Society of Russian Literature; writes his last story: *The Bride.*

1904 January 17: Chekhov's forty-fourth birthday is honored at the premiere of *The Cherry Orchard*, his last play; April: leaves Russia for Germany with Olga Knipper, on doctors' advice. July 2: Chekhov dies at a spa at Badenweiler, German. Buried in the cemetery of the Novo-Devichy Monastery in Moscow.

Please note that the dates of his one-act and full-length plays are set forth in a separate chronology. I have included mention of a few of his almost five hundred short stories, to show that Chekhov wrote stories every year from the ages of seventeen to forty-three, a year before his death. The names of individual stories don't begin in this outline until 1889, since before then, they were so numerous and were published in collections.

Glossary

This glossary contains a brief explanation of selected literary, musical, historical, and cultural allusions in the one-act plays. Its purpose is to enhance the understanding of the texts and their practical usage.

ON THE HIGH ROAD

Vologda
  a town roughly three hundred miles north of Moscow.

Shrine of Tikhon
  the reference here is to a monastery in the Voronezh Province, located in the southern steppes of central Russia, founded in the seventeenth century and named after St. Tikhon Zadonsky.

Holy Mountains
  a monastery in the Kharkov Province of the Ukraine.

Kuban
  the area of the Kuban river, north of the Caucasus.

Poltava
  a town in the Ukraine.

" 'Never mind', as the man in the play says..."
  a reference to a character in the play *The Forest* (1871) by Ostrovsky (1823–86).

Translator's note
  all the characters, especially Fedya, Merik, and Kuzma (and with the exception of Bortsov and Marya Yegorovna, of course) speak in a rough peasant vernacular. I have not translated their speech into any specific regional vernacular in English, but rather have given a suggestion of its roughness.

ON THE HARMFUL EFFECTS OF TOBACCO

Nyukhin

One great source of amusement for Chekhov, in writing the vaudevilles, was endowing the names of his characters with suggestive meanings. Here, the derivation of this character's name is from the verb "to sniff."

blini

a type of Russian pancake.

"Dixi et animam levavi"

"I have spoken, and I am much relieved." (Latin)

Translator's note

Chekhov wrote the first draft of this monologue in 1886, and subsequently revised it five times during his lifetime. This translation is of the final (1902) version.

SWAN SONG

Calchas

the original title of this play, adapted from Chekhov's short story of the same name. Chekhov retitled it, with the following explanation: "I have renamed *Calchas* as *Swan Song*. It's a long, bittersweet title, but I couldn't think of another one, though I spent a long time trying." *(From Chekhov to Lensky, 10/26/88.)* A likely explanation for the original title is that on the evening when the play takes place, Svetlovidov had been performing in Shakespeare's *Troilus and Cressida*. He was playing the minor role of "Calchas," father of Cressida, an old and dignified Trojan priest.

King Lear
Hamlet
Othello

It is interesting to note that the texts of Shakespeare's plays were known to Chekhov in Russian translation only. (Chekhov himself did not read English.) Chekhov loved Shakespeare, and his passion for Shakespeare's plays is evident both in *Swan Song* and *In Moscow (A Moscow Hamlet),* as well as in his full-length plays.

"A quiet night in the Ukraine"
This stanza is from the second canto of the narrative poem *Poltava* (1829), written by Aleksandr Pushkin, Russia's greatest poet (1799–1837).

Translator's note:
I have only made two omissions from Svetlovidov's recitations, both from Russian literature (see below). Chekhov had included them because they are readily identifiable by a theatre-going Russian audience, and therein lie their relevance and poignancy in the play's context. However, they would not be recognizable to the vast majority of English-speaking audiences. On the other hand, Svetlovidov's recitations from Shakespeare, all of which I have preserved, are certainly familiar to English-speaking audiences, and will therefore produce the effect that Chekhov desired.

For the benefit of those interested in the original text, these two omitted quotations are: l) from *Boris Godunov,* Aleksandr Pushkin's (1799–1837) neo-Shakespearean history play (written in 1825, published in 1831). It has survived in the contemporary theatre only in the form of Mussorgsky's opera of the same name; 2) from *Wit Works Woe* (1822–1824), a satire by Aleksandr Griboedov (1795–1829), Chatsky's exit lines in Act IV, scene xiv, in the final scene.

Chekhov's original text reads as follows, with the quote from *Godunov* (see p. 74):

"Hey, listen to this, old fellow…wait, let me catch my breath…How about something from *Godunov:*

> "Ivan the Terrible blessed me as his son,
> His ghost named me Dmitri from his grave.
> Because of me the people rise as one,
> Because of me Boris will not be saved.
> I am the Tsarevich. That is my name,
> And Poland's daughter cannot bring me shame!"

Not bad, eh? *(Animated.)* Wait, here's something from King Lear…Imagine it — black sky, torrent, thunder…" (etc.)

Similarly, for the ending, I have substituted the familiar quote from *Richard III* (Act V, sc. 4): "My horse, my kingdom for the horse" for the following quote from *Wit Works Woe*, again for the reasons given above (see p. 77):

> "Away from Moscow! Never to return,
> My feelings wounded, and my pride disparaged,
> I'll search the wide world over, for I yearn
> To find a quiet place. Bring me my carriage!"

I have provided these original texts here, should any actor or director wish to use them.

THE BEAR

dedicated to N. N. Solovtsov

The idea for *The Bear* occurred to Chekhov after seeing his childhood friend Solovtsov (1856–1902) play the part of a boorish suitor in a French vaudeville *Les Jirons de Cadillac* (1865) by Pierre Berton. Solovtsov was a huge actor with a roaring voice, and reminded Chekhov of a Russian bear. The play was the most successful of Chekhov's vaudevilles, and a continuous source of income over the years. (See pages 16–18 of the introduction to this collection.)

"a state of deep mourning"

observed by those who mourn parents, a spouse, or a child, it involves wearing only black (and for a woman, veiling her face — a possible costuming choice for a production), and lasts for the duration of a year.

Luka

a biblical name with an old-fashioned tenor to it, most commonly found among the peasant class.

"a regiment in town"

in nineteenth-century Russia, the regiment stationed in a small provincial town was the center of social and cultural life for the landed gentry, as many works of literature have depicted. The regiment became the centerpiece of Chekhov's later play, *The Three Sisters*.

"Matushka"

literally, "little mother," in affectionate terms. It is used as an exclamation or an expression of dismay, such as: "Heavens!" or "Good gracious!"

kvass

a (slightly alcoholic) beverage made from fermented cereals.

"ochi chornye, ochi strastnye"

(translation: "dark eyes, passionate eyes"): the first lines of the famous Russian "romanz" ("romance"), a ballad form popular in nineteenth century Russia, consisting of tunes often set to the lyrics of famous Russian poetry.

"whispers, timid sighs..."

the first lines of a "romance," whose lyrics are from a poem by A. A. Fet (1820–92).

"chef d'oeuvre"

masterpiece (French).

"progressive-minded women"

a term coined by Pisarev (1840–68, a political thinker) in *The Realists* (1864), used in the late nineteeth century to label a man with progressive views; here, Chekhov "recoins" the phrase, with playful and satirical intent, by having it pertain to women.

Tamara

Tamara (1841), a poem of the great Russian poet Lermontov (1814–41), is a reworking of the Georgian legend about the mysterious and beautiful queen in a dark tower who lures men to their doom.

THE PROPOSAL

cast of characters

The playful Chekhov is again at work, with the suggestive names of his characters. Here, **Chubukov** suggests a long-stem Turkish tobacco pipe (a "choobook") with a clay bulb. The derivation of **Lomov** is from the verb meaning "to break, fracture."

etcetera etcetera…and so on and so on…yes, indeed…

these are "verbal tics" in Chubukov's speech, i.e., phrases that embellish his conversation. No matter how they are translated, the joke is that they dominate his speech patterns. Chekhov loved using these idiosyncracies of speech in his plays. In *The Seagull,* for example, Sorin's speech is laced with such pedantic expressions, always ending with "and that's all." Yepikhodov's speeches in *The Cherry Orchard* are literally a minefield of verbal tics!

the land registry

the publication of statutes in the 1860s and 1870s, which clarified the issue of land ownership after the emancipation of the serfs in 1861.

"O, what a trial it is, dear Lord, to be the father of a full-grown daughter."

Famusov's exit line at the end of Act I of the famous verse comedy *Wit Works Woe* (1822–24) by Aleksandr Griboedov (1795–1829), well-known to Russian audiences of Chekhov's day.

"lying on top of the stove"

the shelf above the stove made a warm bed in a Russian peasant's hut, traditionally reserved for the old, the disabled, or the children of the household.

TATYANA REPINA

Tatyana Repina

the title of Suvorin's own new play, *Tatyana Repina*, a four-act (report-edly) turgid melodrama, written in 1886. Suvorin had based his play on a true story (occuring in 1881) of the well-known Russian actress Eulalia Kadmina, who actually poisoned herself intentionally so that she could die onstage in a production of Ostrovsky's *Vasilisa Meletyeva* in Kharkov — and all this to punish her unfaithful lover who was present in the audience. Chekhov's parody of his publisher's play was meant to be a practical joke. He never intended to have it performed. (See pp. 20–21 of the introduction to this collection.)

cast of characters

Translator's note: in this particular one-act, perhaps because it was a parody of Suvorin's play, Chekhov only listed the names of the characters on the cast page. I have therefore filled in their identification based on the text.

wedding and crowning ceremony
in this one-act play, Chekhov uses, *verbatim*, the text of the service entitled "The Rite of Holy Matrimony" from *The Service Book of the Holy
Orthodox-Catholic Apostolic Church*. (See acknowledgments in Notes from
the Translator, p. *x.*)

A. S. Suvorin
wealthy, powerful, and influential publisher of the journal *Novoe Vremya
(New Times);* considered to be the most important and influential colleague and friend of Chekhov's career. He began to publish Chekhov's
work in 1885, and convinced Chekhov to publish under his true name
instead of "Antosha Chekhonte." They became close friends, and
Chekhov's intimate correspondence to Suvorin, particularly during the
period 1887–89, contain some of Chekhov's most eloquent and significant passages on life, art, literature, and the theatre.

patchouli
a heavy perfume made from a fragrant oil derived from an East Indian
shrubby mint.

Prokimenon
part of the text of the Russian Orthodox church service.

"qu'est-ce que c'est"
means "what is it" (French).

THE TRAGEDIAN IN SPITE OF HIMSELF

"dacha"
a summerhouse or cottage in the country.

"Don't say that our youth has been wasted…"
a line from a poem by Nekrasov (1821–78) entitled "A Heavy Cross
Became Her Lot in Life" (1855), set to music in a "romance" (popular
Russian love song of the day).

"Again before you I stand…"
the opening line of the poem "Stanzas" (1841) by V I. Krasov, set to

music in a "romance." Both these "romances" must have special meaning to Chekhov — or else they must have been particularly popular in his day, because Dr. Dorn also sings these songs in *The Seagull.*

THE WEDDING

collegiate registrar

The rank system was created by Peter the Great who in 1722 set up the hierarchy of fourteen official ranks, of which "collegiate registrar" is the fourteenth (i e., the lowest). Each official (and his wife) had an appropriate honorific title. The officials were also given decorations. Civil servants and their ranks were often the object of Chekhov's satire in his stories (a Gogolian tradition), as in *Fat and Thin*, for example, where he satirizies the sychophancy of a member of a lower rank towards a higher one.

cast of characters

One great source of amusement for Chekhov, in writing the vaudevilles, was endowing the names of his characters with humorous meanings. In this vaudeville, such names abound. Here, for examples **Revunov** suggests "howl"; **Karaulov** suggests the cry for "help!"; **Zmeyukina** suggests "serpent"; **Aplombov** suggests "aplomb"; **Nyunin** suggests "sniveler or whimperer"; **Mozgovoy** suggests "cerebral"; **Yat** is the name of an old letter in the Russian alphabet, which is now obsolete.

Volunteer Fleet

merchant ship and crew, which could be mobilized in case of an emergency.

"I loved you once…"

the opening lines of well-known poem by Pushkin, set to music in a "romance."

"and while we're on the subject of drinking, why not have a little drink…"

a Russian proverb.

"He sought the ocean's mighty role…"

from the famous poem "The Sail" (1832) by Lermontov.

"make it sweet!"

The Russian toast at a wedding is "gorko!" — meaning "bitter"; the kiss of the bride and bridegroom will make it sweet.

piqué
> An elegant, ribbed fabric of cotton, rayon, or silk (French).

"Hands aloft, to the foresail and mainsail" etc.
> All Revunov-Karaulov's sailing terminology pertains to large nineteenth century Russian sailing vessels of the Imperial Navy fleet.

THE JUBILEE

cast of characters
> again, the playful Chekhov is at work with the suggestive names of his characters. In this vaudeville, the name **Shipuchin** suggests "sparkling" or "fizzy"; the root of the name **Khirin** suggests the Russian verb meaning "to grow sickly," "to wither."

profession de foi
> means "credo" (French).

Jack the Ripper
> a notorious murderer who was believed to have been responsible for the stabbing and mutilation of at least six London women in 1888. One of the theories was that he may have been a Russian doctor.

"Onegin, I'll confess it gladly…"
> from the famous bass aria "Young and old do love obey…" from Act IV of Tchaikovsky's opera *Eugene Onegin* — well known to Russian audiences. Vershinin also sings a line from this aria to Masha in Act III of Chekhov's *The Three Sisters.*

"One night two friends…"
> from the fable *The Passers-by and the Geese* by I. A. Krylov (1769–1844). Solyony quotes from this fable again in Chekhov's *The Three Sisters.*

"Don't say that our youth…"
> a "romance" of a poem by Nekrasov. Tolchakov refers to this romance in *The Tragedian in Spite of Himself.* Dr. Dorn also sings this romance in *The Seagull.*

THE NIGHT BEFORE THE TRIAL

Sic transit; gloria mundi; aqua destillatae
> "Sic transit gloria mundi" is a well-known saying in Latin, meaning, literally "and so passes the glory of the world," i.e., things of this earth are fleeting. "Aqua destillatae" means "distilled water." In the context of the one-act play, they are prescriptions given by "Doctor" Zaytsev to the object of his affections, Zinochka! Dr. Chekhov must have taken delight in concocting them.

Translator's Note
> **GUSEV: "Please accept my heartfelt expression of gratitude, doctor…"**
> Herein ends the unfinished one-act play by Chekhov. As I have explained in my introductory "Notes from the Translator," I have finished the play from this point on, in faithful accordance of the short story from which Chekhov adapted it (*The Night before the Trial*, 1886), for the benefit of theatre artists who might wish to perform it.

IN MOSCOW

Testov's
> a famous restaurant in Moscow. (In *The Three Sisters*, Andrey, exiled in a remote provincial town, longs to sit in Testov's again.)

Queen of Spades
> written in 1834 by Pushkin, it is a fantastic, melodramatic tale of the supernatural.

Yermolova
> leading lady of the Maly Theatre in the 1880s. Chekhov submitted *Platonov,* his first full-length play, to her in 1881, and was so upset when it was rejected that he destroyed the manuscript.

Maly Theatre
> the preeminent theatre of the 1880s. Stanislavsky and Nemirovich-Danchenko felt that the acting style of the Maly company was outdated and stultified, and that a whole fresh, new, inspirational approach to acting was necessary for the Russian stage.

Calderon

Spanish dramatist (1600–1681), successor to Lope de Vega, and considered the most celebrated Spanish dramatist of the latter part of the seventeenth century.

Lope de Vega

famous Spanish dramatist (1562–1635), and considered to be the most prolific dramatist of all time. He himself claimed to have written 1500 plays! — although the actual number of surviving texts is about 470.

mauvais ton

Means "in poor taste, unstylish" (French).

Belinsky

a leading Russian literary critic, political thinker, and philosopher (1811–1848).

Vaganka

a well-known cemetery in Moscow.

Pronunciation Guide

For the actor, the most significant aspect of the pronunciation of Russian names is the accentuation of the correct syllable, indicated below by an accent mark (') after the syllable to be stressed. Once the actor masters this, the narrative will flow, and the names will provide the richness that resonates in the original Russian. Note that the Russian name and patronymic is used for formality in address. Occasionally, the patronymic is contracted in the dialogue (e.g., "Sergeevich" sometimes becomes "Sergeich"). In general, accented "a" is pronounced as in "father", accented "e" as in "yet"; accented "o" as in "for". Note: This guide is only approximate, since the pronunciation of many Russian letters and vowels changes slightly, based on whether they are accented or not, or depending on their position in a word.

ON THE HIGH ROAD

CAST OF CHARACTERS:
Tikhon Yevstigneev (Tisha)
    Tee'-khon Yev-steeg-**nye'**-yev (**Tee'**-sha)
Semyon Sergeevich (Sergeich) Bortsov (Senya)
    Sye-**myon'** Syer-**ge'**-ye-veech (Syer-**ge'**-yeech) Bor-**tsov'** (**Sye'**-nya)
Marya Yegorovna
    Ma'-rya Ye-**go'**-rov-na
Savva (Savvushka)
    Sa'-va (**Sa'**-vush-ka)
Nazarovna
    Na-**za'**-rov-na
Yefimovna
    Ye-**fee'**-mov-na
Fedya
    Fye'-dya
Yegor Merik
    Ye-**gor' Mye'**-reek
Kuzma
    Kuz-**ma'**

OTHER NAMES:
Vologda
    Vo-**log'**-da

Andrey Polikarpov
    An-**drey'** Po-lee-**kar'**-pof
Kuban
    Koo-**ban'**
Khamonvesky
    Kha-mo-**nyev'**-skee
Bortsovka
    Bor-**tsov'**-ka
Yergovsky
    Yer-**gov'**-skee
Mikishkinsky
    Mee-**keesh'**-keen-skee
Senya
    Syen'-ya
Poltava
    Pol-**ta'**-va
Tisha
    Tee'-sha
Varsonofyevo
    Var-so-**no'**-fye-vo
Denis
    Dye-**nees'**

ON THE HARMFUL EFFECTS OF TOBACCO

CAST OF CHARACTERS:
Ivan Ivanovich Nyukhin
    Ee-**van'** Ee-**va'**-no-veech **Nyoo'**-kheen

OTHER NAMES:
Varvara
    Var-**var'**-a
Natalya Semyonovna
    Na-**ta'**-lya Sye-**myo'**-nov-na

SWAN SONG

CAST OF CHARACTERS:
Vasily Vasilyich Svetlovidov (Vasyusha) (Vasyushka)
    Va-**see'**-lee Va-**seel'**-yeech Svyet-lo-**vee'**-dof (Va-**syu'**-sha) (Va-**syush'**-ka)
Nikita Ivanich (Nikitushka)
    Nee-**kee'**-ta Ee-**va'**-nich (Nee-**kee'**-toosh-ka)

OTHER NAMES:
Yegorka
    Ye-**gor'**-ka
Petrushka
    Pye-**troo'**-shka
Aleksey Fomich
    A-lyek-**syey' Fo'**-meech

THE BEAR

CAST OF CHARACTERS:
Luka
    Loo-**ka'**
Yelena Ivanovna Popova
    Ye-**lye'**-na Ee-**va'**-nov-na Po-**po'**-va
Grigory Stepanovich Smirnov
    Gree-**go'**-ree Stye-**pa'**-no-veech Smeer-**nof'**

OTHER NAMES:
Nikolai Mikhailovich
    Nee-ko-**lai'** Mee-**khai'**-lo-veech
        ("lai" rhymes with the word "why")
Matushka
    Ma'-toosh-ka
Ryblova
    Ri'-blo-va
Korchagin
    Kor-**cha'**-geen
Vlasov
    Vla'-sof

Gruzdev
    Grooz'-dyef
Yaroshevich
    Ya-**ro'**-she-veech
Kuritzyn
    Koo'-ree-tsin
Mazutov
    Ma-**zoo'**-tof
Semyon
    Sye-**myon'**
Dasha
    Da'-sha
Pelagea
    Pye-la-**ge'**-ya

THE PROPOSAL

CAST OF CHARACTERS:
Natalya Stepanovna
    Na-**ta'**-lya Stye-**pa'**-nov-na
Ivan Vasilevich (Vasilich) Lomov
    Ee-**van'** Va-**see'**-lye-veech (Va-**seel'**-yeech) **Lo'**-mof
Stepan Stepanovich (Stepanich) Chubukov
    Stye-**pan'** Stye-**pa'**-no-veech (Stye-**pa'**-nich) Chu-bu-**kof'**

OTHER NAMES:
Nastasya Mikhailovna
    Na-**sta'**-sya Mee-**khai'**-lov-na
        ("khai" rymes with the word "why")
Mironov
    Mee-**ro'**-nof
Volchanetsty
    Vol-cha-**nyet'**-skee
Marusky
    Ma-**roo'**-skee

TATYANA REPINA

CAST OF CHARACTERS:
Olenina
 O-**lye'**-nee-na
Sabinin
 Sa-**bee'**-neen
Kotelnikov
 Ko-**tyel'**-nee-kof
Volgin
 Vol'-geen
Matveev
 Mat-**vye'**-yef
Kokoshkin
 Ko-**kosh'**-kee-n
Kokoshkina
 Ko-**kosh'**-kee-na
Patronnikov
 Pa-**tron'**-nee-kof
Ivan
 Ee-**van'**
Nikolai
 Nee-ko-**lai'**
  (*"lai"* rhymes with the word "why")
Aleksey
 A-lek-**syey'**
Kuzma
 Kooz-**ma'**

OTHER NAMES:
Pyotr
 Pyo'-tr
Vera
 Vye'-ra
David Solomonovich
 Da-**veed'** So-lo-**mo'**-no-veech
Altukhov
 Al-**tu'**-khof

Mashenka Ganzen
    Ma'-shen-ka **Gan'**-zen
Feofile
    Fe-**o'**-fee-le
Tatyana Petrovna Repina
    Ta-**tya'**-na Pye-**trov'**-na **Rye'**-pee-na
Konstantin
    Kon-stan-**teen'**
Yelena
    Ye-**lye'**-na
Zipunov
    Zee-**poo'**-nof

A TRAGEDIAN IN SPITE OF HIMSELF

CAST OF CHARACTERS:
Ivan Ivanovich Tolchakov
    Ee-**van'** Ee-**va'**-no-veech Tol-cha-**kof'**
Aleksey Alekseevich Murashkin
    A-lek-**sey'** A-lek-**sye'**-ye-veech Moo-**rash'**-keen

OTHER NAMES:
Sonichka
    So'-neech-ka
Vlasin
    Vla'-seen
Volodya
    Vo-**lo'**-dya
Vikhrin
    Vee'-khreen
Krivuyla Ivanovna
    Kree-**voo'**-lya Ee-**va'**-nov-na
Olga Pavlovna Feinberg
    Ol'-ga **Pav'**-lov-na **Fein'**-berg
Petrushka
    Pye-**troo'**-shka
Marya
    Ma'-rya

THE WEDDING

CAST OF CHARACTERS:
Yevdokim Zakharovich (Zakharich) Zhigalov
    Yev-**do'**-keem Za-**khar'**-o-veech (Za-**kha'**-rich) Zhee-**ga'**-lof
Nastasya Timofeevna
    Na-**sta'**-sya Tee-mo-**fye'**-yev-na
Dashenka (Darya Yevdokimovna)
    Da'-shen-ka (**Da'**-rya Yev-**do'**-kee-mov-na)
Epaminond Maksimovich (Maksimich) Aplombov
    Eh-pa-mee-**nond'** Mak-**see'**-mo-veech (Mak-**see'**-mich) A-**plom'**-bof
Fyodor Yakovlevich Revunov-Karaylov
    Fyo'-dor **Ya'**-kov-lye-veech Rye-vu-**nov'** Ka-ra-**oo'**-lof
Andrey Andreevich (Andryusha) (Andryushenka) Nyunin
    An-**drey'** An-**dre'**-ye-veech (An-**dryoo'**-sha) (An-**dryoo'**-shen-ka) **Nyu'**-neen
Anna Martynovna Zmeyukina
    An'-na Mar-**tin'**-ov-na Zme-**yoo'**-kee-na
Ivan Mikhailovich Yat
    Ee-**van'** Mee-**khai'**-lov-na Yat
    ("khai" rhymes with the word "why")
Kharlampy Spiridonovich (Spiridonich) Dymba
    Khar-**lam'**-pee Spee-ree-**do'**-no-veech (Spee-ree-**do'**-nich) **Dim'**-ba

OTHER NAMES:
Dmitry Stepanovich Mozgovoy
    Dmee'-tree Stye-**pa'**-no-veech Moz-go-**voy'**
Osip Lukich Babelmandebsky
    O'-seep **Loo'**-keech Ba-byel-man-**dyeb'**-skee

THE JUBILEE

CAST OF CHARACTERS:
Andrey Andreyevich Shipuchin
    An-**drey'** An-**dre'**-ye-veech Shee-**poo'**-cheen
Tatyana (Tanyusha)
    Ta-**tya'**-na (Ta-**nyu'**-sha)
Kuzma Nikolaevich Khirin
    Kooz-**ma'** Nee-ko-**la'**-ye-veech **Khee'**-reen

Nastasya Fyodorovna Merchutkina
    Na-**sta'**-sya **Fyo'**-do'-rov-na Myer-**choot'**-kee-na

OTHER NAMES:
Dryazhsko-Pryazhsky
    Dryazh'-sko - **Pryazh'**-skee
Boris Matveich
    Bo-**rees'** Mat-**vye'**-yeech
Katya
    Ka'-tya
Vasily Andreich
    Va-**see'**-lee An-**dre'**-eech
Zina
    Zee'-na
Seryozha
    Se-**ryo'**-zha
Grendilevsky
    Gren-dee-**lyev'**-skee
Berezhnitsky
    Bye-ryezh-**neet'**-skee

THE NIGHT BEFORE THE TRIAL

CAST OF CHARACTERS:
Fyodor Nikitich Gusev
    Fyo'-dor Nee-**kee'**-tich **Goo'**-syef
Zinochka (Zina)
    Zee'-noch-ka (**Zee'**-na)
Aleksey Alekseich Zaytsev
    A-lek-**syey'** A-lek-**sye'**-eech **Zai'**-tsef
        ("Zai" rhymes with the word "why")

OTHER NAMES:
Cheprakov
    Che-pra-**kof'**
Turgenev
    Toor-**ge'**-nyef

Samara
   Sa-**ma'**-ra
Shervetsov
   Sher-vet-**sof'**

IN MOSCOW (A MOSCOW HAMLET)

CAST OF CHARACTERS:
Testov's
   Tyes'-tof
Aleksandrov
   A-lek-**san'**-drof
Fedotov
   Fye-**do'**-tof
Shpazhinsky
   Shpa-**zheen'**-skee
Tretyakov
   Tre-tya-**kof'**
Yermolova
   Yer-**mo'**-lo-va
Maly
   Ma'-lee
Protopopov
   Pro-to-**po'**-pof
Ivan Ivanich (Ivanov)
   Ee-**van'** Ee-**va'**-nich (Ee-**va'**-nof)
Belinsky
   Bye-**leen'**-skee
Vaganka
   Va-**gan'**-ka

Selected Bibliography

The following sources were consulted for some of the biographical and literary information included in the introduction to this collection.

Chekhov, Mikhail. *Vokrug Chekhova*. Moskva, Moskovsky Rabochy, 1960.

Gottlieb, Vera. *Chekhov and the Vaudeville*. Cambridge, Cambridge University Press, 1982.

Hingley, Ronald. *A New Life of Anton Chekhov*. New York, Knopf, 1976.

Magarshack, David. *Chekhov the Dramatist*. London, John Lehmann, Ltd., 1952.

Mirsky, D. S. *A History of Russian Literature*. New York, Knopf, 1958.

Nemirovich-Danchenko, V., transl. by John Cournos. *My Life in the Russian Theatre*. London, Geoffrey Bles, 1968.

Simmons, Ernest J. *Chekhov: A Biography*. Chicago, The University of Chicago Press, 1962.

Troyat, Henri. *Chekhov*. New York, Fawcett Colombine, 1986

Worrall, Nick. *File on Chekhov*. London, Methuen, 1986.

The texts of Chekhov's one-act plays and the excerpts from his letters were newly translated from the Russian for this collection from the following:

Chekhov, Anton Pavlovich. *Polnoe sobranie sochineniy i pisem v tridtsati tomax*. Moskva, Izdatelstvo 'Nauka', 1974–82.

The excerpted quotations from reminiscences of his contemporaries were newly translated from the Russian for this collection from the following:

Gorky, M. "A. P. Chekhov," *Polnoe sobranie sochineniy; khudozhestvennye proizvedenia v dvadtsati pyati tomakh*. Moskva, 1970.

Korolenko, V. G. "Anton Pavlovich Chekhov," *Izbrannye Proizvedeniya*. Moskva, 1947.

In addition to these, the following books are also recommended to actors and theatre artists as valuable source material for enriching their understanding of the four major plays. They are only a few of the many sources available in English about Chekhov and his work:

Hackett, Jean. *The Actor's Chekhov*. Lyme, NH, Smith & Kraus, 1992.

Magarshack, David. *Chekhov: A Life*. New York, Grove Press, 1952.

Magarshack, David. *The Real Chekhov*. London, George Allen & Unwin, Ltd., 1972.

Miles, Patrick, ed. and transl. *Chekhov on the British Stage*. Cambridge, Cambridge University Press, 1993.

Pritchett, V. S. *A Spirit Set Free*. New York, Vintage, 1988.

Chekhov, Anton Pavlovich. *Four Plays*. Translated by Carol Rocamora. Lyme, NH, Smith & Kraus, 1996.

Stanislavsky, Konstantin, transl. by J. J. Robbins. *My Life in Art*. London, Methuen, 1989.

Valency, Maurice. *The Breaking String*. New York, Oxford University Press, 1966.